T0278318

PCs & Laptops

by Dan Gookin

A Wiley Brand

PCs & Laptops For Dummies®

Published by: **John Wiley & Sons, Inc.**, 111 River Street, Hoboken, NJ 07030-5774, www.wiley.com

Contents at a Glance

Table of Contents

Introduction

S ince the first IBM PC rolled off the assembly line in 1981, tremendous leaps in technology have taken place. Who would have thought you could purchase a sophisticated, high-speed computer or laptop in the same place where you buy tires and booze? Despite these advancements, computers remain a daunting, intimidating piece of machinery. They can make you feel like a dummy.

This book's job is to convince you that you're not a dummy. Computers are intimidating only when you believe them to be. Peel back that sleek case and you find a shy, frightened beast that desires only to help you. Oh, and I'm speaking metaphorically: Try to avoid peeling off the computer's case.

This book covers desktop PCs and laptops. The information here runs the gamut, from assembling a desktop to taking your laptop out to a swanky cybercafé. Across the desktop and from laptop to lap-bottom, it's all covered here.

About This Book

I'm glad you're still reading this introduction. Most people stop reading after a few paragraphs, probably from the fear that I'll regale them with dull details about 19th century French poetry or describe the effect of cubism on honeybee migration. Regardless, I appreciate your dedication.

This book covers both laptops and desktop computers. These categories define two different configurations of what is essentially the same device: a personal computer, or PC. The term *PC* applies to both, though it traditionally refers to the desktop model. Regardless, these devices run Windows, the most popular and hated computer operating system in history.

Topics here cover computer tasks and duties, from setup and identification of parts and basics such as turning the thing on and off to other subjects like networking, printing, computer security, and maintenance. These are concepts that were once contained in the computer manual, though this book isn't as serious and has less of a chance of giving you a paper cut.

Foolish Assumptions

You have a computer, desktop or laptop, or you intend to purchase one before you read the last word in this sentence. Good. The computer you have or desire to obtain is a PC, as described earlier. It is not a Macintosh. It is not a Cray supercomputer. It is not an ENIAC.

The term *desktop* applies to all desktop PCs, from the behemoth under-the-desk powerhouses to those tiny models that are slightly larger than a deck of cards. These are nonportable computers.

I use the word *laptop* to refer to all types of portable computers, from traditional notebooks to tablets and various models in between. These are all easily flung out a window.

Here's what I think of you: Beyond being clever and handsome, you are a human being and not a cleverly disguised owl. You may have some experience with a computer or none at all. But you're not a Vulcan or a superintelligent gerbil desiring to program an Arduino in FORTRAN.

This book covers both Windows 10 and Windows 11, the two current and most fashionable versions of the Microsoft Windows operating system. Previous editions of this book cover Windows 7, and even older versions cover the horrid Windows 8, for which several Microsoft employees are still paying penance. Windows 9 doesn't exist for reasons that are understandable only to Germans.

When this book refers to Windows without a specific edition or version, the information applies to both Windows 10 and Windows 11.

Though using Windows is necessary to performing many tasks in this book, I do not cover the Windows operating system directly. For details on using Windows, I recommend *Windows For Dummies*, by my pal Andy Rathbone (Wiley Publishing). For helpful tomes on using various software applications, hunt down a *For Dummies* title on that specific program.

Where to Start

This book is a reference. You can start reading at any point because, unlike books on reassembling cats, this book doesn't assume that you've already read previous chapters or even some of the current chapter. After you read the information, you're done; there's no need to read any further. The book has no plot, the characters are one-dimensional, and the conclusion is predictable.

Each of this book's 28 chapters covers a specific aspect of the computer. Sample sections include:

» Restarting the PC

» Ejecting storage media

» Stopping a printer run amok

» Accessing a Wi-Fi network

» Understanding cloud storage

» Things to pack in your laptop bag

» Doing a virus scan

Each section is designed to be read independently of other information in the book. Read the information quickly, digest what you have read, and then put down the book and get on with using the computer — or instead choose to do something beneficial to humanity, such as play pickleball.

Conventions Used in This Book

Menu items, links, and other controls on the screen are written using initial-cap text. So, if an option is labeled "Turn off the computer," the text Turn Off the Computer (without quotes or commas) appears in this book.

If you must type something, it looks like this:

Type me

You type the text *Type me* as shown. You're told when and whether to press the Enter key. You're also told whether to type a period; periods end sentences written in English, but not always when you type text on a computer.

Windows menu commands are shown like this:

Choose File ⇨ Exit.

This line directs you to choose the File menu and then choose the Exit command.

Key combinations you may have to press are shown like this:

Ctrl+S

This line says to press and hold down the Ctrl (Control) key, type an *s*, and then release the Ctrl key. It works the same as pressing Shift+S on the keyboard to produce an uppercase *S*. Same deal, different shift key.

 The Windows key on the keyboard is labeled with the Windows icon, lurking in the margin. This key may instead be adorned with the keyboard manufacturer's logo. It's used by itself to pop up the Windows Start menu, though it can also be used like a shift key with other keys on the keyboard. See Chapter 10 for exciting keyboardy stuff.

Icons Used in This Book

TIP

The Tip icon indicates helpful advice or an insight that makes using the computer interesting. For example, when you're dunking the computer into liquid nitrogen, be sure to wear protective goggles.

REMEMBER

This icon indicates something to remember, like wearing trousers when you address a large crowd.

WARNING

When you see this icon, pay careful attention to the text. It flags something that's bad or that can cause trouble. For example: "The enormous sea monster slithering toward your village won't be using the courts to settle its grievances."

TECHNICAL
STUFF

This icon alerts you to a technical topic, an aside or a trivial tidbit that I simply cannot suppress the urge to share. For example: "My first laptop was a steam-powered, 8-bit 6502 that I breadboarded myself." Feel free to skip over any text tagged with this little picture.

Where to Go from Here

Thank you for making it through the introduction. See? I didn't cover French poetry at all and only barely mentioned honeybee migration.

What's next is up to you: Open the table of contents and pick a spot that amuses you or concerns you or piques your curiosity. Everything is explained in the text, and topics are carefully cross-referenced so that you don't waste your time reading repeated information. Again, everything is carefully cross-referenced so that you don't waste your time reading repeated information.

My email address is dgookin@wambooli.com. Yes, this is my real address. I reply to all email I receive, though you get a quick reply if you keep your question short and specific to this book. Although I enjoy saying hi, I cannot answer technical support questions or help you troubleshoot your computer. Thanks for understanding.

With this book in hand, you're now ready to go out and conquer your desktop or laptop PC. Try not to read all of it, which would embarrass me because I've never finished reading a book, let alone

1

Hello, Computer!

Chapter **1**

Computer 101

Y ou must accept two important facts about a computer: It can't blow up and it's not evil.

Computers explode in the movies. They excel at it. You see fire, smoke, and little pieces flying everywhere. Real life is sadly less dramatic.

Though it's stimulating to believe that computers are evil, and such a belief explains many confusing things nicely, it just isn't true. Computers are innately indifferent, almost disappointingly so.

Sad to say, computers are handy tools — just frustrating to use at times. This chapter helps ease you into understanding these useful and often misunderstood gizmos.

The enrollment application for dogs to join the Marines in WW2 was designed to be filled out from the dog's perspective:

The Fast Idiot

Computers aren't smart; they're just fast. If you slow down time and observe deep inside the computer's bosom, you find a calculator. That's it. But surrounded by lots of helpful electronics, and cranking out billions of computations per second, the computer seems amazing. It's like your drooling nephew building a Lego Eiffel Tower in two seconds. You'd think he's a genius, but he's just moving quickly. That's essentially how the computer fools you into thinking it's smart.

What a computer does

A computer's core mission statement is to consume input, process it, and generate output. In this manner, the computer operates like a cow but one that's less expensive to feed and with less odorous output. Figure 1-1 illustrates the basic computer operation, which coincidentally also applies to a cow.

FIGURE 1-1:
What a computer does at its simplest level.

To perform its basic task, the computer occupies itself with three activities:

>> I/O

>> Processing

>> Storage

I/O: I/O stands for input and output. It's pronounced "I owe," like *Io*, the third-largest moon of Jupiter. The computer receives input from devices such as the keyboard, a pointing device (mouse), and the Internet. It generates output displayed on the screen, printed, or returned to the Internet. I/O is also a popular subject for songs sung at computer camp.

Processing: Between input and output you find *processing*. The input is somehow manipulated, mangled, or munged. Then it's spewed out in a modified form. Minus any processing, the computer is like a tube, and computer science would be identical to plumbing. Processing is covered in Chapter 6. Plumbing is covered in *Plumbing For Dummies*.

Storage: The final computer activity is storage. Storage can be temporary or long-term. Temporary storage is the computer *memory*, or *RAM*, covered in Chapter 7. Long-term storage is provided by the computer's storage media, covered in Chapter 8. Overhead storage is designed for luggage that doesn't fit below the seat in front of you.

Hardware and software

All parts of a computer system can be classified as either hardware or software.

Hardware is the physical part. Anything you can touch or see — or that smells like burning plastic — is hardware.

Software is the computer's instructions. It tells the hardware what to do.

For example, consider a symphony orchestra. The hardware consists of the musicians and their instruments. Their software is music. As with a computer, the music (software) tells the musicians and their instruments (hardware) what to do.

Without software, hardware just sits around bored. Like a symphony orchestra without music, that can be an expensive waste of time, especially at union scale. No, it's software that makes the computer system work. It's in charge. Software determines the computer's personality and potential.

>> If you can toss it out a window, it's hardware.

>> If you can toss it out a window and it comes back, it's a cat.

>> Computer software includes all the programs you use on the computer.

>> The most important piece of software is the computer's operating system. It's the main program in charge of everything.

Doubtless, You Have Some Questions

Rather than bore you with further exploration of the dry and dull world of computer technology, I thought I'd save some time and get some burning questions you may have out of the way.

"What is a PC?"

A *PC* is a personal computer. The name applies to pretty much all computers these days, though historically a PC is related to the original IBM PC (personal computer), introduced in the early 1980s. Today, a PC is any computer system that isn't a Macintosh, though a Mac is technically also a personal computer.

"Do I need a laptop?"

Probably.

"Can you be more specific?"

Okay. The two main styles of personal computers are desktop systems and laptops.

A desktop PC dwells in one location. It's not portable. These systems are often more powerful and expandable than laptops. They can also be upgraded, which isn't possible with most laptops.

Laptops go anywhere, thanks to their light weight and battery power. They are powerful but sacrifice features and expandability for their portability. They can also be more expensive than comparable desktop systems.

TIP

>> You can use a laptop as a desktop system, expanding it with a full-size keyboard and monitor. This setup has the advantage of your still being able to take the computer with you to work remotely or when the building is on fire.

>> Many people opt to use both systems: a powerful desktop for the office or home and a laptop to take on the road.

>> Laptops are also a near necessity for students. Colleges and universities offer guidelines for student computers — specifically, laptops. Heed this advice.

"Why not just use a tablet or smartphone instead of a computer?"

The quick answer is that mobile devices such as smartphones and tablets are designed for data *consumption*, not data production. If you're merely passing through this digital life, you can get by with a phone or tablet and never own a computer. If you need to create something, however, a computer is a better tool than a tablet or smartphone.

- As someone who detests typing on a touchscreen, I can assure you that typing on a real keyboard is the best reason to own a computer.

- If you enjoy using a tablet with a removable keyboard, you would probably be happier with the full power of a laptop instead.

- Mobile devices lack a computer's potential for expandability.

- A typical computer lasts for years. Mobile devices are usually replaced on an average 2-year cycle.

"Seriously, can a computer explode?"

A computer cannot spontaneously explode. Even if you accidentally spill a fish tank of water on it, the device most likely will short out and die, flipping the circuit breaker, but it won't explode.

My first PC had a 65-watt power supply that failed. I heard a pop and the computer died. Then I saw a puff of smoke rise from behind the monitor. I replaced the dead power supply with a beefier model and the computer worked fine after that. No drama, though I delighted in the experience, knowing that I would write about it later in this book.

Buy That Computer!

If you don't yet have a computer, you must rush out and buy one! Or, if your current computer is so old that it can access the DuMont Network, get a new one right now! This order carries no urgency, despite what you just read.

Buying a complex piece of electronics like a computer isn't the same as purchasing a vase or cement mixer. To make your purchase a successful one, consider my friendly, 5-step method for buying a computer.

1. **Know what it is that you want the computer to do.**
2. **Choose between a desktop and laptop.**
3. **Determine how much hardware is required.**
4. **Locate service and support.**
5. **Buy the computer!**

If you heed these steps, you'll be a lot more satisfied with your computer purchase than if you just saunter into an upscale store to buy something with the Apple logo on it.

Step 1: Determine what you want the computer to do

Computers are best used to create something: to write a novel, edit video, generate graphical designs, compose music, devise a spreadsheet to monitor gambling debts, and so on. On the antiproductivity side, computers are great for playing high-end video games. Many gamers prefer computers over the various gaming consoles, primarily because computer hardware is easily upgraded.

The point of this step is to understand how you plan on using the computer. What do you see yourself doing? How are you going to use the computer: as a tool to get work done or to professionally waste time?

TIP

>> Gaming consoles are considered specifically engineered computers.

>> Even if you decide to use your computer for one task, you can expand to other creative activities later. For example, you can perform office tasks as well as play horrifically graphic video games.

>> If you just need to check email, browse the web, or waste time with a serious expression on your face, consider buying a smartphone or tablet instead of a computer.

Step 2: Choosing between a desktop and a laptop

Desktop computers stay in one place. They're powerful, expandable, and less expensive than laptops. They're more difficult to lose in a stack of magazines on the coffee table and then accidentally tossed out in a rush because guests are coming over.

Laptop computers go anywhere. They're wireless, though the battery must be charged and can last only so long (usually, several hours). They lack expandability. Due to their small size and other specifics, laptops are generally more expensive than desktop computers.

>> Laptops offer you freedom to compute anywhere. Desktops offer you power.

>> Laptops occupy less space than desktops. This condition makes sense because it's awkward to balance a desktop computer on your lap.

>> Desktop computers offer full-size keyboards and larger monitors.

>> Some laptops are expandable, but most all desktop systems can be upgraded with new hardware.

>> You can use both a laptop and a desktop. My desktop is my main computer, but I take my laptop on the road — or even out to work in a café when the smell from the neighbor's meth lab becomes too intense.

Step 3: Calculate how much hardware you need

Software makes the computer go, so before you discuss PC brand names or big box stores, you must consider the programs you plan on using. That's because some software — games, video production, graphics — requires specific computer hardware. To determine how much hardware you need, read the software requirements.

For example, a game may recommend a specific video adapter and quantity of memory to run. Graphics software may demand a specific processor. Video editing uses a lot of computer storage. Gather this information to understand how much computer hardware you need.

REMEMBER

>> Computer software controls computer hardware.

>> For general computer use, any system that can run the Windows operating system works great. When you have specific software you plan on running, however, ensure that the computer you get has the hardware to handle the software's needs.

TIP

>> Specific hardware nonsense is covered in Part 2 of this book. Don't worry about trying to understand software requirements when you're just starting out. Use this book's index to help you learn about the various PC hardware thingies.

Step 4: Locate service and support

You must know where to take your computer should it break. You may also need to know whom to turn to should you have questions about the computer. These items are known as "service and support," and they're often overlooked when buying a computer.

Service means one thing: Who fixes the computer? For the best service, I recommend buying your computer from a local dealer, a mom-and-pop type of store. If you buy at one of those big box stores, you must ask to discover who actually fixes your computer and where it gets fixed.

Support is about getting help for your computer. Some people need lots of help. If that's you, buy from a place that offers free classes or has a toll-free support number. That support may add to the purchase price, but it's worth every penny if it saves you aggravation in the future.

TIP

>> Computers generally come with a 90-day warranty. This length of time is sufficient. If anything electronic is going to break, it does so right away. You're well-covered with a 90-day warranty.

>> Avoid buying an extended warranty on a desktop computer. For a laptop computer, a 3-year warranty is ideal. Keep in mind that due to wear and tear most laptops tucker out after about three years. Furthermore, because laptop parts are teensy and specialized, they're more expensive to replace.

>> Avoid service contracts. They are a waste of money.

Step 5: Buy it!

The final step to getting a new computer — or your first computer — is to buy it. Do it! Don't hesitate because you think a newer, faster model is coming out soon. A newer faster model is *always* coming out soon. Don't let this ongoing condition deter your purchase.

What to Do with Old Computers

A computer can last for years. But like that Venus flytrap you brought home from the county fair, eventually it dies. What to do with a dead or dying computer or one that's old enough to collect Medicare depends on whether the system is a desktop or a laptop.

REMEMBER

Toss out old electronics per the disposal rules of your jurisdiction. Be especially careful with laptop batteries: They cannot just be thrown in the trash.

Disposing of a geezer desktop PC

A computer is a system. When part of it goes, you need not toss out the rest. Beyond the computer box, you can reuse the keyboard, mouse, monitor, printer, and other hardware with your new computer system. And, if the new computer comes with these parts, keep the old ones around as spares.

>> Desktop PCs can last six years or longer. After about eight years or so, the technology becomes too old to be compatible and too slow to be useful.

>> Turn in an old computer box to a computer recycling center. Many of the circuit boards can be stripped for precious metals or turned into festive windchimes.

>> Old desktops can be donated to charities, but call first to see whether they want yours.

>> One item you might not want to recycle is the old computer's mass storage device — the hard drive or SSD. If possible, remove it and have it destroyed. Outfits that shred documents offer such destruction services, should security be a concern to you or your presidential campaign.

Discarding that old laptop

Laptops last for a good three years — or longer if you're kind to them. As they age, the laptop's battery life dwindles, which is a sure sign you need a replacement. When you get a new laptop, I recommend keeping the old one around for a bit longer as a spare. Once you're certain that the new laptop is worthy, you can dispose of the old one.

>> Before you slip the laptop into the mail slot of eternity, I recommend removing its mass storage device — the hard drive or SSD. This gizmo may still contain sensitive data. Dispose of it at a data recycling center. If the mass storage device cannot be removed, dispose of the entire laptop at a data recycling center.

>> Remove a laptop's battery before getting rid of it. If you cannot remove the battery, ensure that the entire laptop is properly disposed of.

A Final Thing to Remember

Computers aren't evil. They harbor no sinister intelligence. In fact, when you get to know them, you discover that they're rather dumb.

This rule doesn't apply to robots.

IN THIS CHAPTER

» Reviewing PC hardware design

» Discovering goobers on a PC case

» Locating pluggable-innable places

» Finding the I/O panel

» Identifying items on a laptop

Chapter 2

The PC Tour

f you're to believe television and film, computers are fancy, futuristic devices with hundreds of buttons, blinking lights, and cool sound effects. The text on the screen appears one character at a time, coupled with an annoying teletype noise. Hackers never use a mouse; they type wildly and — in a matter of moments — the Pentagon is hacked. O, if only computers were so flashy.

The truth is that computers are dull. Beyond the keyboard, few buttons are found. Your car's dashboard has more lights than a modern computer. Even so, it's good to know what the buttons, lights, and doodads are called and what they do. Time for your computer tour.

The Many Shapes of PC

Thanks to major conspiracies and a snide sense of humor in the computer industry, not all computers look the same. To keep you confused, manufacturers like to shake it up a bit when it comes to PC design. Figure 2-1 shows typical computers in their various incarnations, along with their official names that I made up.

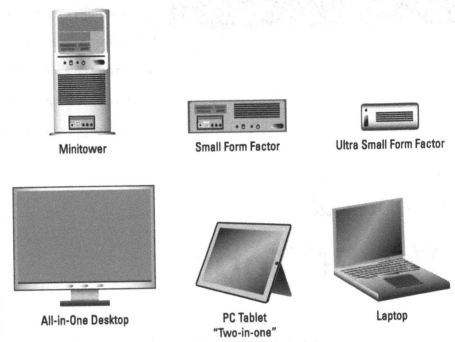

FIGURE 2-1:
PC shapes and sizes, also known as "form factors."

Minitower   Small Form Factor   Ultra Small Form Factor

All-in-One Desktop   PC Tablet "Two-in-one"   Laptop

Minitower: The minitower is the most popular desktop PC type. It sits atop a desk (duh), or it can be tucked away out of sight below the desk.

Small form factor (SFF): These tiny PCs pack a lot of power but lack expandability. They're about the size of a large, hardbound book. You find them in office settings where they can double as coffee warmers.

Ultra small form factor (USFF): The smallest of the small, these desktop computers are as teeny as a deck of cards. They lack expandability due to their diminutive size. Sadly, they don't generate enough heat to warm a cup of coffee.

All-in-one (AIO): This popular and trendy computer design combines both the computer box and monitor into a single unit. From the front, the system looks like a monitor, though it's thicker. On the sides, you find the myriad of fun connectors, knobs, buttons, and lights.

PC tablet: Also known as a *two-in-one*, this ultrathin, portable PC comes in two pieces: screen and keyboard. The keyboard detaches and is easily lost. Once you give up looking for it, you're forced to endure using the PC tablet's touchscreen for input.

Laptop: The traditional portable computer, the laptop, is a handy, lightweight package, ideal for slowing down the security checkpoints in airports. Laptop PCs work just like the other systems but lack the dedication demonstrated when you set up your desktop PC at a Starbucks.

>> No matter what size the computer, the amount of clutter you have always expands to fill the available desk space.

>> A larger version of the minitower is called "the tower." It's used for high-end workstations, and it provides acres of room inside for expensive electronics and for smuggling.

>> The computer box is often referred to as a *console*. I use the term "computer box" to avoid confusion with gaming consoles. Also confusion with the word *console*, which means to comfort in times of woe — which is also applicable to computers that run the Windows operating system.

>> The amount of space a PC console occupies is often referred to as its *footprint*. Smaller consoles are *small-footprint* PCs.

Around the Desktop PC

Due to their history, power, and expandability, desktop PCs feature a lot more goobers on their box than laptops do. Therefore, an official tour is necessary. These items are more than fancy decorations, and knowing their purposes and official names is necessary if you don't want to sound like a dweeb.

Exploring a typical computer system

Figure 2-2 lovingly illustrates a typical desktop PC. It may not match the specific computer you have, because my purpose is to label the pieces and not to stalk you.

Here are the important items to note in a typical computer system:

Computer box: The main computer box is the centerpiece of the computer system. It is *not* the CPU, though plenty of dweebs out there refer to it as such. Inside the computer box you find the system's electronic guts. Outside you find various buttons, lights, and holes into which you attach the rest of the computer system.

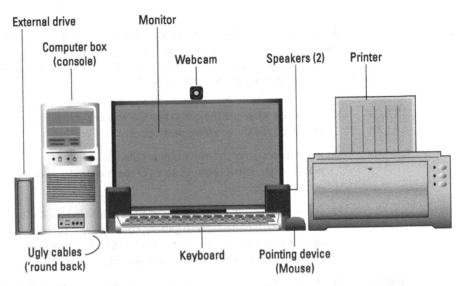

External drive　　　Monitor

Computer box
(console)　　　Webcam　　　Speakers (2)　　Printer

FIGURE 2-2:
A typical
computer system.

Ugly cables
('round back)　　　Keyboard　　　Pointing device
(Mouse)

Monitor: The monitor is the device where the computer displays information — its output. On an all-in-one PC, the monitor and box are the same thing. Otherwise, don't assume that the "computer" dwells inside the monitor. The monitor merely displays stuff. Some computers may sport two monitors, one for each eye. See Chapter 9 for the specifics.

Keyboard: The keyboard is the thing you type on and is the primary way you communicate with the computer. This gizmo has the most buttons — over 100 — including many you'll never use.

Pointing device: Computers need a pointing device, generically called a *mouse*, to help manipulate graphical goobers on the monitor. Pointing devices come in many shapes and sizes, from the traditional computer mouse to weird science-fictiony things. And yes, *graphical goober* is official computer jargon.

Speakers: Computers bleep and squawk through a set of stereo speakers, which can be separate devices (refer to Figure 2-2) or built into the computer box or monitor. You can also use headphones or just duct-tape the speakers to the side of your head. For more realistic sound, you can obtain computer surround sound hardware and a subwoofer to sit under your desk. It's worth the extra cost just to frighten the neighbors.

Webcam: The webcam is used for online chat and virtual meetings, and to make you nervous that someone is spying on you. It can be part of the monitor or perched atop the monitor like a creepy electronic bird.

External drive: You may not have one (yet), but an external hard drive is necessary to *back up*, or create a safety copy of, the important stuff you store on your computer. See Chapter 22 for details on computer backup.

Printer: The printer is where you get the computer's printed output, also called *hard copy*. This device is connected directly to your computer or is found on the local network. Chapter 12 covers computer printers.

One thing deliberately not shown in Figure 2-2 is the ganglion of cable that dwells behind all computers. What a mess! These cables are required in order to plug things into the wall and into each other. No shampoo or conditioner on Earth can clean up those tangles, though keep in mind that wireless connection options are readily available.

>> Items outside the computer box are known as *peripherals*. Even the keyboard, mouse, and monitor are considered "peripheral," despite their being an essential part of the computer system. Nerds debate me on this point, but I'm writing the book. So there.

>> Take a moment to identify the basic computer parts in your own computer system.

>> CPU stands for central *processing* unit. It's another term for the computer processor, not for the computer box. See Chapter 6 for the deets.

**TECHNICAL
STUFF**

Finding interesting things on the box's front

You would think it would be logical to place controls and connections useful for humans on the front part of a computer. Alas, there is no logic in the computer industry. For years, computers set all the interesting items on the back. Only recently have computer designers determined that humans sit in front of a computer and might need access to those items shown in Figure 2-3.

Optical drive: A few minitower PCs come with an optical drive, though the technology is sorely dated. CDs and DVDs don't hold enough data for them to be useful, which is why many new computers lack this feature.

Future expansion: Desktop-model PCs feature blank spots on their front panel. These are hole covers for future expansion.

Media card slots: Into these slots and slits you insert media cards, such as those used by digital cameras and other portable electronics. Your PC may have only one media card slot, or, as shown in Figure 2-3, it can sport a 19-in-1 card reader to accept all media card formats. See Chapter 8 for details on all computer storage devices.

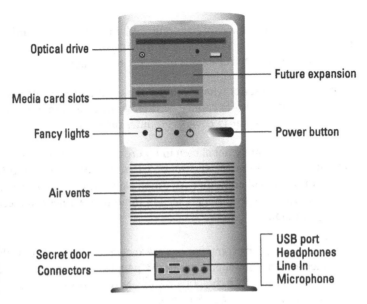

Optical drive

Future expansion

Media card slots

Fancy lights

Power button

Air vents

FIGURE 2-3:
Items of note
on the front of
the console.

Secret door
Connectors

USB port
Headphones
Line In
Microphone

Power button: No longer a plain on–off button, the power button does more than just turn the computer on or off. Chapter 4 discloses the power button's secrets.

Lights: Computers in the movies are festooned with lights, but in the real world you may find only one: the power lamp. A second lamp may flicker as storage is agitated, which is primarily for festive purposes.

Air vents: Air vents keep the console cool by helping air circulate inside. Do not set anything in front of the computer's air vents, not even as a joke.

I/O panel: The most interesting item found on the front of a desktop PC is the I/O panel. In this location you find various connectors useful to humans who operate computers: audio connectors, USB ports, and more. These are gizmos you may need to plug and unplug from time to time. See the section "The I/O panel," later in this chapter.

Don't be disappointed should your computer lack any of these features or you can't find them as shown in Figure 2-3. For example, an all-in-one PC has similar items but on the side of the monitor. And, if you truly desire an optical drive, you can obtain one from the local antique shop.

Stuff found on a desktop PC's rump

Just like an exotic dancer, a desktop PC's backside is a busy place. This is where you find connectors for the many devices in the computer system. Use Figure 2-4 as a guide for discovering these important items on the back of the PC box. Their location and visual appearance may look different from what's shown, and some may be missing; not every PC is the same.

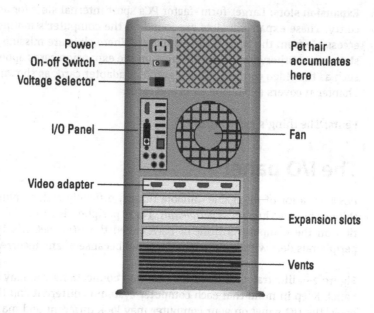

Power

On-off Switch

Voltage Selector

Pet hair accumulates here

I/O Panel

Fan

Video adapter

Expansion slots

FIGURE 2-4:
Important
doodads on
the computer's
backside.

Vents

Power: Computers crave power. The power connector is where you plug in the PC's power cord. Computers work faster when connected to power.

Fans: You may find two fans on the PC's rump, as illustrated in Figure 2-4. One belongs to the power supply. The other cools the computer box. Air gets sucked or blown out, I forget which.

On–off switch: The power supply's on–off switch isn't the computer's power button. Don't use it to turn off the computer! Its purpose is to disable the power supply for troubleshooting or repair. Keep the switch in the On position. Not every PC features this switch.

Voltage selector: Use this switch to change power frequencies to match the specifications for your country, region, or planet. This switch is part of the power supply.

I/O panel: Aside from the power cord, and anything attached to an expansion card, the rest of your PC's plug-in-type things are connected on this panel, which I call the I/O panel. Details of what you can find there are covered in the next section.

Video adapter: This item is the rear end of an internal expansion card — an extra piece of circuitry — designed to control one or more monitors connected to the computer. See Chapter 9 for more information.

Expansion slots: Larger form-factor PCs sport internal slots for adding new circuitry. These expansion slots are found on the computer's motherboard but are accessible from the back of the computer. Where slots are missing, you see blank slot covers. Otherwise, any connectors on the expansion cards appear in this area, such as the video connectors on a graphics adapter card, as shown in Figure 2-4. Chapter 11 covers expansion slots and cards.

Vents: The thing's gotta breathe.

The I/O panel

PCs host a lot of pluggable-innable things, officially called "pluggable-innable things" but also known as *peripherals*. These peripherals connect to a central location on the computer's front or back called the *I/O panel*. It's I/O because the peripherals deal with input and output, not because of any incurred debt.

Figure 2-5 illustrates some of the common connections you may find on the I/O panel. Keep in mind that each computer system is different and that, unlike this book, the I/O panel on your computer may look different and many of the items are in color.

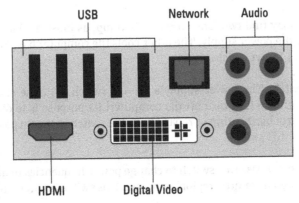

USB   Network   Audio

HDMI   Digital Video

FIGURE 2-5: Stuff to find on the I/O panel.

Here are some I/O panel highlights:

USB: The keyboard, mouse, printer, scanner, and just about everything else plugs into these Certs-size Universal Serial Bus (USB) ports (holes). That's why the standard is "universal." See Chapter 10 for more information about USB.

Network: Connect the network (local-area network, or LAN) cable here. Part 3 of this book covers networking.

Audio: Into these colorful holes you connect the computer's speakers and microphone. Multiple audio connections allow for surround sound.

Video: The PC's monitor connects to one of the video adapters on the I/O panel, which can be an HDMI connector or a DV (digital video) connector, as illustrated in Figure 2-5. Other connectors include DP (DisplayPort) and possibly the antique VGA connector. See Chapter 9 for details.

The good news about connecting cables to the PC's rear I/O panel is that it's typically done only once. Then the computer's butt faces the wall for the rest of its life and you never have to look at it again — well, unless you add something in the future or you just enjoy looking at PC butts.

>> USB connectors are also present on the front of the computer, as illustrated earlier, in Figure 2-3. Use these connections for thumb drives and other items you attach and remove frequently.

>> The video connection on the I/O panel uses the system's display adapter. It's better to use a display adapter card, which provides high-power video output. See Chapter 9.

>> Connectors for a microphone and headphones are also found on the PC's front I/O panel, illustrated earlier, in Figure 2-3. You can use either set.

>> Audio connections are color-coded to help identify what-plugs-into-what but also to confound people who are colorblind. The speakers or headphones connect to the lime green jack; microphones connect to the pink jack. Other connectors' color codes are inconsistent, which keeps everyone guessing.

Laptop Exploration

If a laptop were merely a miniaturized desktop PC, writing this chapter would be a lot easier. Then again, you'd need super tiny hands and long skinny fingers to use the device. Though such an image is hilarious, it's best that a laptop is its own computer, capable like a desktop system but with its own set of features worthy of exploration.

Major parts on a typical PC laptop are shown in Figure 2-6. These are the same items found on a desktop PC, but not in the same location nor with the same abundance. Some items are missing, in fact. For example, rare is the laptop that has a wired network connection; all laptops use Wi-Fi (wireless) network access, which helps boost their light, carefree, wireless existence.

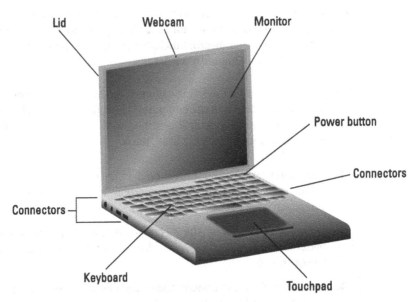

FIGURE 2-6:
Laptop things and
their names.

Major parts of a laptop include:

Lid: This top part of the laptop swings upward, allowing you to access the keyboard and view the screen. Some laptop lids swing right up. Other laptops require that you press a button or slide a release to free the hinged lid.

Webcam: Center-top on the screen is the webcam, used for online meetings and taking goofy pictures of yourself.

Monitor: The laptop's lid serves as its monitor, the screen on which computer information appears. Many laptops feature touchscreen monitors, which allow you to use your fingers to smear and smudge the display.

Power button: The laptop's power button might masquerade as a key on the keyboard, or it may be a separate button lurking elsewhere. Chapter 4 discloses the secrets.

Keyboard: The laptop's keyboard tries its best to work just like a full-size keyboard found on a desktop. Alas, it falls short. See Chapter 10 to review the differences between the two keyboard types.

Connectors: External items use holes (*ports*) on the laptop's edges and back. These include USB ports, power cord connectors, audio jacks for headphones or speakers, external monitor connections, and other mystery holes.

Touchpad: This area serves as the laptop's pointing device — its "mouse." Chapter 10 describes its use.

TIP

>> See Part 3 of this book for details on accessing the network and Internet from your laptop.

>> For security reasons, many laptop users conceal the webcam. I recommend using a Band-Aid to cover the webcam because the soft part won't damage the webcam lens. Remove the Band-Aid whenever you need to use the webcam.

>> Be aware that covering the webcam lens doesn't mute the laptop's microphone. See Chapter 21 for details on system security.

>> The USB C port can be used to connect not only various peripheral gizmos but also an external monitor. On some laptops, the USB C port also serves to charge the laptop. The USB galaxy of ports is covered in Chapter 11.

>> One of the holes on your laptop might be an SD card slot, into which you can insert a media card.

>> Larger-format laptops may include a full-size keyboard, including the numeric keypad. These gunboat-sized laptops are designed for high-end uses, like playing video games. Their battery life is dismal.

>> Some laptops may feature a replaceable battery and even a spot to add or remove a mass storage device. Look on the laptop's bottom for these features.

IN THIS CHAPTER

» Setting up your desktop or laptop

» Connecting computer cables

» Attaching things to the computer

» Using a power strip

» Managing with a UPS

Chapter **3**

Setup, Connections, and Power

I could lie to you and cheerfully extol how setting up a PC is so simple that a child could do it. A Vulcan child, perhaps. Even so, it's possible for a mere mortal to assemble a computer. You may find this task more enjoyable than assembling backyard play equipment or setting the time on your microwave oven. The process all boils down to what-plugs-into-what.

Desktop PC Assembly

Getting a new desktop computer is a time of both delight and dread. The lure of new technology is always exciting; the fresh smell of overseas air as you unpack the box can be intoxicating. The chore of assembling the thing may not be as thrilling, but it's a necessary step.

» Your computer runs faster when you take it out of the box.

» Ensure that you sift through all packing materials inside the computer box. Sometimes, manufacturers stick important items, such as power cables or remote controls, inside the packing material.

>> Keep all boxes and packing materials. You need them should it be necessary to return the computer or ship it elsewhere to be fixed. Also, use the box to store the computer when you move; some movers don't insure a computer unless it's packed in the original box.

Finding a place for the computer box

The main computer box is the locus of all PC activities, so you should set it up first. Clear a swath of your desk for the box. Set aside space for the monitor and any peripherals. If you plan to place the box beneath the desk, put it there now.

If possible, pull the desk away from the wall so that you have room to squeeze back there and get work done. All computers need space between the desk and the wall to hang cables. If the desk has a hole in it, gently shove the cables through this hole.

>> The computer must breathe! Don't place it in a confined space or inside a cabinet without proper air circulation.

>> Avoid setting the computer by a window where the sun can heat it. Like city road crews, computers don't like to operate in extreme heat — or extreme cold, for that matter. A PC is happiest when it operates at temperatures between 40°F (4°C) and 80°F (27°C).

>> If you compute in an area with high humidity, ensure that the computer room is air-conditioned. Yes, computers can grow mold in the proper environment.

Setting the monitor

After setting up the computer box, it's time to position other items — the *peripherals* — around the main computer box, like small deities worshiping a larger, angrier main deity. Chief among these peripherals is the monitor.

The monitor sits next to a minitower PC or atop one of the smaller form-factor computers. Do not set the monitor on top of the computer box unless it resides there safely without wobbling. Also be aware that some smaller computer boxes aren't designed to support the heft of a large computer monitor.

As far as positioning the monitor, remember that it normally sits behind the keyboard. Place it an arm's length or greater from the edge of the desk. You can always adjust it later, if need be, but make room for it now.

TIP

Very large monitors can be affixed to a wall by using a special arm-hangy-bracket-thing. The special arm-hangy-bracket-thing is extra and should be affixed to the wall by trained arm-hangy-bracket-thing professionals.

Laptop Setup

Laptops are delightfully self-contained and mobile. You can use a laptop computer anywhere — including your lap. Unlike a desktop PC, after the laptop is freed from its box, it's ready to go. Well, you must charge its battery, so:

Look for the power cord in the laptop's shipping box. The power cord may come in two pieces: the cord itself and a box-thing that the cord plugs into. The box-thing has its own cord that connects to the laptop. Figure 3-1 illustrates how these connections might look.

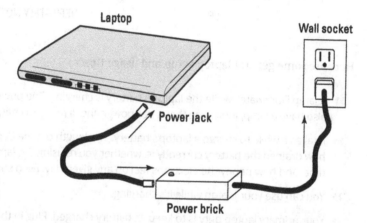

FIGURE 3-1:
Charging
the battery.

Charge the battery: Connect the power cord to the laptop and a power source. There. You're done with laptop setup.

You can start using the laptop as it charges. See Chapter 4 for details. But before then, consider where to stow your laptop when you're not on the road. As you do so, consider the well-being of your back or neck, which can suffer unduly if you abuse them while using a laptop.

Ensure that your arms are extended level with the keyboard for the best typing posture. Adjust the lid so that the laptop's screen presents itself at an appropriate angle. Use Figure 3-2 as your guide.

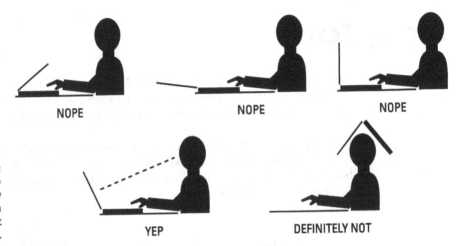

FIGURE 3-2: Adjust the lid so that you can view the screen at an angle that's just right for you.

Here are some general laptop setup and usage tips:

TIP

REMEMBER

>> A lamp illuminates while the laptop's battery is charging. The power cord may also have a lamp, indicating that it has power and is ready to charge.

>> It takes a while to charge a laptop's battery. The length of time depends on how drained the battery currently is, whether you're using the laptop at the time, and how peppy the electrons feel on any given day. Even so:

>> You can use your laptop while it's charging.

>> Your primary laptop duty is to keep its battery charged. Plug in the laptop when you're not using it. When you're using it and power is available, keep it plugged in. Doing so doesn't diminish battery life.

>> Chapter 18 offers oodles of tips and suggestions for getting the most from your laptop's battery.

>> Use the laptop on a flat, steady surface. The laptop's underside has air vents to help keep it cool. Setting the laptop on a pillow or another uneven surface makes the laptop run hotter than it would like.

>> Keep the laptop away from the sun, if possible. Heat isn't good for any computer, but you can't see the screen in direct sunlight (or else you'll waste battery power turning up the screen-brightness level).

>> Keep Mr. Laptop away from, or out of spilling range of, any drinks or food you might be consuming.

>> Have a place to store your laptop when it's not in use: in a drawer, on a shelf, or as part of an art mural you purchased at a street fair, titled "Technology is making us less human." Keeping your laptop in the same location means that you can always find it when you need it.

>> See Chapter 19 for information on finding a good laptop bag, perhaps the most important laptop accessory.

TIP

The Plug-In Guide

Both desktop and laptop computer designs feature holes into which you can connect various electronic gizmos to expand the system's hardware potential. Desktops feature more pluggable-innable items, but laptops aren't entirely free from these technological tethers.

>> All major parts of a desktop computer system plug directly into the main computer box.

>> Wait to turn on the main computer box until after you've connected all the pieces.

>> Plug powered peripherals into the computer box before you plug them into the wall.

>> It's generally okay to plug something into a computer while the system is on, though for first-time setup, I recommend keeping everything off.

>> See Chapter 11 for information on using USB devices, which includes just about every peripheral known in the PC kingdom. That chapter also covers using Bluetooth to wirelessly connect peripherals to your computer.

>> A hole into which you plug a computer cable is called a *port*. This word defines not only the shape of the hole and the connector type but also the technology used to control the connected device.

TECHNICAL
STUFF

KNOW YOUR COMPUTER CABLES

A computer cable is known by which port it plugs into. For example, USB cables plug into USB ports.

The ends of a computer cable are configured so that you cannot plug in the cable incorrectly: The connectors insert only one way. When the connectors are the same shape, it doesn't matter which end plugs in where.

All cables fasten snugly. Network cables have little tabs on them that snap when the cable is properly inserted. You must squeeze the tab to remove the cable. Antique video connectors have tiny thumbscrews on the side, which help cinch the cable into the connector.

Some devices, such as the keyboard and mouse, are permanently attached to their cables. Other cables are connected at both ends: one for the computer and the other for the attached device.

If needed, extra cables can be purchased at any office supply store. As a suggestion, measure the distance for which you need a cable, and then double it to get a cable of the proper length. For example, if it's 2 feet between your computer and printer, you need at least a 4-foot cable.

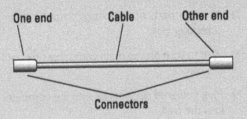

Plugging in the monitor

Monitors have both a power cable and a data cable. The *power cable* connects to a wall socket. The *data cable* connects to the main computer box. These cables may be permanently connected to the monitor, or they may exist as their own cables, free to wander Earth in search of religious fulfillment.

Two popular ports are used for the monitor's data cable: HDMI and DisplayPort (DP). These two cables have similar connections, so be mindful of the differences.

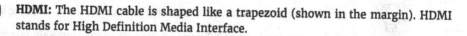 **HDMI:** The HDMI cable is shaped like a trapezoid (shown in the margin). HDMI stands for High Definition Media Interface.

DisplayPort (DP): The DP cable is shaped like a rectangle with a cut corner.

The monitor's cable may be attached or come separately. If it's separate, first attach the cable to the monitor, which is an awkward process and may require a flashlight and goggles. Next, connect the monitor's cable to the graphics adapter port on the computer. If the computer features a display adapter card, connect the cable to a port on the expansion card — do not use the adapter on the I/O panel. When multiple ports are available on the expansion card, you can choose any one.

You can also plug in a monitor to your laptop for use when the laptop is stationary, though this technique is also how projectors are connected to laptops for giving those mind-numbing PowerPoint presentations. Laptops use either the USB-C or Mini DisplayPort connections to attach a monitor. USB-C adapter/converters are available to connect DisplayPort or HDMI cables to a laptop's USB-C port.

>> The monitor also requires power. See the later section "It Must Have Power."

>> Some monitors act as a USB hub, hosting one or more USB ports. This feature requires that the monitor also connect to a USB port on the computer box (or on any other connected USB hub). See Chapter 11 for more information on USB connections and hubs.

TECHNICAL STUFF

>> DisplayPort (DP) is considered the superior technology to HDMI, preferred by gamers who enjoy quick graphics. Whether a monitor has HDMI or DP connections is up to the manufacturer.

>> See Chapter 9 for more information about PC monitors and graphics.

Attaching the keyboard and mouse to a desktop PC

The traditional location for a desktop computer's keyboard is between you and the monitor. The mouse (pointing device) dwells to the right or left of the keyboard, depending on whether you're right- or left-handed.

>> Wired keyboards and pointing devices use a USB cable to connect to the main computer box.

>> Wireless keyboards must be configured to work with the computer. See Chapter 11.

>> If the keyboard features its own USB port, connect the mouse to this USB port.

>> I recommend using USB ports on the back of the computer box for connecting the keyboard and pointing device. This location means the cable is less likely to be accidentally disconnected.

>> Don't use the blue-colored USB 3.0 ports to connect a keyboard or mouse — unless the keyboard or mouse cable features a blue USB connector. Save the USB 3.0 ports for high-speed devices, like external drives.

Connecting to a wired network

The cable for a wired computer network connects to a desktop PC's I/O panel located on the box's rump. Laptops primarily use Wi-Fi, though if a wired connection is available, it's found on the laptop's side or back. The wired connection attaches only one way and snaps into place.

More networking information is offered in Part 3 of this book, including details on making a wireless connection.

Hooking up a printer

A printer is either added directly to the computer or accessed over the network, which is more common. For a home or office with only one computer, use a USB cable to plug the printer into the main computer box or the laptop. That's it.

Printers also require power. As with other powered devices, connect the printer's data cable (the USB cable) first before plugging in its power cord.

See Chapter 12 for printing duties.

Adding audio stuff

Desktop and laptop PCs have built-in speakers. These devices are remarkable in that the sound quality is extremely bad. Therefore, you probably want better audio output devices.

For a laptop, you can use the single audio jack (hole) to connect a set of earbuds, headphones, or speakers.

For a desktop, you can add headphones or speakers. For speakers, I recommend connecting them to the rear audio jacks. For headphones, use the audio jacks on the front of the box. Speakers and headphones connect to the lime green audio jack.

Laptops also feature built-in microphones, so you have no need to purchase an extra one. A desktop, however, has no microphone. You can purchase a separate microphone or buy a headset, which is a combination of headphones and microphone.

Microphones connect to the pink audio jack. A headset plugs into both the green (speaker) jack as well as the pink (microphone) jack.

TIP

>> As an alternative to using the audio jacks, you can connect USB speakers, microphones, or headsets. Oftentimes, these devices are far more reliable than those using standard audio jacks.

>> Some desktops have special audio hardware, which you can determine by looking at the back of the computer box for audio connectors on an expansion slot cover. If your system is configured this way, plug the speakers into the audio card's output jacks, not those on the I/O panel.

It Must Have Power

Computer devices seek three sources for power:

>> Wireless gizmos use batteries.

>> Some devices use their USB cable for power.

>> Greedy peripherals require a wall socket for power.

This section covers those devices that require wall socket power and how best to connect them to complete your computer system.

Plugging everything into a power strip

A computer system has far more devices than available wall sockets. This deficiency is why Thomas Edison invented power strips. The idea is to plug everything into a power strip and then plug the power strip into the wall, as illustrated in Figure 3-3.

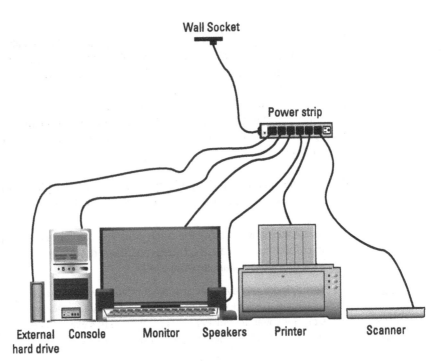

Wall Socket

Power strip

FIGURE 3-3:
Plug in computer
stuff like this.

External   Console   Monitor   Speakers   Printer   Scanner
hard drive

Follow these steps:

1. **Ensure that all the gizmos have their on–off switches in the Off position.**

   Don't worry if the device has a power button where you can't determine whether it's on or off. If it's not plugged in, it's off.

2. **Ensure that the power strip is in the Off position.**

3. **Plug everything into the power strip.**

Directions for turning on the computer system are provided in Chapter 4.

TIP

>> Try to find a power strip with line noise filtering. Even better, pay more to buy a power strip that has line conditioning! Such technology defends delicate electronics from the savage electrical beasts roaming the power lines. See the nearby sidebar, "Surges, spikes, and lightning strikes."

>> Try to find a power strip that arranges its sockets in a manner to accommodate the bulky plugs and connectors used by computer equipment — for example, where the sockets are perpendicular to the power strip.

WARNING

>> Don't plug one power strip into another power strip. Doing so is electrically unsafe!

>> A laser printer must be connected directly to a wall socket. It says so in your laser printer's setup directions — if you ever get around to reading them.

SURGES, SPIKES, AND LIGHTNING STRIKES

The power that comes from the wall socket into your computer isn't composed of pure energy, not like Trelane in the *Star Trek* episode "The Squire of Gothos." No, the power may be corrupted by some of the various electrical nasties that, every now and then, come uninvited into your home or office. Here's the lowdown:

Line noise: Interference on the power line, often caused by an electric motor on the same circuit. For example, an AM radio turns staticky when you use the blender. That's line noise.

Surge: A gradual increase in power.

Sérge: Some guy from Europe.

Spike: A sudden increase in power. Spikes happen when lightning strikes nearby. Always shut down computer equipment and even unplug it from the wall should a lightning storm rage nearby.

Dip: The opposite of a surge; a decrease in power. Some electrical motors don't work, and room lights are dimmer than normal. Dips are referred to as *brownouts*.

Power outage: An absence of power coming through the line, commonly called a *blackout*.

Taking advantage of a UPS

Forget about overnighting that fancy new slow cooker. For your computer's power supply, UPS stands for uninterruptible power supply. Basically, a *UPS* is a power strip combined with a battery to keep your computer running when the power goes out.

Figure 3-4 illustrates the proper way to connect a computer system to a UPS and power strip. Not shown is the USB cable that connects the UPS to the console to alert the computer about a power outage. Yes, in addition to being a fancy power strip, the UPS is yet another computer peripheral.

Please dash those visions you have of continuing to use your computer while the rest of the neighborhood is watching Netflix on their smartphones in the dark. No, the UPS is designed to keep your basic computer components — the main box and monitor — up and running just long enough for you to save your work and properly shut down the system. The goal is not to lose anything due to a sudden power outage.

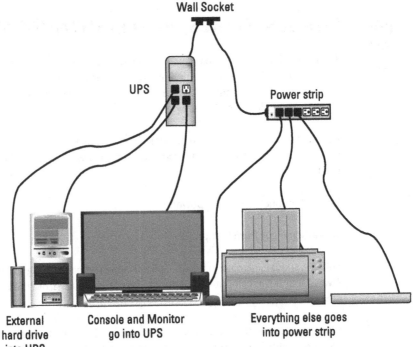

Wall Socket

UPS

Power strip

FIGURE 3-4:
Hooking
up to a UPS.

**External
hard drive
into UPS**

**Console and Monitor
go into UPS**

**Everything else goes
into power strip**

Come to think of it, all power outages are sudden. Anyway, the point is to save your data, not to keep computing, which would quickly drain the UPS battery anyway.

>> Ignore what it says on the box: A UPS gives you *maybe* 5 minutes of computer power. Most often, you get only 2 minutes of power.

>> Some UPS systems also have non-battery-backed-up sockets where you can plug in noncritical peripherals. Just ensure that the monitor and console are plugged into the battery-backed-up sockets.

>> I also recommend plugging external drives into the UPS's battery-backed-up sockets.

TIP

>> Leave the UPS on all the time. Turn it off only when the power is out and the computer has been properly shut down.

>> In addition to providing emergency power, a UPS provides higher levels of electrical protection for your equipment. Many models offer surge, spike, and dip protection, which keeps your PC running smoothly despite any nasties the power company may send your way.

» Laptops do not need to be plugged into a UPS. Laptops have their own battery backup.

Using the UPS (a short play)

Interior upscale kitchen. A thunderclap is heard. The lights flicker and then go out. ROGER, 40ish and nerdy, is left sitting in the dark, his computer still on. The UPS beeps once every few seconds. FELICIA rushes in. She is pretentious, but not insufferably so.

FELICIA: The power is out! The brioche I put in the toaster oven is ruined! Did you lose that urgent doodle you were creating in Windows Paint?

ROGER: No, darling, I'm still working on it. See? Our UPS has kept the computer and monitor turned on despite this dreadful power outage.

FELICIA: Oh! That explains the beeping.

ROGER: Yes, the UPS beeps when the power has gone out. It does that just in case I failed to observe the pitch darkness.

FELICIA: Well, hurry up and print your doodle!

ROGER: Not now, sugarplum! Printing can wait, which is why I didn't connect the printer to the UPS. It's as powerless as the toaster oven.

FELICIA: What can you do? Hurry! The UPS battery won't last forever!

ROGER: Relax, gentle spouse. I shall save the doodle to the PC's main mass storage device, thus. *(He presses Ctrl+S on the keyboard.)* Now I may shut down the computer, assured with the knowledge that my glorious artwork is safely stored. There. *(He turns off the computer and monitor. He shuts off the UPS and the beeping ceases.)* Now we can weather the storm with peace of mind.

Two hours later, after the power is back on, FELICIA and ROGER are sipping wine.

FELICIA: Honey, you certainly demonstrated your Ivy League pedigree with the way you used that UPS.

ROGER: Well, I'm just thankful I read Dan Gookin's book *PCs For Dummies*, from Wiley. I think I shall buy more of his books, as well as visit his website at wambooli.com and like his page on LinkedIn.

FELICIA: Who knew that we could find such happiness, thanks to a computer book?

They canoodle.

IN THIS CHAPTER

» Turning on a desktop computer

» Starting up a laptop

» Getting into Windows

» Exploring parts of the
operating system

» Accessing the Action Center

» Using the Settings app

Chapter 4

To Turn On a Computer

ike certain staple-pierced models of times gone by, your computer has a zodiac sign and measurements, as well as a list of turn-ons and turn-offs. The biggest turn-on for a computer is its own power button. In fact, in various cultures, the power button must be concealed behind a heavy curtain in the adults-only section. Truly, touching a power button causes all sorts of things to happen.

Turn On the Computer

In the book *Lamps For Dummies* (Wiley), the author devotes two entire chapters to the topic of turning on a lamp, which I feel is a tad excessive. In this book, which covers a far more technologically challenging topic, I devote only this single section to the vital topic of turning on the complex device called a computer.

Powering on a desktop PC

The term "powering on" accurately describes turning on a desktop computer. It's the noise that makes the difference. Fans whirring to life gives Mr. PC a sense of power. Your digital day is dawning.

When the computer system is connected to separate wall sockets, follow these steps to get things started:

1. **Turn on everything but the main computer box.**

   Press the power button or flip the on–off switch on the peripheral items. Look for the monitor's power button on the bottom edge, though manufacturers do enjoy hiding the monitor's power button. See Chapter 9 for monitor mayhem.

2. **Turn on the main computer box.**

   Press the power button on the front of the box.

When the computer system's gizmos are all plugged into a power strip, turn on the power strip. Some items may come to life instantly. For others, you may need to press the power button.

REMEMBER

>> By turning on the main computer box last, you allow time for the other devices in the computer system to initialize and get ready for work. This way, the system recognizes these peripherals faster and more consistently.

>> Not all computer devices have their own on–off switches. For example, some USB devices — scanners and external storage — use the USB port's power. These devices are on when the computer system is on.

>> Some devices can be left on all the time. For example, the printer may have an energy-saving mode that allows you to keep it on all the time. It's often better to keep these devices on than to turn them on or off several times a day.

>> Power buttons are marked with the universal on-off icon, shown in the margin. Enjoy the fact that computer designs like to color this icon dark gray and set it on a black background.

TIP

>> When something doesn't turn on, ensure that it's plugged into power or properly connected to the computer box. Cables must be connected at both ends.

Turning on a laptop

The *laptop* is the entire computer, though it may be connected to various peripherals when you keep it in one spot. There or on the road, the steps for firing up a laptop are as follows:

1. **Orient the laptop.**

   The lid opens away from you, but the tricky part is that any logo on the lid appears upside-down when you're looking at the laptop. This orientation means that the logo is right side up when the lid is open. This way, people know that you're working on an ASUS laptop instead of a S∩S∀. Yes, people are that dumb.

2. **Open the lid.**

Some laptops may have a latch you must release. Otherwise, the lid swings up and away from you.

3. **Locate and press the power button.**

Some laptops may turn on automatically when you open the lid.

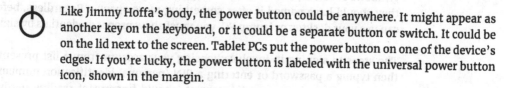

Like Jimmy Hoffa's body, the power button could be anywhere. It might appear as another key on the keyboard, or it could be a separate button or switch. It could be on the lid next to the screen. Tablet PCs put the power button on one of the device's edges. If you're lucky, the power button is labeled with the universal power button icon, shown in the margin.

Upon success, the laptop comes to life. If nothing happens when you punch the button, the laptop's battery is most likely dead. Use the AC adapter to plug the laptop into a wall socket.

Here Comes Windows

Computer hardware is dumb. It needs software to make it work. The main piece of software in charge of all the hardware and all the other software is the *operating system*. For PC laptops and desktops, the operating system is Microsoft Windows, which you may recognize as a punch line from the jokes that nerds like to tell.

>> As a PC starts, you first see the manufacturer's brand logo. As the operating system takes over, you see the Windows logo.

>> When you first turn on a brand-new computer, or after a Windows system update, you find yourself confronted with a series of questions and configuration options. These include items such as the language you use, the time zone, your user account information, and where you hide your valuables.

>> Though you don't need a Microsoft account to sign in to Windows, using or creating such an account has advantages. For example, Windows remembers your settings across multiple computers when you sign in with the same account.

>> Another key step to a computer's initial configuration is to connect to the Internet. See Part 3 of this book.

>> Laptops use the same version of Windows that's used on desktop PCs. Extra options are available for laptops; specifically, for power management and battery monitoring.

>> When creating a user account, *do not* forget your password! The password cannot be recovered if it's lost. I recommend writing it down in a secure place.

Identifying yourself

Windows is so suspicious that you might not be who you say you are that I think they should have named it after something more opaque. Regardless, before you can use your desktop or laptop PC, you must show proper credentials by signing in.

The steps to signing in involve choosing your account from a list presented and then typing a password or entering a PIN (personal identification number). On a laptop, you can also scan a fingerprint, should fingerprint reading hardware be available.

Press the Enter key if you use a password to sign in. You don't need to press Enter when typing a PIN or using the fingerprint reader.

Figure 4-1 illustrates the Windows 11 sign-in screen. Other versions of Windows look similar.

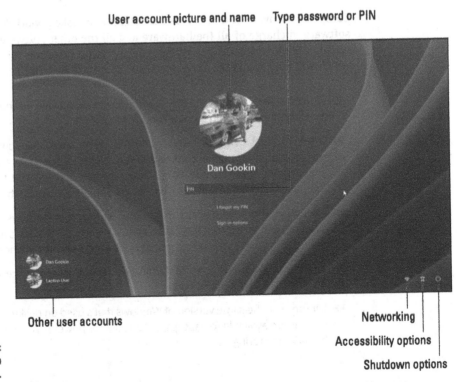

FIGURE 4-1:
Signing in
to Windows.

If the computer hosts multiple users and your account isn't the one shown center screen (refer to Figure 4-1), choose your user account from the list in the lower left corner of the screen. For some versions of Windows, if you don't see your account name listed, choose the Switch User option.

When all goes well, you're signed in and can start using the computer.

>> The process of identifying yourself to the computer is called signing in, logging in, or logging on, depending on the version of Windows installed and whether you're from timber country.

>> The fingerprint reader works whether your finger is attached or not. And yes, you watch too many spy movies.

>> Mind the Caps Lock key on the keyboard! Passwords are case-sensitive.

TIP

Staring at the desktop

After you sign in, the next thing that appears is the Windows desktop. This glorious graphical gateway presents the way the computer attempts to interface with you, a human. Figure 4-2 illustrates the Windows desktop and the interesting items you may find there.

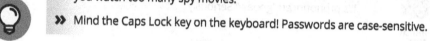

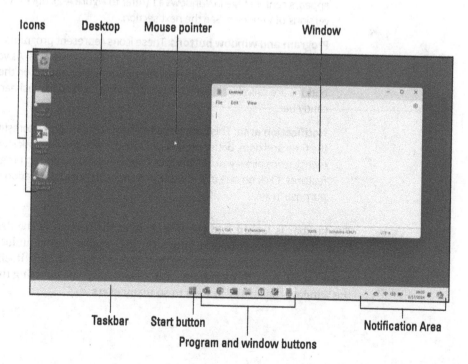

FIGURE 4-2:
The Windows desktop and all its trappings.

Icons   Desktop   Mouse pointer   Window

Taskbar   Start button   Notification Area

Program and window buttons

Despite all the distractions, the *desktop* is the place where the actual windows appear in Windows. These are the graphical containers for your programs, games, and other frivolity.

>> If the desktop is overburdened with windows or other distractions, press the Win+D keyboard shortcut: Press and hold the Windows key and tap the D key. The detritus blows away to reveal the full Windows desktop.

>> The desktop is called a *desktop* for traditional reasons. Early graphical operating systems featured an interface that really did look like a desktop, complete with paper pad, clock, glue, scissors, and other desktop-y things.

>> The Windows operating system is known as a GUI, or graphical user interface. It's pronounced "gooey." Seriously.

Working the taskbar

The action in Windows takes place on the desktop, but everything starts at the taskbar. It appears as a ribbon lurking at the bottom of the screen, as shown in Figure 4-2. Here are some fun things to identify on the taskbar:

Start button: This icon is where you start programs and control Windows. It appears center stage in Windows 11 (refer to Figure 4-2), but off to the left in older versions of Windows. See the next section.

Program and window buttons: These icons represent programs you can quickly start: Click once on an icon to launch its associated programs. As you open programs and windows, corresponding buttons also appear on the taskbar. These buttons are called *tasks*, which is why this area is called the taskbar and not the candy bar.

Notification area: This part of the taskbar is chock-full of interesting trivial tidbits: the time and date, battery status, volume control, and network status. Other teensy icons allow you to control or check on various running programs or features. Click on one of the wee icons to glean more information about its purpose in life.

The taskbar is locked into position, held at the bottom of the desktop by digital bolts made of the strongest bits. Still, the taskbar can be unlocked and moved wantonly to any screen edge. Further, the taskbar can hide itself, so it may not appear at all. It's this marvelous capability to keep you guessing that has endeared the Windows operating system to so many users.

Accessing the Start menu

The Start button abides on the taskbar. For Windows 11 it's located near the center, as shown back in Figure 4-2. For older versions of Windows, it lurks off to the left. It wanders.

Clicking the Start button pops up the Start menu, illustrated in Figure 4-3. Use this menu to start programs in Windows, but also to access various features.

Pinned or favorite apps   Display all apps (programs)

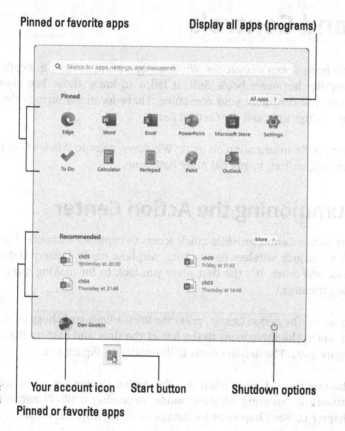

Your account icon   Start button   Shutdown options

Pinned or favorite apps

To view all programs installed on your computer, click the All Apps button, shown in Figure 4-3. Choose a program to start from the list that's displayed. Some programs are found in folders on the All Apps list: Open the folder, and then click the icon to start a program.

> **»** Computer programs are now referred to as *apps,* which is short for *application.* Using this abbreviation makes older computer industry executives feel more in touch with the kids.

>> The All Apps button is titled All Programs in earlier versions of Windows. Computer industry executives weren't so hip back then.

>> A quick way to pop up the Start button menu is to press the Win key on your computer's keyboard.

>> Press the Esc key to dismiss the Start menu when it bores you.

Settings and Controls

This book doesn't cover the Windows operating system in depth, because it's a computer hardware book. Still, it helps to know those key places in Windows where you configure your computer. These locations include the Action Center, the Settings app, and the Control Panel.

For specific information on using Windows, refer to *Windows For Dummies* (Wiley Empire), written by my pal Andy Rathbone.

Summoning the Action Center

The Action Center provides quick access to common computer hardware features. These include wireless networking, Airplane mode, battery status, volume controls, and more. It's the first place you look to for making quick adjustments to the computer.

To access the Action Center, press the Win+A keyboard shortcut. You can also click on any of the three icons to the left of the time and date on the taskbar (refer to Figure 4-2). The Action Center is illustrated in Figure 4-4.

The two times I most often use the Action Center are when accessing a Wi-Fi network or entering Airplane mode. Accessing a Wi-Fi network is covered in Chapter 14. See Chapter 19 for details on using Airplane mode.

>> The variety of controls shown in the Action Center depends on whether you're using a desktop or laptop. For example, in Figure 4-4 you see the Project button (as in slide show projector) and a slider to control display brightness. These items may not appear on a desktop computer's Action Center.

>> The battery status appears on a desktop computer if a UPS is connected. Refer to Chapter 3.

>> Use the Edit icon (refer to Figure 4-4) to add or remove items from the Action Center.

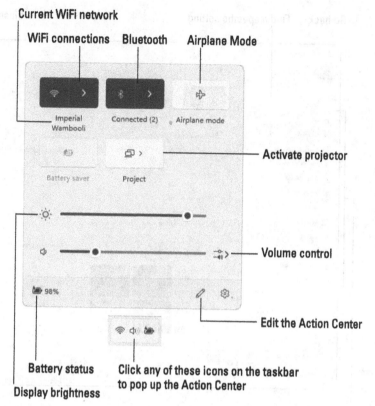

Current WiFi network

WiFi connections   Bluetooth   Airplane Mode

Imperial   Connected (2)   Airplane mode
Wambooli

Activate projector

Battery saver   Project

Volume control

98%

Edit the Action Center

FIGURE 4-4:   Battery status   Click any of these icons on the taskbar
The Action   to pop up the Action Center
Center.   Display brightness

TIP

>> If your desktop, laptop, or tablet features a touchscreen, swipe inward from the right edge of the screen to view the Action Center.

>> The Action Center looks different in Windows 10, though all the controls are present, as illustrated in Figure 4-4.

Using the Settings app

In the battle between the Settings app and the original Windows Control Panel, the Settings app is winning. You must know how to get to this vital location where all sorts of computer features are controlled and manipulated. Despite its new-found prominence, The Settings app may occasionally (and bashfully) send you off to the Control Panel. See the next section.

To summon the Settings app, press the Win+I keyboard shortcut. Why the letter I? *I* dunno. Perhaps it's this: "*I* summon the Settings app!" Anyway, the Settings app changes its look from time to time. Figure 4-5 shows its current incarnation as this book goes to press.

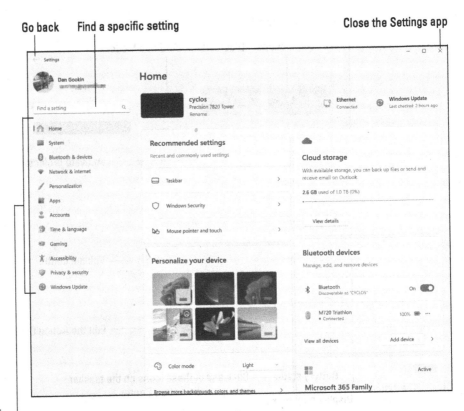

Go back   Find a specific setting   Close the Settings app

FIGURE 4-5:
The Settings app.

Categories

The Settings app window lists major categories on the left side of its window. The main window, Home, shown in Figure 4-5, provides an excellent summary of your PC's condition plus some shortcuts to popular settings and a few advertisements because Microsoft enjoys pleasing its shareholders.

Choose a category from the left, and then navigate to specific settings. Use the Back button (upper left) to return to the previous category.

TIP

Use the Search bar in the Settings app (refer to figure 4-5) to quickly locate a specific setting. This approach is often easier than wading through the menus, trying to guess where a specific setting is buried.

After you've changed or checked a setting, close the Settings app: Click the X button in the upper right corner of the window.

Visiting the Control Panel

For generations, the Control Panel has been the go-to spot for adjusting PC hardware and changing Windows settings. Then that new kid, the Settings app, barged in. Old programs get no respect.

To summon the Control Panel, heed these directions:

1. **Tap the Windows key on the keyboard to pop up the Start menu.**

2. **On the keyboard, type** control panel **— or just enough of it until you see the Control Panel item displayed on the left side of the Start button menu.**

3. **Choose the Control Panel (System) item.**

   The Control Panel appears, looking like Figure 4-6.

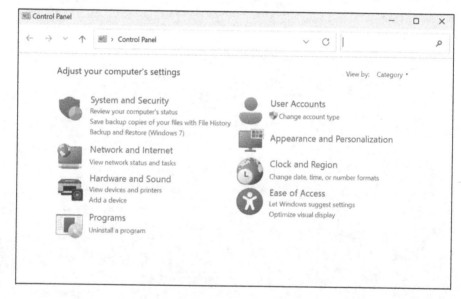

FIGURE 4-6:
The Control
Panel, Category
view.

To operate the Control Panel, choose a category or link. Sometimes, you need to click a few links to drill down to the specific spot you need. For example, to view a list of hardware devices available to your computer, below the heading Hardware and Sound, click the View Devices and Printers link.

Just to annoy you, some items available in the Control Panel are hidden from direct access. To view them, click the View By menu (refer to Figure 4-6) and choose one of the Icons views, Small or Large. In this view, you see all the Control Panel items.

IN THIS CHAPTER

» **Locating shutdown options**

» **Sleeping the computer**

» **Shutting down a PC**

» **Signing out of your account**

» **Changing the power button's function**

» **Leaving the computer on all the time**

Chapter **5**

To Turn Off a Computer

The first thought I had when I turned off my first computer was, "Will it be okay?" Turning off a strange, powerful, and expensive piece of hardware is scary! So after I flipped the on–off switch, I waited and then turned the machine back on to ensure that it survived. It did. But I went through a few more cycles, just to be sure.

Computers today lack on–off switches. They have a power button, which can be fickle. You can tell the Windows operating system what to do when you punch the power button — including the option of having the computer not do anything! This chapter covers the possibilities.

Goodnight, Computer

Nothing is more satisfying than turning off a computer by ripping its power cord from the wall. I've done it several times myself. Each time is met with a brief, mirthful smile. And although yanking out the cord works, it's not the best way to turn off a computer.

Finding the Windows power options

You don't really turn off a computer. No, Windows turns off the computer. It's a software operation. Remember that software controls hardware. In this instance, the software tells the computer to turn itself off.

Rather than be straightforward, Windows presents a slate of power options for turning off the system. Like most illogical things, these options appear on the Start menu: start to stop. Makes sense. Obey these directions:

1. **Summon the Start menu.**

   Click the Start button on the taskbar or tap the Windows key on the keyboard.

2. **Choose the Power icon on the Start menu.**

   Use Figure 5-1 as your guide. The figure shows the Windows 11 Start menu, though Windows 10 looks similar.

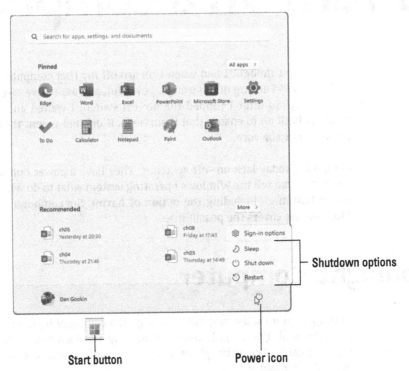

FIGURE 5-1:
Windows
power options.

Start button

Power icon

Shutdown options

The three power options shown in the figure are

>> Sleep

>> Shut Down

>> Restart

These options aren't the only way to end your Windows day. Other options appear on the left side of the Start menu, where you click your account button to review choices, as illustrated in Figure 5-2.

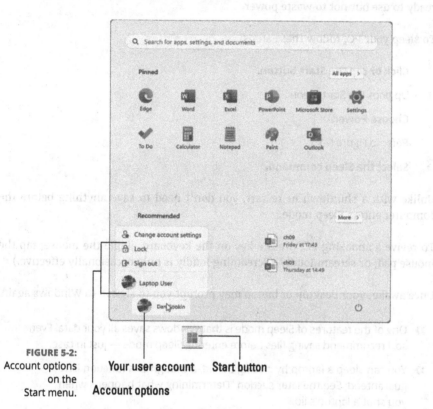

FIGURE 5-2:
Account options
on the
Start menu.

Your user account   Start button

Account options

The account options are

>> Lock

>> Sign Out

>> Switch to Another User

These are your choices for ending your Windows day. The sections that follow describe the details.

Putting the computer to sleep

(If you're reading this book out loud, now is the time to whisper.)

Sleep mode refers to a computer's low-power operating state. In this mode, the system is still on, but the screen goes dark, the processor throttles back to low speed, and activity reduces to a low simmer. The idea is to keep the computer ready to use but not to waste power.

To sleep your PC, follow these steps:

1. **Click or tap the Start button.**

Up pops the Start menu.

2. **Choose Power.**

Refer to Figure 5-1.

3. **Select the Sleep command.**

Unlike with a shutdown or restart, you don't need to save anything before the computer enters Sleep mode.

To revive a snoozing PC, press a key on the keyboard, jiggle the mouse, tap the mouse pad, or scream loudly. (Screaming loudly is only occasionally effective.)

Once awake, your desktop or laptop may prompt you to sign in to Windows again.

TIP

>> One of the features of Sleep mode is that Windows saves all your data. Even so, I recommend saving files before entering Sleep mode — just in case.

>> You can sleep a laptop by closing the lid, although this function isn't guaranteed: See the later section "Determining what happens when you shut a laptop's lid."

>> If a laptop is conditioned to sleep when you close its lid, opening the lid wakes it up.

>> Your computer may automatically go to sleep after a period of inactivity — say, 30 minutes or so. Setting this timeout is part of the system's power management scheme, which is covered in Chapter 18.

» Sleep mode isn't the same as locking the computer, which does not reduce its power.

» Some computers feature a sleep button. This button is configurable just as the power button can be configured. See the later section "Setting the power button's function."

» The PC doesn't snore while in Sleep mode.

» You can stop whispering now.

Hibernating the computer

A stealthy option for both desktops and laptops is to hibernate the system as opposed to entering Sleep mode. This choice isn't available on the Power menu (refer to Figure 5-1) unless you know the secret to activating it. The following steps reveal the secret. Please! Do not let them fall into enemy hands:

1. **Pop up the Start menu.**

2. **Type** control panel.

   Or type enough of it until you see the Control Panel (System) item displayed.

3. **Choose the Control Panel item.**

4. **Ensure that Category view is chosen.**

   You find this option in the upper right corner of the Control Panel window.

5. **Choose the heading Hardware and Sound.**

6. **Below the title Power Options, click the link Change What the Power Buttons Do.**

   At the bottom of the window, below the Shutdown Settings heading, you see a list of items you can activate for the Power menu.

7. **Place a check mark by the Hibernate item.**

   Not every PC is capable of hibernation. If this option is unavailable, the system doesn't support hibernation.

Upon success, the Hibernate item appears on the Power menu.

The Hibernate option works like Sleep mode. The difference is that all your data is saved and the computer is turned off. When you wake up the computer and sign in again, all your data is restored.

Hibernate mode saves more power than Sleep mode, though it does take the computer longer to start back up again.

Shutting down the computer

It's the end of the day and you must flee the digital realm and enjoy the benefits of the real world. Time to turn off the computer. The official term is *shutdown*, because lots of tasks must take place before the computer turns itself off. Heed these steps:

1. **Save your work and close all programs.**

   The generic Save command is Ctrl+S.

2. **Summon the Power menu.**

   Pop up the Start menu and choose the Power item.

3. **Choose Shut Down.**

   The computer turns itself off.

Say you skipped Step 1 because you think I'm just being silly. Ah-ha! The computer stubbornly prompts you to save unsaved documents as part of the shutdown process. If you're unable to do so, you can force a program to quit, though I recommend waiting a few impatient moments before choosing to do so.

TIP

>> You can configure the computer to shut down when you press its power button. See the later section "Setting the power button's function."

>> Always properly shut down a laptop upon seeing a critical battery warning. If you don't do so, the laptop turns itself off automatically at some point.

>> Shutting down might trigger Windows to install updates. If so, the shutdown process takes longer than anticipated and may require an Internet connection.

>> If a desktop computer is improperly shut down — say, during a power outage or in a fit of rage — you're scolded when Windows restarts. It takes a while for Windows to clean up your mess, but the computer eventually starts normally.

REMEMBER

>> Closing the lid doesn't necessarily turn off your laptop! See the later section "Determining what happens when you shut a laptop's lid."

TECHNICAL STUFF

>> The emergency way to turn off a computer that's frozen or otherwise stuck is to press and hold its power button for about 12 seconds. The computer turns itself off. This trick is the only way to power off a stubborn laptop; unlike with a desktop PC, you can't just yank a laptop's power card from the wall, which I don't recommend anyhow. Use this press-and-hold trick only for situations when you are otherwise unable to control the computer.

Restarting the PC

You need to restart your computer in two instances. First, Windows may direct you to restart after you install something new or change a setting. Second, restarting is a good idea whenever something strange happens, like the mouse starts giggling. For some reason, a restart clears the computer's head like a good nose blow, and things return to normal.

To restart, obey these directions:

1. **Save your work and close all your programs.**

   This is the step everyone forgets, so let me repeat it:

2. **Save your work and close all your programs.**

3. **Pop up the Start menu.**

4. **Choose Power.**

5. **Choose Restart.**

The computer behaves as if you chose the Shut Down command, but instead of turning itself all the way off, the computer starts up again.

TIP

» Windows may initiate a restart on its own, such as after an update. If you're lucky, a prompt is displayed, allowing you to restart the computer. Sometimes, however, a restart is automatic. See Chapter 21.

» Rather than restart to fix a problem, sign out instead. See the later section "Signing out of Windows."

Locking Windows

A quick way to protect your computer when you're away for a spell is to lock it: Press the Win+L keyboard shortcut. The Windows lock screen appears. Only by signing in again can you regain access.

To unlock the computer, sign in to Windows.

TIP

» Lock the computer whenever you need to step away for a bit.

» I have a home office, yet I still lock my desktop when I step away. It's not to keep family members out of my system. No, I do it to keep my cat out of the system.

>> You don't need to save any files or close any programs when you lock the computer. Locking doesn't turn off anything or suspend any activities.

>> The Lock command is also found on the Account Options menu, illustrated earlier, in Figure 5-2.

Signing out of Windows

Another option to end your computer day is to sign out. This choice is used primarily on desktop computers (workstations) with multiple users, though anyone can sign out at any time. To do so, follow these steps:

1. **Save your work and close your programs.**

   If you forget to save your work, Windows reminds you in a suitably rude fashion.

2. **Pop up the Start menu.**

3. **Choose your account name, found at the lower left of the Start menu.**

   Refer to Figure 5-2 for the location.

4. **Choose the Sign Out command.**

   Windows stops your programs, prompting you to save any unsaved documents. Eventually, you see the main sign-in or lock screen again.

Once you sign out, another user on the same machine can sign in, though I typically sign out to clear the computer of a bug or other annoyance. For example, when Windows says that a file is "busy" when I know that it's not, signing out and then signing back in again often fixes the problem.

REMEMBER

Signing out of Windows does not turn off the computer.

Switching to another user

Windows is designed to host multiple users on a single computer, which is more popular for a desktop system than a laptop. For example, you may have a kid's account on your system at home. To switch to the other account, heed these directions:

1. **Pop up the Start menu.**

2. **Choose your account picture in the lower left corner of the Start menu.**

   Refer to Figure 5-2 for its location.

3. **Select the other user from the Account Options menu.**

You're signed out of Windows, and the computer immediately displays the other user's sign-in screen.

One problem with these steps is that your account is still signed in. It remains active on the computer while the other person is using it. Therefore, rather than switch to another user, I recommend you first sign out (refer to the preceding section) and then let the other user sign in.

Though it's best to sign out, I have followed the steps in this section to let other users sign in briefly to perform some activity, such as check mail or upload a file. Then they sign out and I can continue using the computer.

Shutdown Options and Configuration

The power button always turns on a computer. That's a given. Of course, if a laptop has a dead battery, you can press all day long and nothing happens. Still, the real mystery surrounding the power button is what happens when you punch it while the computer is on.

Setting the power button's function

Five things could happen when you press the power button while the system is on. It can

>> Do nothing

>> Sleep the computer

>> Hibernate the computer

>> Shut down the computer

>> Turn off the display

Not every computer supports all these options. For example, my laptop has only Do Nothing, Sleep, and Shutdown options.

By default, pushing the power button when a desktop PC is on starts the shutdown operation. On a laptop, the default differs depending on whether the laptop is plugged in. Regardless, you can change the power button's function by obeying these steps:

1. **Pop up the Start menu.**

   Tap the Windows key on the keyboard.

2. **Type** control panel **to locate the Control Panel app.**

3. **Choose the Control Panel app.**

   The Control Panel window opens, a relic of Windows versions gone by.

4. **Choose the Hardware and Sound category.**

5. **From beneath the Power Options heading, click the link labeled Change What the Power Buttons Do.**

   You see the Power Options System Settings window, illustrated in Figure 5-3. It has two columns: one for when the computer is battery-powered and another for when it's plugged into the wall.

Laptop's lid

Sleep button function   Battery power options   Choose a function from the menu

Power button function   Plugged into the wall options

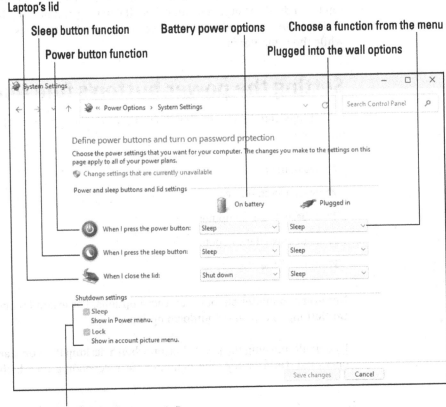

FIGURE 5-3:
The Control
Panel's power
button settings.

Options for the Start menu's Power menu

The top two rows in Figure 5-3 represent the power button and sleep button's function. The sleep button item appears even when this button is unavailable. The third row appears only on laptop PCs.

6. **Choose what happens when you press the power button on battery power.**

   You see options displayed pertaining to the computer's capabilities.

   Battery power also applies to a desktop computer when it's connected to a UPS. Refer to Chapter 3.

REMEMBER

7. **Choose what happens when you press the power button while the system is plugged in.**

8. **After choosing the various options, click the Save Changes button.**

9. **Close the window.**

For my desktop system, the power button is set to Shutdown for both items: On Battery and Plugged In. For my laptop, the power button is set to Sleep for both items. See the next section for my advice on how to deal +with shutting the laptop's lid.

TIP

>> The sleep button's row may not appear on all systems.

>> If you're leery of accidentally pressing the power button and having your computer react in an unexpectedly brutish manner, set its function to Do Nothing.

REMEMBER

>> The power button always turns on the computer. You cannot alter this primary function.

Determining what happens when you shut a laptop's lid

It's your pleasure to set what the laptop does when you shut its lid. My choices are shown in Figure 5-3: When the laptop is on battery power and I shut the lid, the laptop turns itself off. When the laptop is plugged in, shutting the lid activates Sleep mode.

You can make your own choices about what happens with your laptop's lid: Follow the directions in the preceding section to access the Power Options System Settings window. Set the laptop's lid action according to your whims.

TIP

Setting the close-lid action to Do Nothing is a legitimate option for a laptop. For example, if the laptop is connected to an external monitor and keyboard, you can shut the lid and use the laptop like a desktop with the lid closed. Even so, I like having two monitors on my laptop, so I leave the lid open.

Should You Leave the Computer On All the Time?

I've been writing about computers since my first book, *Eniac For Dummies* (Wiley), published in 1947. The burning question back then was, "Should we ever turn the thing off?" People have their opinions.

"I want to leave my computer off all the time"

It's an excellent solution, recommended by computer security experts.

"I want to leave my computer on all the time"

For a desktop PC, it's good to keep it on all the time — but only when you use your computer often. Especially when you find yourself turning the computer on and off several times during the day, just leave it on all the time.

The only time I ever turn off my computers is when I'll be away for longer than a weekend.

Does this method waste electricity? Yes, but not as much as you think. Computers have an energy-saving mode that keeps the power low when they're not in use. See Chapter 18 for details on implementing an energy-saving plan customized for how you use your PC.

More importantly, computers do enjoy being on all the time. Having that fan whirring keeps the console's innards at a constant temperature, which avoids some of the problems caused by turning the system off (cooling) and on (heating) again.

>> Keeping your PC on all the time doesn't raise your electric bill grotesquely, not like the Jacuzzi or the kids' Tesla coil does.

>> If you use your PC only once a day (during the evening for email, chat, and the Internet, for example), turning it off for the rest of the day is fine. And if you're really that casual about your computer, consider replacing it with a tablet.

>> Most businesses leave their computers on all the time, though medium-size businesses can save thousands of dollars a year by shutting down their computers overnight. Just a thought.

WARNING

>> If you leave your computer on all the time, don't put it under a dust cover. You'll suffocate the thing.

Keeping a laptop on all the time

If you leave a laptop on for a long time, it eventually enters Sleep mode, which keeps the screen dark and saves power. Even so, unlike leaving a desktop computer on all the time, I don't recommend doing so for a laptop. The primary reason is that laptops run hot. It's a good idea to shut it down when you're done working.

2

A Non-Nerdy Guide to Computer Hardware

IN THIS CHAPTER

» Studying the PC's insides

» Supplying the system with power

» Examining the motherboard

» Understanding the processor

» Checking your PC's processor

» Telling the time

Chapter **6**

A Peek Inside the Box

Desktop PCs are designed for expansion, but not laptops. You can open a desktop PC to add a new component, replace something, or amaze yourself with all the accumulated dust and crud. Even so, most people never open their computer — which is good because you don't open the furnace or the cat, both of which can work just fine without looking inside.

Despite a lack of necessity, and with a laptop a lack of access, it helps to know about the electronic gizmos lurking inside your computer. You may even know some of the terms: *motherboard, processor, power supply,* and so on. It's time to take a peek inside the box.

Computer Guts

Science fiction television in the 1960s had a clever way to reveal when someone was, in fact, an android and not a human being. At some point in the episode, the character would open a conspicuous hatch on his belly. Revealed was a mess of wires and blinking lights. The visual impact was ominous and believable. Computer guts today are dull by comparison.

Looking under the hood

Buried in your computer's bosom is a maze of mysterious technology, from large metal boxes to tiny pointed, dangerous, raw electronics. In Figure 6-1, I provide a safe and lovely illustration of what you might see inside a typical desktop PC. A laptop contains similar items, but all smooshed flat, like a pancake.

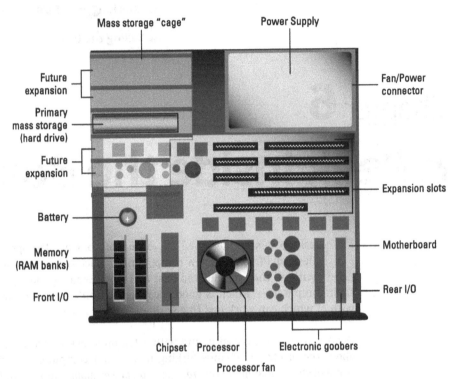

Mass storage "cage"

Power Supply

Future expansion

Fan/Power connector

Primary mass storage (hard drive)

Future expansion

Expansion slots

Battery

Memory (RAM banks)

Motherboard

Front I/O

Rear I/O

Chipset   Processor

Electronic goobers

Processor fan

FIGURE 6-1: A peek inside the console.

To put things in perspective, Figure 6-1 illustrates the side view of a typical minitower PC. The front of the computer is on the left. What you don't see in Figure 6-1 are the cables that festoon the box's interior space like a spilled bowl of pasta. Also missing is a thin layer of dust and perhaps some pet hair.

Of all the things wonderful and terrifying inside the computer's tummy, three are worthy in the big picture:

» The power supply

» The motherboard

» The mass storage cage

The *power supply* feeds the console all-important electricity.

The *motherboard* is the computer's main circuitry board. It's important, as are its many residents, which include the processor, memory, and stuff like that.

Finally, the *mass storage cage* is a contraption that corrals internal storage devices, such as hard drives and SSDs, plus maybe a media card reader. The cage also has room for even more computer storage — the so-called future expansion — usually right behind some knockout panels on the computer's front.

>> Because they're designed for portability, laptops lack the roominess and expansion of the typical desktop PC illustrated in Figure 6-1. Beyond the mass storage cage and expansion slots, a laptop's guts are the same but smaller, hotter, and more expensive.

>> Laptops also house the all-important battery, which keeps the system running when it has wandered away from wall power. See Chapter 18.

>> The wee battery illustrated in Figure 6-1 is for powering the computer's onboard clock. See the later section "Your Computer is Also a Timepiece."

Powering Mr. Computer

The least intelligent part of your computer is also the most important. No, that's not *you*. Silly. It's the power supply. It does the following wonderful things for Mr. Computer:

>> Brings in electricity from the wall socket and converts the electricity from wild, untamed, wishy-washy AC current into calm, collected DC current

>> Provides electricity to the motherboard and everything dwelling thereupon

>> Provides juice to the internal storage devices

>> Charges a laptop's battery

>> Uses fans to help cool the computer's viscera

The power supply is also designed to take the brunt of the damage if your computer ever suffers from electrical peril, such as a lightning strike or power surge. Like the hero that it is, the power supply is designed to die, sacrificing itself for the good of your PC. For a desktop PC, you can easily have the power supply replaced. Your computer will be fine. For a laptop, however, a damaged power supply means that you need a new laptop.

Here are some fun power supply facts:

>> Thanks to the fan, the power supply is the noisiest part of any computer.

>> Power supplies are rated in *watts*. This yardstick is important for desktop PCs because the more internal hardware you cram inside — mass storage, memory, and expansion cards, for example — the greater the quantity of watts are required. A typical desktop PC has a power supply rated at 150 or 200 watts. More powerful systems may require a power supply upward of 750 watts.

>> Because laptops aren't internally expandable, their power supply is considered Goldilocks: It's *just right*.

>> One way to keep a desktop computer from going poof (even in a lightning strike) is to invest in a UPS. Refer to Chapter 3 for details.

Lurking on the motherboard

The largest circuitry board inside a PC is called the *motherboard*. It's a term of endearment and, yes, motherboards are celebrated in May.

All that aside, the motherboard is home to the computer's most important electronics. There you find the following essential PC components, some of which are illustrated in Figure 6-1:

>> Processor and its fan

>> Chipset

>> Memory

>> Battery

>> Expansion slots

>> I/O connectors

>> Electronic goobers

Many of these items are covered elsewhere in this chapter or they have a chapter of their own in this part of the book. Yes, they're that pretentious.

The *I/O connectors* are locations on the motherboard where various cables connect to communicate with the rest of the computer system. For example, on the motherboard, you find a connector for mass storage, the power supply, and the I/O panels on the computer's case.

THE CHIPSET

Rather than refer to the tossed salad of computer chips on the computer's motherboard as The Tossed Salad of Computer Chips on the Computer's Motherboard, technicians wearing white lab coats and holding clipboards have devised a single descriptive term. All those computer chips constitute the *chipset*.

The *chipset* is what makes up your computer's personality — it contains instructions for operating the basic computer hardware: keyboard, mouse, networking interface, sound, video, and whatever else I can't think of right now.

Various chipsets are available, depending on which types of features the computer offers. For example, some motherboards contain advanced graphics in the chipset or maybe wireless networking. The chipset isn't anything you can change, but it is occasionally referenced in the computer's parts list.

An older term for the chipset is BIOS, which stands for Basic Input/Output System. There's a BIOS for the keyboard and mouse, one for the video system, one for the network, and so on. Altogether, they make up the chipset.

The electronic goobers that festoon the motherboard are added because they look impressive. If the motherboard were a cupcake, these items would be like sprinkles on top. They're that good.

Storing mass storage devices

To allow for adding more mass storage, as well as to keep these devices from jostling around like that clacky thing in a spray paint can, desktop computers include a mass storage cage. This location consists of a series of slots into which storage devices are inserted.

The primary mass storage device, a hard drive or SSD, is anchored into one of the slots. Other mass storage can be added, including an optical drive or even a gramophone if you're feeling nostalgic.

>> Some slots are accessible from the front of the console. These are best used for gizmos that require direct access, such as an optical drive or a media card reader.

>> Storage devices are anchored to the cage to keep them stable.

- » A laptop's mass storage device is permanently affixed inside the case. Some laptops offer removable storage. Look under the laptop for access to such storage — if available.

- » Mass storage devices require two cables: a power cable and a data cable. The power cable finds the power supply; the data cable plugs into the motherboard.

- » See Chapter 8 for more information about mass storage devices.

The Processor Rules the Motherboard

The main chip inside a computer, king of the motherboard, is the computer's processor. It is *not* the computer's brain. Software is the computer's brain because it tells the hardware what to do. But it's the processor that carries out those orders and has the loyalty of nearly all other hardware in the computer system.

- » Just about every other gizmo on the motherboard exists to serve the processor, save for that one capacitor that seems a bit dodgy.

- » Another term for a processor is *CPU. CPU* stands for *central processing unit.*

- » Processors run very hot and therefore require their own cooling. To keep the king processor cool, he wears a tiny fan as his crown. It's like those propeller beanies you see the kids wear, but wholly practical and stylish.

Understanding the processor's role

Despite its importance and outrageous cost, what the processor does is rather simple. It handles three basic tasks:

- » First, it does simple math — addition, subtraction, multiplication, and division.

- » Second, the processor reads from and writes to memory.

- » Finally, it performs input and output (I/O).

This list is dreadfully unimpressive until you consider that the processor performs these basic tasks *very fast.*

For a visual image, picture the processor as a traffic cop, though the traffic is traveling 64 lanes wide and at the speed of light.

Naming PC processors

Once upon a time, computer processors were named after famous numbers, like 8088 and 386. The trend now is toward names, but not human names, like John or Mary, or even dog names like Rover or Abednego. No, now processors are named after potential science fiction heroes, pharmaceuticals, or sounds made by a baby rhinoceros in distress. None of these details matter to your computer — unless the software you use demands a specific processor. In this instance, the software tells you which specific name brand to use. That's all you need to know.

>> The two big PC processor companies are Intel and AMD.

>> Intel uses the Core brand to name its processors, followed by a letter and number, such as Core i7.

>> AMD opts for science fiction names with its product line. For example, the AMD Ryzen processor is comparable to the Intel Core i7.

>> Truth be told, outside a courtroom, little difference exists between Intel and non-Intel processors. As far as your PC's software is concerned, the processor is capable no matter who made it.

Measuring processor speed

Processors are judged by their speed. Because they don't move, the measurement is based on the number of cycles per second (hertz, or Hz) at which the processor performs its calculations. The higher the hertz value, the faster the processor. Because the processor is fast, its speed is measured in billions of cycles per second, or *gigahertz (GHz)*.

>> The faster the processor, the more it costs.

>> Sadly, processor speed is relative. For example, an Intel Core i7 running at 3.4 GHz is technically slower than a Core i7 running at 4.0 GHz. Even so, you probably wouldn't notice any difference between the two in performance, appearance, or smell.

Discovering your PC's processor

You may not know which processor spins busy inside your PC's thorax, but Windows does! The System window shows a technical inventory, like the one shown in Figure 6-2.

Memory   Processor

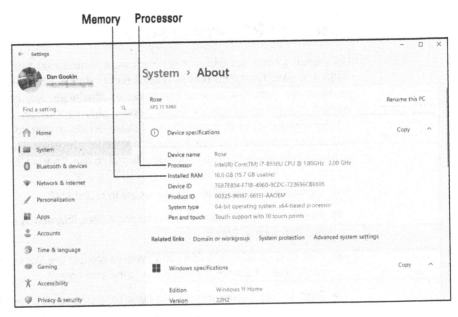

FIGURE 6-2:
The System
window.

To summon the System window, follow these directions:

1. **Press the Win+I keyboard shortcut to summon the Settings app.**

2. **Choose the System category.**

3. **Scroll to the bottom of the list to choose About.**

In Figure 6-2, the laptop sports an Intel Core i7 CPU running at 2.0 GHz. It features 10GB of memory (RAM). All this information jibes with what I paid for, so my dealer is off the hook.

>> The details shown in Figure 6-2 are for Windows 11. The Windows 10 Settings app screen looks similar.

>> The keyboard shortcut to summon the About screen is Win+Break. The Break key may be labeled Pause on some keyboards. Sadly, laptops often lack a Break key.

>> See Chapter 7 for details on computer memory.

Your Computer Is Also a Timepiece

If you were born on January 1, 1980, you share something in common with your computer. This date is what the PC assumes "today" to be unless its internal clock is properly set. Fortunately, your PC comes equipped with an internal clock that features a battery backup. It always knows the correct time — more or less.

The point of the clock isn't just to feature a handy date-and-time display in the lower right corner of the screen. No, computers use clocks for scheduling, to timestamp information and events, and generally to prevent everything from happening all at once.

Both desktop and laptop computers have a battery backup for their internal clock. Desktop PCs use a tiny battery on the motherboard (refer to Figure 6-1). Laptops might also feature a separate battery or use the main battery to power the clock. This battery helps the computer keep track of the date and time when the system is unplugged or the laptop's battery dies.

Alas, the battery backup doesn't help the computer keep *accurate* time. Computers make lousy timepieces, typically losing about a minute or two by the end of the day. Why? Who knows! Fortunately, the clock is set automatically while your computer is connected to the Internet. It even knows about the dratted daylight saving time and adjusts the clock automatically.

TIP

>> Clock circuitry exists somewhere on the motherboard. You cannot hear it ticking.

>> To see a pop-up clock and calendar in Windows, click the time display on the right end of taskbar.

>> A desktop PC's clock battery lasts for about six years, possibly more. When it dies, the computer's date and time go screwy or you see a message informing you that the motherboard's battery needs replacing.

>> Though the Internet updates the PC's clock, it may not reset the time zone when you travel with your laptop. To adjust the time zone, right-click on the time display in the lower right corner of the screen. Choose Adjust Date and Time. In the Settings app, choose the correct time zone from the drop-down menu.

REMEMBER

>> If you do reset the laptop's time zone, remember to set it back when you return from your trip. See Chapter 19 for more laptop travelling information.

TECHNICAL STUFF

>> The reason the computer doesn't automatically set the time zone is that all computer time is based on Coordinated Universal Time (UTC), once known as Greenwich Mean Time (GMT). The computer adjusts the time display output based on the time zone you select. This option was chosen when you first configured the Windows operating system, but for a peripatetic laptop, it must be manually updated whenever you hop time zones.

IN THIS CHAPTER

» **Understanding memory**

» **Measuring memory quantity**

» **Using chips and dips (and DIMMs)**

» **Discovering how much memory is in your PC**

» **Adding memory to your computer**

» **Understanding virtual memory**

Chapter **7**

Computer Memory

They say that a goldfish has a two-second memory, which means that any goldfish reading this sentence has already forgotten how it started. It also means that you can tell a goldfish the same joke repeatedly and they'll always give a hearty laugh. Fun can be had with a lack of memory.

Alas, no fun can be had with a computer that lacks memory. No, your PC needs digital elbow room to handle a variety of tasks easily and swiftly. When the computer lacks a sufficient quantity of memory, things get cramped worse than a tour bus overflowing with sweaty-drunk engineers returning from an all-you-can-eat kimchi bar. But I digress. When it comes to computer memory, more is better.

Random Access Memory

Computer memory is officially known as random access memory, or RAM. The random part has nothing to do with unpredictability.

In computer jargon, *random* means that it's possible to access memory at any location as opposed to reading memory front-to-back, like a book. So, the computer can dive into memory at location nine zillion and say, "Look! I found the letter *P* right here." It's impressive.

For the computer, memory is the field upon which the digital realm is built. It's where stuff happens. The more memory inside the computer, the more ably it can perform its various duties. Less memory means things slow down, like trying to play a game of football on a squash court.

The reason a computer sports hectares of RAM is that the processor has very little storage. For example, a processor can store your weight, height, and IQ, but not a picture of the Eiffel Tower or a video showing Leonardo da Vinci stabbing Michelangelo with some chopsticks. Your computer needs oodles of memory to do these things — and more.

>> All computers need memory.

>> Memory is where the processor saves and stores its work.

>> Computer memory is often referred to as *temporary* storage. The reason is that RAM requires electricity to maintain its information. Long-term storage is provided by media such as a hard drive or SSD. Information is saved from memory to this long-term storage so that it's only lost when you need it the most. See Chapter 8 for information on long-term storage.

>> I know nothing about the size of a squash court, nor do I know how to play squash. I just know that it's a funny word. Squash.

>> People from the Midwest say, "Squarsh."

REMEMBER

>> Turning off the power makes the *contents* of memory vanish. The memory chips themselves aren't destroyed, but without electricity to maintain their contents, the information stored on the chips is lost.

>> Computer memory is *fast*. The processor can scan millions of bytes of memory — the equivalent of Shakespeare's entire folio — in a fraction of a second, which is far less time than it took you to trudge through *Hamlet* in the 11th grade.

>> Memory is reusable. After you create something and save it, the computer allows that memory to be used again for something else. It's like a magic erase tablet but without that soothing sound when you pull up the plastic.

TECHNICAL STUFF

>> Yes, Mr. Smartypants, some types of computer memory do not require electricity to maintain information. Called *flash memory*, this type of memory isn't fast enough to get real work done. It is used, however, in media cards and thumb drives. See the nearby sidebar, "Boring details on RAM, ROM, and flash memory."

BORING DETAILS ON RAM, ROM, AND FLASH MEMORY

RAM, or random access memory, refers to memory that the processor reads from and writes to. When you create something in memory, it's created in RAM. RAM is memory, and vice versa.

ROM stands for *read-only memory*. The processor can read from ROM, but it cannot write to it or modify it. ROM is permanent, like some members of Congress. ROM chips contain special instructions or other information that the computer uses — important stuff that never changes. For example, the chipset on the motherboard is in ROM (refer to Chapter 6). The processor can access information stored on a ROM chip, but unlike with RAM, the processor cannot change that information.

Flash memory is a special type of memory that works like both RAM and ROM. Information can be written to flash memory, like RAM, but like ROM the information isn't erased when the power is turned off. Sadly, flash memory isn't as fast as RAM, so don't expect it to replace standard computer memory anytime soon.

One Byte at a Time

Computer memory is measured by the byte. So, what is a byte?

A *byte* is a tiny storage unit, like a small box. Into that box fits a single character. For example, the word *cerumen* is seven letters (characters) long, so it requires seven bytes of storage. That's seven bytes of computer memory, which isn't a lot these days, thanks to inflation.

Individual bytes aren't very useful. Only when you have lots of bytes can you store interesting and wonderful things.

Back in the 1970s, having a few thousand bytes of computer storage was *really something!* The Apollo lunar module computer had 2,048 bytes of memory. Today's PCs demand *millions* of bytes just to run the operating system. That works because today's PCs typically have *billions* of bytes of storage available.

Because the words *million* and *billion* represent values too large for the human mind to comprehend, but not large enough for the government to spend, computer scientists use special terms to reference large quantities of computer storage. Such jargon is presented in Table 7-1.

TABLE 7-1   **Memory Measurements**

Term	Abbreviation	About	Actual
Byte		1 byte	1 byte
Kilobyte	K or KB	1 thousand bytes	1,024 bytes
Megabyte	M or MB	1 million bytes	1,048,576 bytes
Gigabyte	G or GB	1 billion bytes	1,073,741,824 bytes
Terabyte	T or TB	1 trillion bytes	1,099,511,627,776 bytes

Although it's handy to say "kilobyte" rather than mouth out "1,024 bytes," it's difficult to visualize how much data this quantity represents. For comparison, think of a kilobyte (KB) as a page of text from a novel. That's about 1,000 characters.

One *megabyte* (MB) of information is required to store one minute of music in your computer, a medium-resolution photograph, or as much text information as in a complete encyclopedia.

The *gigabyte* (GB) is a huge amount of storage — 1 billion bytes. The computer can store about 30 minutes of high-quality video in a gigabyte.

The *terabyte* (TB) is 1 trillion bytes, or enough RAM to dim the lights when you start the PC. Although I can think of no single item that requires 1TB of storage, though lots of 1GB items float and fit happily into that 1TB of storage.

A *trilobite* is an extinct arthropod that flourished in the oceans during the Paleozoic era. It has nothing to do with computer memory.

Other trivia:

» The term *giga* is Greek and means *giant*.

» The term *tera* is also Greek. It means *monster!*

» Long-term mass storage media is also measured in bytes; see Chapter 8.

» Microsoft recommends at least 4GB of RAM to run the Windows 11 operating system. More is better.

TECHNICAL STUFF

» The terms used to describe computer memory (storage) in Table 7-1 aren't technically correct, but they're traditional. In 1998, the International Electrotechnical Commission (IEC) decided that, due to confusion or possibly boredom, a kilobyte would be exactly 1,000 bytes. The correct quantity, 1,024, would be called a kibibyte. Likewise, a megabyte is officially 1 million bytes, but a mebibyte is 1,048,576 bytes, and so on. I freely ignore the IEC's attempt to rewrite computer history.

THE HOLY NUMBERS OF COMPUTING

Computer memory comes in given sizes. You see these same numbers over and over:

1, 2, 4, 8, 16, 32, 64, 128, 256, 512, 1024, 2048, 4096, and so on

Each of these values represents a power of two — a scary mathematical concept that you can avoid while still enjoying a fruitful life. To quickly review: $2^0 = 1$, $2^1 = 2$, $2^2 = 4$, $2^3 = 8$, and then skip a few to: $2^{10} = 1024$. These values grow larger until you get a nosebleed.

The values of two happen because computers count by twos — ones and zeros — the old binary counting base from medieval times. So, computer memory, which is a binary-like thing, is measured in those same powers of two. Memory chips come in quantities such as 512MB, 1GB, 2GB, and so on.

Note that, starting with 1024, the values take on a predictable pattern: 1024 bytes is really 1K; 1024K is really 1M; and 1024M is 1G. So, really, only the first ten values, 1 through 512, are the magical ones.

Enough of that.

Memory Chips and Dips

Physically, memory dwells on the PC's motherboard, sitting very close to the processor for fast access and boon companionship. The memory itself resides on a tiny memory expansion card, or *DIMM*. On the DIMM, you find the actual memory chips.

DIMM stands for *dual inline memory module*, and it's pronounced "dim" with the first *M* silent.

A typical DIMM is illustrated in Figure 7-1, although in real life you'll find chips on both sides. That's why it's a *dual* inline memory module and not a *single* inline memory module (SIMM).

Each DIMM contains a given quantity of RAM, measured in megabytes or gigabytes using one of the magical memory quantities of 1, 2, 4, 8, 16, 32, 64, 128, 256, or 512. These quantities must match the motherboard's specifications, which also include the memory chip's speed, type, and political affiliation.

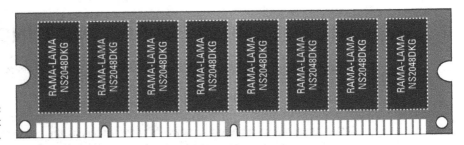

FIGURE 7-1:
A semisweet
DIMM.

DIMMs are plugged into slots on the motherboard, where they form a *bank* of memory. For example, a computer with 4GB of RAM may have four banks of 1GB DIMMs installed or two banks of 2GB DIMMs. All these details are trivial, however. The only time you need to give a rip is when you upgrade memory. I write more about that task later in this chapter.

>> The most common type of memory chip installed in a PC is the DRAM, which stands for *dynamic random access memory*. It's pronounced "dee-ram."

>> Half a byte is a nibble. I'm not making that up.

>> The word *byte* is the source of many computer puns — real thigh-slappers that keep the nerds from doing real work. Only the word *modem* is used to make more puns.

Memory Q&A

It doesn't matter where I am — greeting people at church, gesturing to my fellow drivers on the freeway, or leaving rehab — folks stop and ask me questions about computer memory. Over the years, I've collected the questions and distilled the answers in this section. They should help clear up any random access thoughts you may have about computer memory.

"How much memory is in my PC right now?"

You may not know how much RAM resides in your computer's carcass, but the computer knows! Summon the Settings app to find out. Obey these directions:

1. Press the Win+I keyboard shortcut to bring forth the Settings app.

2. Choose System from the categories listed.

3. **Choose About.**

The RAM data appears in the Device Specifications area, labeled as Installed RAM.

Refer to Figure 6-2 in Chapter 6 for a visual reference.

"Do I have enough memory?"

If you have to keep asking this question, the answer is no.

"Does my PC have enough memory?"

Knowing how much memory is in your PC is one thing, but knowing whether this quantity is sufficient is entirely different.

The amount of memory your PC requires depends on the demands of installed software. Some programs, such as video editing apps, require lots of memory. Just check the software's hardware requirements to see how much memory is needed. For example, the Adobe Premiere Pro video editing program prefers at least 16GB of "fast" RAM, though it can hobble by with 8GB.

>> Not enough memory? You can upgrade! See the upcoming section "'Can I add memory to my computer?'"

>> One sure sign that your computer needs more memory is that it slows to a crawl the more you do. See the next section.

"Can I test whether my PC has enough memory?"

Your computer can function when it lacks a sufficient amount of memory — it just does so with a snotty attitude.

To test whether the PC has enough memory, you must make the system *very* busy: Start several big programs, such as Photoshop and Excel (if installed). While these lumbering programs are doing their thing, switch between them: Press the Alt+Esc keyboard shortcut to switch program windows.

As you use the Alt+Esc keyboard shortcut, observe how quickly the windows change on the screen. If you detect a noticeable pause between programs — a big, sluggish pause — the computer is swapping memory. This swapping is a sign that the PC lacks enough RAM to do its job. Close any programs you have opened.

>> See the next section for details on adding more memory to your computer.

>> See the later section "'What is virtual memory?'" if you dare to understand why the computer slows down as you swap programs.

"Can I add memory to my computer?"

For a desktop PC, the answer is yes! Some laptops do let you swap out or add more memory, but most don't. Even so, the best thing you can do for any computer is to add more memory. It's like putting garlic in a salad. *Bam!* More memory provides an instant performance boost to the system.

Adding memory to your computer is LEGO-block simple. Well, if LEGOs cost a few hundred dollars each and required electricity, then it would be LEGO-block simple. Knowing how much memory and which type to buy is the tough part. Because of that, I highly recommend that you have a computer expert do the work for you.

If you opt to perform your own PC memory upgrade, I recommend Crucial at www. crucial.com. The website uses special software to determine which type of memory you need and how much. You can then buy the memory upgrade directly from the site.

"Will the computer ever run out of memory?"

Nope. Unlike mass storage, which can fill up like that trash can in the kitchen that everyone refuses to empty, your PC's memory can never truly get full. At one time, back in the dark ages of computing, the "memory full" error was common. That doesn't happen now, thanks to something called virtual memory.

"What is virtual memory?"

Virtual memory is a fake-out. It lets the computer pretend that it has much more memory than it has physical RAM.

To make the scheme work, Windows swaps out chunks of memory to mass storage. Because Windows manages both memory and mass storage, it keeps track of things quite well: Chunks of data are swapped back and forth between memory and mass storage. *Et, voilà!* — you never see an "out of memory" error, thanks to virtual storage.

Alas, a problem with virtual memory is that the swapping action slows things down. Although the swapping can happen quickly and often without your noticing, when memory gets tight, virtual memory takes over and things start moving more slowly.

>> Swapping virtual memory is the trick you're trying to entice the computer into performing when you follow the steps outlined in the earlier section "Can I test whether my PC has enough memory?"

>> The solution to avoiding the use of virtual memory is to pack your PC with as much RAM as it can hold. Refer to the earlier section "Can I add memory to my computer?"

>> Windows never says that it's "out of memory." No, you just notice that the hard drive is churning frequently as the memory is swapped into and out of mass storage. Oh, and things tend to slow down dramatically.

TIP

>> You have no reason to mess with the virtual memory settings in your computer. Windows does an excellent job of managing them for you.

"What is video memory?"

Memory used by your PC's video system is known as *video memory*. This memory is separate from the computer's main memory on the motherboard, or it can be shared. Video memory drives the graphics and images you see displayed on the computer's monitor.

Specifically, video memory, also known as VRAM (Video RAM) dwells on a display adapter card. These memory chips are used specifically for the computer's video output and help you see higher resolutions, more colors, 3D graphics, bigger and uglier aliens, and girlie pictures that your husband downloads from the Internet late at night but claims that he doesn't.

When a display adapter card is unavailable, the computer uses graphics circuitry and memory on the motherboard to drive the computer's graphics. This memory is known as *shared video memory*. Laptops without dedicated video memory use shared video memory. Even desktop PCs with rows and rows of dedicated VRAM packed onto a display adapter card also use shared video memory.

See Chapter 9 for more information on display adapters.

IN THIS CHAPTER

» Understanding mass storage

» Inserting and removing media

» Getting to know the drive letters

» Using drive icons

» Finding mass storage in Windows

» Calculating storage capacity

» Using storage devices

Chapter **8**

Disks and Drives

omputers need long-term storage — unless you plan on writing all the software yourself each time you turn on the beast. If so, I applaud your pluck. But because most users prefer to avoid this chore, long-term storage is a vital part of any computer system.

The evolution of PC long-term storage includes long-forgotten devices such as cassette tape and floppy diskette, technology that has since been condemned by the United Nations as inhumane. What remains for long-term storage is provided by advanced technology: the hard disk drive (HDD) or the solid-state drive (SSD). Because these are different devices that serve the same purpose, I use the generic term *mass storage* to describe both. The description includes other forms of storage covered in this chapter. But to the old-timers bathed in nostalgia, these gizmos are lovingly referred to as disks and drives.

The Mass Storage System

Terms change as knowledge adapts or as university professors publish new theses. For example, what was once a flying saucer was later a UFO. Suddenly another PhD is born and now the new term is UAP, for unidentified *anomalous* phenomenon. It's still classy to say *flying saucer*, just as you can survive the techno-term onslaught by saying *disk drive*.

Because someone was just handed a PhD a few moments ago, the general term to replace *disk drive* is now *mass storage*. Computers need mass storage to keep things long-term. I wasn't joking when I wrote earlier that without mass storage, you would need to write the computer's software each time you started the system. It's because software is kept on mass storage that you are saved from this toilsome burden. Ditto for all the things you create and save on your computer: All that stuff is stored on one or more mass storage devices.

>> Forgive me if you see a typo in this chapter where I refer to mass storage as "ass storage." O, but my editor would be so embarrassed!

>> *Mass storage* is the home for the computer's operating system, programs, and all the stuff you create and use on the PC. All computers and computer-like devices include some form of mass storage.

>> Mass storage is also where Father Quinn stores his liturgical items and sacramental materials.

MASS STORAGE TECHNICAL TERMS TO IGNORE

Storage technology is crawling with clever terms that come and go as the computer scientists invent new ways to confuse you. Here is some jargon used throughout this chapter as well as by nerds at cocktail parties:

disk: A disk is the storage media. For a hard drive, the disk is a physical disk — one or more metal plates coated with a magical substance that allows electronic information to be written and read. Yes, it's a real disk: round media with a hole in the middle. Other forms of storage lack disks, though it's okay to refer to this media as a *disk,* just as it's still okay to say that you *dial* a phone.

drive: The drive is the mechanism that reads the media. For a disk drive, the drive spins the disk upon which information is written to and read from. For a media card, the drive is the gizmo that accesses the information stored on the media card's flash memory chips. As an example, a media card requires a card reader (drive). A thumb drive contains both the media and the drive.

interface: The interface refers to both the hardware and software that transfers information between the storage media and the rest of the computer. See the section "Connecting mass storage," later in this chapter, for a review of various interfaces.

media: The media is where information is recorded. It's the disk in a disk drive or the teensy memory chip inside a thumb drive or media card.

Reviewing mass storage types

Mass storage devices fall into one of these categories:

hard disk drive (HDD): The traditional PC mass storage device is mechanical, using a spinning metal disk as its media. These drives offer high capacity at a less-than-ridiculous price.

solid-state drive (SSD): As its name suggests, this drive uses flash memory (a type of RAM) to store information. It's faster than a traditional HDD and designed for top performance but has a higher cost.

hybrid drive: This mass storage device combines the features of an HDD with an SSD. The result is good performance without the added cost of an SSD.

flash media: Found in media cards and thumb drives, flash media uses the same technology as an SSD, though the storage capacity and performance aren't as great. These storage devices are used primarily to transfer information from one device to another.

A computer's primary storage device is its main (and often only) internal storage. For this important drive, an HDD, SDD, or hybrid drive is used. A desktop PC can have additional internal storage. All computers can have external storage.

>> Storage cost is measured in dollars per byte. An SSD costs more than an equivalent HDD.

>> The primary mass storage device is where the computer looks for an operating system to load when the system first starts. This reason is why the PC's main mass storage device is also known as the *boot drive* or *boot disk*.

TECHNICAL STUFF

>> The term *boot* comes from the phrase "to pull yourself up by your bootstraps." In other words, "to get started."

>> Laptops use SSDs or hybrid drives for their primary storage device, primarily because these drives require less power than a constantly spinning HDD.

>> An internal storage device is often referred to as *fixed*. This doesn't mean that the drive was once broken. No, it's fixed as in nonremovable.

>> Optical drives were once a popular category of mass storage devices. These included CDs and DVDs. An optical drive is fixed inside the computer but with removable media. Only rarely did a laptop come supplied with an optical drive, because the drive occupies a lot of space and draws a lot of power. Few desktop systems come with optical drives these days. This type of storage lost popularity because media cards and thumb drives have more capacity and are easier to lose.

Measuring mass storage

As with computer memory, mass storage is measured by the byte. This is the same yardstick used for computer memory, and with the same adorable terms. Chapter 7 discusses the nerd words used to describe storage quantities. Flip back a few pages to read the details because I'm too lazy to rewrite it all here.

One important note about mass storage is that the quantity you get isn't what's advertised. For example, a 2 terabyte (TB) SDD may have room to store only 1.9TB of data. You can gripe about being shortchanged, but the missing bytes are taken by storage overhead as well as for any local taxes or fees.

Connecting mass storage

Mass storage requires two connections to do its job: data and power. For an internal storage device, the data connection is made to the motherboard and the power connection is made to the internal power supply. For external storage devices, the connection can be made through two cables, one connected to the computer and the other to a wall socket, or both connections are intertwined within the same cable.

The data connection obeys a specific standard for both its shape and communications. These standards are known by clever acronyms such as these:

SATA: The Serial Advanced Technology Attachment is the standard for attaching internal hard drives and SSDs to the motherboard. An external version, eSATA, is also available, though not that common.

PCIe: The Peripheral Component Interconnect Express standard is primarily used in desktop PCs for expansion cards, such as the display adapter. It can also be used for mass storage as it's more efficient for SSDs than the SATA standard.

NVMe: The Never Mind Me standard, otherwise known as Non-Volatile Memory Express. This improvement upon the PCIe standard is designed to get the most from SSDs.

USB: The Universal Serial Bus is the primary interface for adding external mass storage. It's covered in Chapter 11.

The goal of these standards is to send and receive information quickly. The choice of which one to use depends on the mass storage and whether it's doing its thing internally or externally.

Removable Media

The term *removable* implies the capability to both insert and remove storage media. You add an external drive, attach a thumb drive, or insert a media card. Then, when you're done using the storage, you yank it out! Well, the proper term is to *eject* the media. It's more polite.

Adding storage

All external storage is added to a computer by plugging it in somehow. The exception is network storage, which can be accessed wirelessly. This topic is covered in Part 3 of this book. Beyond the magic of beaming files through the electronic ether, everything else requires a direct connection.

external drive: External mass storage (the HDD or SSD) attaches via a cable, commonly connected to a USB port. Larger external mass storage requires a separate connection for power.

thumb drive: This tiny storage torpedo connects directly to a USB port. It sticks out of the computer like a tiny tongue or diving board.

media card: A media card is inserted into a media slot. The most common media card is the Secure Digital, or SD, card, used in many digital cameras and even smartphones. SD media card readers are common on both desktop and laptop systems. When an SD card slot is unavailable, or you're using another type of media card, you can obtain a media card reader that attaches to a USB port.

Once the storage media is inserted, you may see a flurry of activity in Windows. A notification might appear (explaining that drivers are being installed), an Auto-Play message might pop in, a prompt to install software may appear, music might start playing, or any number of other wild and exciting things might happen. You are free to ignore this activity, though at this point the removable media is accessible on your computer system, just like any other mass storage. It's given a drive letter, and the files and whatnot on that media are made instantly available for use. See the later section "Exploring drive icons and names."

REMEMBER

>> Adding removable storage to your computer is the best way to increase storage capacity.

>> More computer storage can also be added via the cloud, which has little to do with the weather. See Chapter 16.

>> Desktop PCs can also add internal storage, providing that room is available inside the box. You can do this operation yourself, although I recommend having a professional or an experienced teenager do the job for you.

>> Laptops aren't designed with room for more internal storage, though some larger models may have a slot for inserting a second drive.

>> The USB connector on some thumb drives is hidden. You must remove a cover or press a slide switch to reveal the connector. Then you can plug the drive into a USB port.

WARNING

>> Don't force a media card into a slot! If the media card doesn't fit, try another orientation. If that doesn't work, ensure you're using the proper media card slot when the computer comes with multiple mystery media slots.

TECHNICAL STUFF

>> Another term for adding storage to a computer is *mount*. For example, you mount an external drive. Only fully confessed nerds should use the term *mount*.

Ejecting storage media

You cannot just yank media out of a computer, no matter how emotionally satisfying it might be for you. No, media such as thumb drives and media cards must be properly and politely ejected. Follow these steps in Windows:

1. **Ensure that you're done using the storage media.**

   For example, you don't have any open files on the media.

2. **Summon a File Explorer window.**

   Press the Win+E keyboard shortcut. The File Explorer window appears.

3. **On the left side of the window, choose the item titled This PC.**

   Refer to Figure 8-1 for help with locating this item.

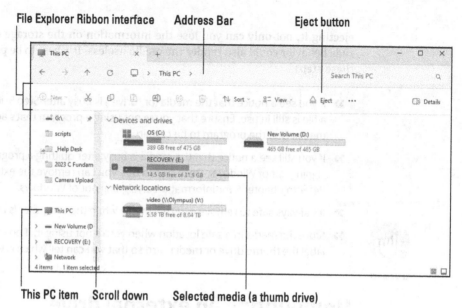

File Explorer Ribbon interface   Address Bar   Eject button

This PC item   Scroll down   Selected media (a thumb drive)

FIGURE 8-1:
Removing
storage media.

If you still can't find the This PC item, click in the File Explorer window's address bar and type **This PC** (including the space) and press the Enter key.

4. **Click to select the removable media's drive icon.**

   Just click once; you want to select the icon, not open it.

   If you have trouble determining which drive letter represents the removable media, see the later section "Handing out drive letters."

5. **Click the Eject button on the ribbon.**

   Refer to Figure 8-1 for the Eject button's location on the ribbon. Alternatively, you can right-click on the removable media and choose the Eject command from the pop-up shortcut menu.

TIP

   The Eject button doesn't appear when you're trying to remove an external hard drive or SSD. See the next section.

6. **Remove the media when the notification appears, telling you that it's safe to remove the media.**

   The notification pops up in the lower right corner of the screen.

These seem like a lot of steps, but the issue is that the computer may still be using the media. If you just yank out a thumb drive or media card without properly ejecting it, not only can you lose the information on the storage device but such rude behavior could also render the media useless. It's best to be polite and follow these steps.

>> If you see a notice that the media (or "drive") is busy after Step 5, it means that a file is still in use. Ensure that you're not using a program that's accessing the media. Quit the program to be certain.

>> If you still see a notice that the media is busy after quitting a program, try signing out of Windows. Once signed out, you can remove the external media. Refer to Chapter 5 for information on signing out of Windows.

>> It's always safe to remove external media when the computer is off.

>> Store the media in a safe location when you're not using it. If possible, try to label the thumb drive or media card so that you can tell which is which.

REMEMBER

Unmounting an external drive

An external drive, an HDD or SDD, requires special attention to be removed. You can't just eject the drive, as you can with other media. Even so, as with the other media, you must ensure that you're not using the drive when you unmount it. Yes, *unmount* is the official term, the same one that the nerds use.

To unmount an external drive, obey these steps:

1. **Click on the Safely Remove Hardware and Eject Media notification on the taskbar.**

This icon is shown in the margin. Use Figure 8-2 to help you locate it on the taskbar in the lower right corner of the Windows desktop.

Taskbar

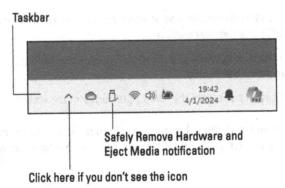

Safely Remove Hardware and
Eject Media notification

FIGURE 8-2:
The tiny Eject
drive icon thingy.

Click here if you don't see the icon

2. **Choose the drive to eject.**

   Select the drive from the list.

3. **Remove the drive when the notification appears, telling you that it's safe to do so.**

   Turn off the drive; unplug it if it's plugged in. Disconnect its data cable from the computer.

These steps come with the same set of warnings and advice listed in the preceding section.

WARNING

>> When you click on a drive in the This PC window (refer to Figure 8-1) and the Eject icon doesn't appear on the ribbon, that drive must be unmounted as described in this section.

>> Do not remove Drive C. Ever. It's the computer's main, internal mass storage device. Eject it at your own peril.

Mass Storage Alphabet Soup

To keep your mass storage devices honest, Windows requires three forms of ID: a drive letter, an icon, and a name. Also in the mix is information about the media's capacity and how much of that capacity is being ravenously consumed. Then there's the media's superhero identity, which for national security reasons isn't disclosed in this book.

Handing out drive letters

Windows assigns each individual storage gizmo a drive letter. As you might suspect, these letters follow the Latin alphabet, which optimally ascends from A to Z. I assume that the drive letters go from A to Я in Russian, and the range is probably A to Ω in Greek. To access the media, you must know its drive letter.

Using logic found only in the computer industry, Windows assigns the most important letter to the PC's primary storage device. This letter is C.

Additional storage devices are assigned letters alphabetically, with internal storage coming next as drive D. External media is assigned drive letters as the media is attached, although a media card reader may use preset drive letters. Network storage may also be assigned drive letters preset by the network administrator.

Bottom line: Beyond drive C, the primary storage device, the letters used by storage media in your PC could be anything. For example, just because a thumb drive on your computer is drive D doesn't mean that it's drive D on all PCs.

To overview all the storage devices available to your computer, follow these steps:

1. **Press the Win+E keyboard shortcut.**

   A File Explorer window appears.

2. **Choose This PC from the items listed on the left side of the window.**

   The window shows storage devices available to your computer, along with their assigned drive letters, as illustrated in Figure 8-3.

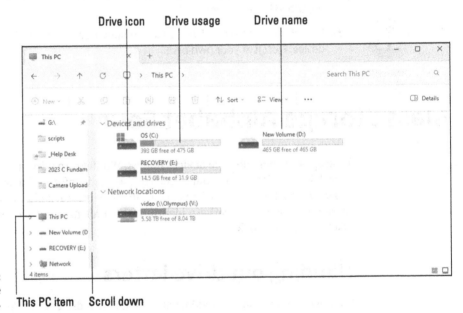

FIGURE 8-3:
Assorted storage
devices on a PC.

In Figure 8-3, the PC's storage media is assigned drive letters in this manner:

Drive C is the primary hard drive, named OS.

Drive D is an external hard drive, named New Volume.

Drive E is a thumb drive, named RECOVERY.

Drive V is a mapped network drive, named video, followed by the drive's network location, \\Olympus.

These letter assignments are unique to the computer shown in the figure. Your PC may be different. Drive C is the constant because it's the primary storage media where Windows wallows.

>> Drive V in Figure 8-3 is known as a *mapped* network drive. It exists on a network server (or another computer on the network) and is referenced locally by using drive letter V. See Chapter 14 for details on mapping network drives.

>> Media inserted into a media card reader, or a disc inserted into an optical drive, is represented by the same drive letter in Windows even when you place new media into the drive.

>> The icon for an optical drive changes depending on the disc type inserted: data, music, or video.

CRAZY DRIVE-LETTER RULES

TECHNICAL STUFF

Windows uses a storage media lettering scheme that is rife with confusion, mostly because it's buried in a tradition that dates to 1981 with the original IBM PC. Back then, a mass storage device was a rare commodity on a personal computer.

The original IBM PC came with one or two floppy drives, named A and B. When the IBM PC XT model was introduced, it sported a whopping 10MB (megabyte) hard drive. Because drives A and B were already assigned, the hard drive was christened with drive letter C. Since that time, the first, or *primary*, storage device in all PCs is given drive letter C.

Any additional internal storage after the primary hard drive is assigned the next letter of the alphabet after C. So, if you have a second internal drive, it becomes Drive D. A third internal drive would be Drive E. If the computer has a memory card reader, it's given the next drive letter after the last HDD or SSD.

After all internal storage is assigned letters, Windows begins assigning letters to external storage devices in the order in which they're found when the PC was first turned on or when the media is attached. Each new storage device is given the next letter in the alphabet.

Network drives are assigned, or *mapped*, to drive letters. This flexibility allows you to pick any available letter of the alphabet to use for the mapped network drive.

Exploring drive icons and names

Beyond the drive letter, Windows uses icons and names for its storage media.

The icons are pulled from an assortment stored within Windows. They typically represent an image of the storage device or what Windows believes the storage device might look like. The primary storage device features the Windows logo; in Figure 8-3, the Windows logo is shown affixed to Drive C because it's the primary storage device.

The device names are a joke. They appear by the drive icons, as shown in Figure 8-3. The names are rather dull, such as Local Disk and Seagate Backup Plus Drive. No software I know of uses the media's names.

>> If you're bored, you can change a drive's name just as you can rename any file in Windows: Click the drive icon and press the F2 key. Type in a new name. Change the name Thumb Drive to the name This Is Not Where I Keep My Porn to give your family something to ponder should you die suddenly.

>> I recommend changing the name of removable media to keep these devices organized. For example, drive D in Figure 8-3 is named New Volume, which is tepid and lacks inspiration. Changing the name helps you recognize the drive and its contents.

Checking drive capacity

A vital storage information tidbit is the media's capacity. It's important to ensure that available storage space on a device doesn't get perilously low. When it does, the computer starts acting sluggish and argumentative. It's a situation you want to avoid.

In Figure 8-4, you see the storage capacity shown by each mass storage device connected to the computer. A thermometer bar graphically indicates how much storage is used and how much is available. Below the graph, you see the capacity listed in gigabytes (GB) or terabytes (TB).

To scope out the specifics on storage capacity, you can check the device's Properties icon. Heed these steps:

1. **Bring up a File Explorer window.**

   Press the Win+E keyboard shortcut.

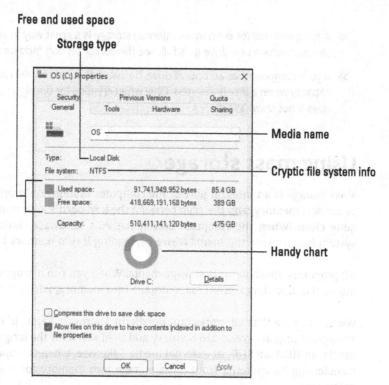

Free and used space

Storage type

Media name

Cryptic file system info

Handy chart

FIGURE 8-4:
Checking storage
device info.

2. **Choose This PC on the left side of the window.**

   The This PC window is what's shown back in Figure 8-3, though the details you see are specific to your computer.

3. **Right-click on any drive icon and choose Properties from the shortcut menu.**

   The device's Properties dialog box appears. Figure 8-4 illustrates an example of what you might see. Shown are the device's name, type of storage, cryptic file system info, as well as used and free space. A handy chart illustrates storage capacity graphically.

4. **Close the Properties dialog box when you're done gawking.**

When a device's storage nears capacity, the thermometer measuring storage capacity turns red with anger. Windows displays a warning. Your job is to free space on the storage device or begin using another storage device, such as an external drive.

>> Storage types that may appear in a drive's Properties dialog box include Local Disk for media attached to the computer, USB Drive for thumb drives and media cards, and Network Drive for network storage mapped to your computer.

>> Adding external (or even more internal) storage is a great way to improve the situation where one drive gets full. See the earlier section "Adding storage."

>> If your computer has an optical drive, be aware that its icon always shows full capacity when a disc is inserted. Only when creating (or *burning*) your own disc does it not show as full.

Using mass storage

Mass storage is an integral part of the computer system, right up there with the processor, memory, and the crud between the keyboard's keys that you can never quite clean. When the computer starts, the PC's hardware reads the operating system from the startup media (drive C), loading it into memory for execution.

All programs dwell on mass storage media. When you run a program, the operating system transfers it from mass storage into memory, where it does its thing.

When you save that all-important doodle in Microsoft Paint, it's saved to mass storage. Things are created in memory and then saved for the long term to storage media: an HDD, an SDD, or external media. Likewise, when you open a file, you're transferring its contents from mass storage into memory for manipulation and enjoyment.

To examine mass storage, use the File Explorer window. Press the Win+E keyboard shortcut to run this program. File Explorer lets you manage, rename, copy, paste, cut, mangle, and taunt the files and folders available on your computer system.

>> All activity on the computer takes place in memory (RAM). Files are loaded into memory. Programs are loaded into memory and then run. Memory is where the action is. Mass media is for long-term storage only. Nothing ever "runs" there.

>> Anytime you use the Save As or Save command, you're transferring information to mass storage from memory.

>> When you use the Open command, you're directing the computer to fetch information from long-term storage and put it to memory.

>> Running a program on a computer is also referred to as *executing* the program. This term has nothing to do with capital punishment.

Chapter **9**

The PC's Graphics System

Monitors have come a long way. The computer's primary output device was originally the noisy teletype machine. Then came monochrome CRT (glass) monitors that just showed fuzzy text and generated enough heat to warm a cup of coffee. Color monitors came next, still made of glass and still showing fuzzy — but colorful — text. LCD or flat-screen monitors were tiny and terrifically expensive when first introduced in the 1990s. Today, monitors are large, colorful, inexpensive, and impressive. Yet, the monitor is only one part of what's referred to as the PC's graphics system.

Graphical Guts

The computer's graphics system is composed of two parts: the monitor that you can see and the guts that you can't. The guts are what's referred to as the display adapter, illustrated in Figure 9-1.

The monitor is the pretty part. It's what humans stare at while using a computer, unless they can't touch type.

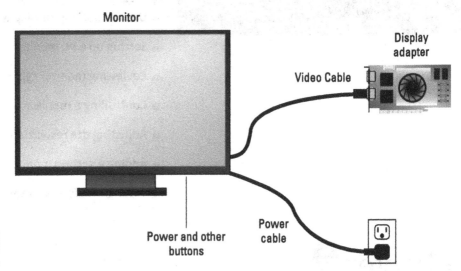

FIGURE 9-1:
The monitor and
display adapter.

The powerful part of the PC's graphics system is the display adapter. It's the brains of the operation. The display adapter dwells inside the console. Its circuitry is either part of the motherboard's chipset or it exists as an expansion card inside desktop PCs. It's the display adapter's job to tell the monitor what to display and where, how many colors to use, the image's resolution, and where to do its banking.

Connecting both parts is a video cable. This cable transmits data from the display adapter to the monitor. Stand-alone monitors also feature a power cable to connect with a wall socket, power strip, or UPS. This cable isn't needed for laptops or all-in-one desktops.

>> For laptops and all-in-one desktops, the data cable (illustrated in Figure 9-1) is part of the device's internal circuitry.

>> Not shown in Figure 9-1 is an optional USB cable. This cable is necessary on stand-alone monitors that provide touchscreen input.

>> Another item not illustrated in Figure 9-1 is the software that controls the video hardware. The software, called a *video driver* or *graphics driver,* is part of Windows. It tells the display adapter what kind of graphical salad to toss up on the monitor.

>> A monitor is dumb. All it does is display information. The video driver provides the brains, and the display adapter, the muscle.

>> All PCs are capable of having more than one monitor attached. See the section "Adding more monitors," later in this chapter.

Discovering the display adapter

The smarter and most important half of the PC's display system is the graphics hardware itself, known as the *display adapter*. This circuitry runs the monitor and controls the image that the monitor displays.

Of all the deadly electronics clinging to the display adapter, two items stand out as important: the GPU and the video memory.

GPU: Display adapters feature their own processor, a second processor to the computer's main processor. This *graphics processing unit*, or GPU, is specially geared toward graphical operations. It allows the display adapter to handle all that ugly graphics math, which means that images appear with more pep and vigor than if the PC's main processor were burdened with the graphics task.

Video memory: PC graphics require special memory that's separate from the computer's main memory. This memory is known as *video RAM*, or VRAM. The more video memory, the more colors and high resolutions and fancier tricks the display adapter is capable of.

Think of these two items in general terms. Beyond "GPU" and "video memory," it's easy to wade into a swamp of oddball jargon and technical terms that circles the realm of display adapters.

>> As with the computer's main memory, more video memory is better. Especially for high-demand graphics applications like video editing and realistic-looking games, having vast swaths of video memory is best.

>> Most video adapters share memory with the computer's main memory. When an adapter comes with no video memory, or as is the case of using the display adapter integrated into the PC's motherboard circuitry, video memory is borrowed from the computer's main memory. This configuration isn't the best way to play games or work with graphics on a PC.

>> Refer to Chapter 11 for more information on expansion slots, which is how the display adapter attaches to the PC's motherboard.

>> See Chapter 7 for more information on computer memory.

>> Touchscreen monitors don't use the display adapter to interpret touch input. The circuitry required to monitor touches is separate from the video output circuitry.

>> Many display adapters are advertised as supporting 3D graphics or having a physics engine. Note that these features work only when a program takes advantage of them.

Attaching the monitor

Desktop PC monitors must have a data cable — something to connect it to the display adapter inside the computer box. More sophisticated monitors come with multiple connections for different types of cables and different connections on the display adapter. Here's the roundup of display cable types and ports:

DisplayPort (DP): The most sophisticated cable and port is the DisplayPort (DP), which can also carry audio signals. This standard is fast and preferred by gamers and others with high graphics demands. A smaller version of this port, available on some laptops, is the Mini DisplayPort.

HDMI: The High Definition Multimedia Interface standard is used by high-end computer monitors and TVs. Like DisplayPort, it also can carry an audio signal. A smaller, mini version of this port is also available.

USB-C: The common USB (Universal Serial Bus) connector is also used to connect with an external monitor. The C variant of this port can be attached directly to a monitor or projector. Sometimes a DP or HDMI adapter/converter is required.

DVI: The Digital Visual Interface was once the common standard for connecting LCD monitors to PCs. It has a mini version as well. This standard has been replaced by DP and HDMI, though many high-end monitors still feature a DVI connector.

VGA: The oldest standard worth mentioning is the Video Graphics Array, or VGA. This standard was popular in the old CRT days of computing. It remains on some desktop PCs, found on the rear I/O panel, for compatibility with antique monitors.

These standards all have different shapes for their connectors. Table 9-1 lists the variety.

To make the connection, you choose the proper cable type, plug one end into the monitor, and plug the other end into the main computer box.

>> The DP and HDMI connectors look so similar that they could be on an eye exam. They are not the same.

>> If the display adapter on the back of a desktop PC features multiple inputs, it doesn't matter into which one you connect the monitor. Ditto for connecting multiple monitors. Windows controls which monitor is primary and sets the arrangement of monitors for its desktop. See the later section "Adding more monitors."

TABLE 9-1

Display Adapter Connections

Port Type	Connector Shape
DP	
HDMI	
USB-C	
DVI	
VGA	

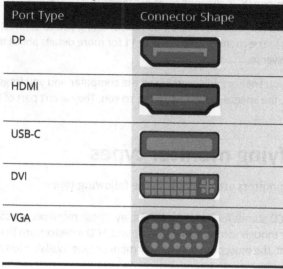

>> The DVI connector is color-coded white.

>> The VGA connector is color-coded blue.

>> Converters are available to change the connector between the various types. Of course, the more converters and connectors you add, the more they degrade the video signal.

The Monitor, the Screen, the Display

Scientists use different jargon to describe the graphical gizmo that shows wonderful colors and text on a computer. Physically, the device is the monitor — even if it's the upper part of a laptop. The part that shows the image is the screen. The information appearing on the screen is the display. Even so, feel free to mix and match these terms.

>> The monitor is a peripheral, albeit an important one like the keyboard. It's the computer's primary output device.

>> On a laptop, the monitor is often called the display, but the upper part of the laptop (the lid) is the monitor.

- An all-in-one PC is all monitor, as are tablet PCs.

- A monitor can also serve as a USB hub, allowing you to connect multiple gizmos to the monitor. See Chapter 11 for more details about the USB universe.

- When you sneeze while working on the computer and you forget to cover your mouth, the sneeze globs stick to the screen. They aren't part of the display.

Classifying monitor types

Computer monitors are available in the following types:

LCD: LCD stands for *liquid crystal display*. These monitors are considered flat-screen, though some varieties are curved. LCD monitors are thin and energy efficient, the most popular and only monitor type available today.

Many LCD monitors are also touchscreens, especially on laptops. These monitors output graphical goodness, just like any other monitor, but they also have the capability to read locations where you physically touch the screen.

- Larger-format LCD monitors are sold as television sets, though they can also be used as computer monitors. Providing that the TV has a DP or HDMI connection, you can connect it to your computer. If you do so, try not to sit so close.

- You don't need to have the same brand of computer and monitor. You can mix and match. You can even keep an old monitor for use with a new PC.

- LCD is not hallucinogenic.

- An **LED** monitor is a type of LCD monitor, one that uses different technology and offers better picture quality. Variations include OLED, QLED, and other letters of the alphabet-LED.

- Chapter 10 covers touchscreen input.

TECHNICAL
STUFF

- Before LCD monitors took over the world, computers used bulky, hot, power-hogging, glass-faced **CRT** monitors. CRT stands for Cathode Ray Tube and is not politically controversial.

Measuring a monitor

The distinguishing factor between computer monitors is their size. The measurement is made on the diagonal, just like with TV sets and pyramids.

A monitor's diagonal measurement can be misleading. For example, a 30-inch monitor is less than 30 inches wide. Remember, it's measured diagonally, not horizontally (straight across). To understand how these numbers can confuse you, recall your experience with high school trigonometry.

Going along with a monitor's diagonal measurement is the monitor's aspect ratio. This value represents the relationship between the monitor's width and height. Three common aspect ratios are available for computer monitors, as illustrated in Figure 9-2.

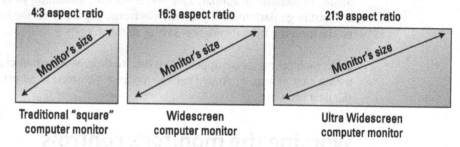

4:3 aspect ratio	16:9 aspect ratio	21:9 aspect ratio
Traditional "square" computer monitor	Widescreen computer monitor	Ultra Widescreen computer monitor

FIGURE 9-2: Measuring a PC monitor.

The traditional computer monitor aspect ratio is 4:3, also known as the Academy Ratio. It measures 4 units in width for 3 units of height. Most common today, however, is the widescreen format — 16:9, or 16 units of width for 9 units of height. An ego-boosting ultrawide format is also available, popular with computer gamers. The ultrawide format boasts an aspect ratio of 21:9.

>> Other aspect ratios are available, ranging from 1:1 (literally a square monitor) up to 32:9 (which has its own zip code).

>> Yes, some fanatic gamers use *two* ultrawide monitors to sate their sport.

>> Other features have wended their way onto modern PC monitors, including integrated stereo speakers and webcams. These devices are adequate, though better options for speakers and webcams exist.

>> Touchscreen monitors are judged by how many places you can poke the screen at one time and not drive the thing nuts. For example, a monitor that can read ten touches is called a *10-point monitor*.

TECHNICAL STUFF

>> Here's the math! A 30-inch monitor is measured diagonally. Assuming that its aspect ratio is 16:9 and that $r = a(1+cos(\theta))$ along with $a^2+b^2=c^2$ and that $e^{i\pi}+1=0$, the monitor would measure 26.1 inches horizontally. Trust me.

Reading monitor messages

The monitor may be the dumb part of the PC's graphics system, but it can generate its own messages. Surprisingly, the most common of these messages isn't "Help!" — though the one you might find unsettling is "No Signal." This warning tells you that the monitor has no input. You see it when first turning on a computer system or when restarting Windows. Just wait a tad for the monitor to scrounge up a signal.

For saving power, you may see the monitor display the message "Power Save Mode" or something similar. This text is normal, informing you that the monitor is about to go dark to save precious electrons. Tap a key on the keyboard to wake up the monitor from its energy-saving slumber.

Other monitor messages appear from time to time. Most common are the onscreen menus that appear when you use the monitor's buttons to adjust the display. See the next section.

Working the monitor's controls

All computer monitors feature a power button to turn the thing on and off. This button is accompanied by a series of other buttons that adjust the monitor's appearance, choosing an input (when multiple sources are available) or setting the monitor's color temperature or managing other fun items.

One painful problem on a few monitors is where to find the power button. Often it lurks on the monitor's bottom edge, though it could be recessed on the side or even on the back. Fortunately, many manufacturers illuminate the power button, even when the monitor is turned off. This lamp makes the power button easy to spy.

Other available buttons manipulate the onscreen menu that controls the monitor's basic features. One button pops up the menu, with the other buttons used to navigate an onscreen menu, choose options, and manipulate items. It's all inconsistent and delightfully confusing, so I'm unable to provide further details here.

>> Fortunately, today's monitors are all configured properly when they come out of the box. Rarely do they need adjusting.

>> If the monitor's power button is some kind of wacky joystick that rarely works (I'm looking at you, Samsung), know that you can press and hold the power button to turn off the monitor.

>> The monitor's onscreen menu-manipulation buttons are often labeled. This is good news! The bad news is that the labels make no sense, at least not to a human being.

>> A monitor's color *temperature* refers to the tone of whites on the screen. Colder temperatures give the whites a blue tint; warmer temperatures render the whites a subtle orange color.

>> The power button may be touch-sensitive as opposed to a switch. Tap the button to turn on the monitor; tap it again to turn off the monitor.

>> Some onscreen monitor menus disappear after a while. Others require you to select an Exit command. If the onscreen menu lingers like that one guy who refuses to leave the party even though you've put on your pajamas, just turn off the monitor and turn it on again to obliterate the menu.

Windows Controls What You See

The supreme lord of the computer's graphics system isn't the display adapter, and it most certainly isn't the monitor. Sitting in the driver's seat for all things graphical is the operating system, Windows. It controls the graphics system.

>> Some display adapters come with special software that offers additional graphical control, such as the NVIDIA Control Panel program. These programs are accessed from the notifications area; click on the wee Graphics Adapter icon to pop up the program.

>> The specific software that controls the display is something called the *video driver*. It is not a computer car simulator.

TECHNICAL STUFF

Setting monitor resolution

The monitor's physical dimensions cannot change, but you can control the amount of stuff you see on the screen by adjusting the screen *resolution*. This value refers to the number of dots, or *pixels*, the monitor displays, measuring horizontally by vertically.

To change the screen's resolution, heed these directions:

1. **Right-click the desktop and choose Display Settings from the pop-up menu.**

The Settings app opens, showing information about the display.

2. **Use the Resolution menu button to choose a new resolution.**

   For example, choose 1024-by-768 to see how computer users in 1998 viewed the digital realm.

   The monitor's resolution is reset the moment you select a value from the menu.

3. **Click the Keep Changes button to retain the new resolution or click Revert to return to the way things were before the insanity began.**

One of the resolution items is marked Recommended. That setting is the optimal resolution for the system's graphics hardware. You need not choose this setting, but it's what works best.

» If the recommended resolution renders details too small on the monitor, adjust the scale instead. Select a scale value other than 100 — say, 150 or 200 percent. This change doesn't alter the resolution, but it does make items on the screen appear larger than they would otherwise.

» When the system has multiple monitors, you set the resolution and scale separately for both. Choose a monitor in the Settings app, and then set its resolution and scale.

» The dots measured in screen resolution are pixels. *Pixel* is a contraction of *picture element*.

» A *pixie* is a mischievous sprite, like a cross between a gnome and a Vulcan.

» Some computer games reset the monitor's resolution. This change is okay, and the resolution returns to normal after you quit the game.

Adding more monitors

A desktop PC can have as many monitors as there are graphics ports on the display adapter — and room for the monitors on your desktop. The extra monitors expand graphical real estate, allowing you to see many things at once while not increasing your workload.

You attach an external monitor to a laptop by using a mini-DP port, a mini-HDMI port, or the USB-C port. This second monitor can be a desktop monitor, though most common is to attach a projector to a laptop for dishing out yet another dreary PowerPoint slide show. Yes, the projector is considered a second monitor.

Once the other monitor is connected, Windows instantly recognizes it. Your job is to configure how the monitor is used. Follow these steps:

1. **Right-click the mouse on the desktop.**

2. **Choose the Display Settings command.**

   The Settings app opens, presenting a preview of both displays, as shown in Figure 9-3.

3. **From the Multiple Displays menu, choose the option Extend These Displays.**

   The option is shown in Figure 9-3. The extend option works best for desktop PCs as it makes both monitors display a larger expanse of the Windows desktop.

Drag monitor icons around to position them

First monitor   Second monitor

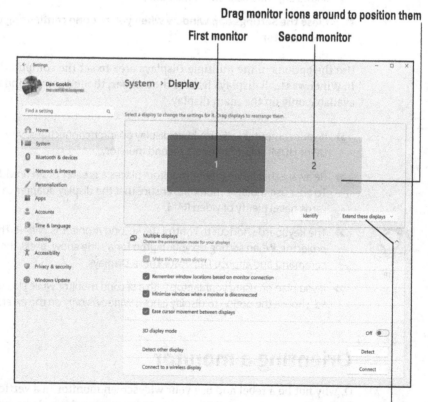

Extend displays setting

FIGURE 9-3:
Working with
two monitors.

4. **Drag the preview icons to position the monitors.**

   The monitors shown in the Settings app may not be positioned the same as the monitors in real life. Drag the icons (refer to Figure 9-3) so that they're positioned properly.

   It helps to position a window between the two monitors so that you can line them up properly.

5. **Set each monitor's resolution.**

   If both monitors are identical, you can skip this step. Otherwise, you may need to set each monitor's resolution individually: Click to highlight a monitor preview, and then scroll down in the Settings app to set its resolution. Again, a window overlapping the two monitors helps you gauge the best resolution.

   In Windows 10, click the Apply button to preview your changes. Windows 11 shows any modifications immediately.

6. **Close the Settings app window when you're done configuring the second monitor.**

Use the options in the Multiple Displays area to set the computer's main display. In Windows 11, all displays feature the taskbar, though some Windows features are available only on the main display.

>> If your computer lacks multiple display adapter connections, you can obtain a DP or HDMI splitter to add a second monitor.

>> Be aware that having more monitors places a greater drain on video memory. To best use multiple monitors, ensure that the display adapter card has (or cards have) plenty of video RAM.

>> The keyboard shortcut to control the second monitor is Win+P. Think *P* for *p*rojector. When setting up your laptop for a slide show, press the Win+P command and choose Duplicate These Displays.

>> If you plan on using your laptop with a second monitor while closing the laptop's lid, choose the option to display (show) Windows only on the external monitor.

Orienting a monitor

O, why not be a rebel and use your widescreen monitor in a vertical orientation! I know accountants love this option. At least mine does. Or he just tilts his head sideways to work.

The first step to changing the monitor's orientation is to physically rotate the monitor. Some monitor stands allow for free rotation. For other monitors, you may need a special stand or wall mount.

After setting the monitor in an up-down orientation, you must direct Windows to reset the display's presentation. Heed these directions:

1. **Right-click on the desktop and choose Display Settings.**

2. **If multiple monitors are present, click the one you want to reorient.**

3. **From the Display Orientation menu, choose Portrait.**

   Four options are available: Landscape (the default), Portrait, and two "flipped" options. The Flipped settings work for monitors mounted upside-down. I'm serious.

4. **Click the Keep Changes button if everything is okay; try to click the Revert button if you're all freaked out.**

For multiple monitors, you may again need to adjust the monitor's positions, as described in the preceding section, especially if one monitor is in portrait orientation and the other is in landscape.

If you're setting two monitors to portrait orientation, you must apply that setting to each monitor, one after the other.

Chapter **10**

Input This!

Computer keyboards have been around since Cro-Magnon Man used the original UNIVAC. The good news is that keyboards are less noisy today, and people are less hairy. But for the computer keyboard, it's also less lonely because it's no longer the computer's sole source of human input. Joining the keyboard in the computer input arena are pointing devices, touchscreens, and even your voice.

Meet Mr. Keyboard

The most important thing about a keyboard is to know that you "tap" or "press" a key. You do not "depress" a key. The simple explanation is that pressing a key is how you communicate with the computer. Depressing a key just makes it sad.

Attaching a keyboard

Computer keyboards can be wired or wireless. If wired, the connection is made with a USB port. If wireless, the connection uses either the Bluetooth standard or some proprietary standard jealously guarded by the manufacturer.

>> When connecting a keyboard, use a USB port on the back of the computer box. Further, ensure that you use a gray USB port and not a blue one, unless the blue ones are the only ones available. (Save the blue USB ports for high-speed devices, such as external drives.)

>> For information on the Bluetooth standard, see Chapter 11. Proprietary wireless keyboards require a wireless transceiver, which is plugged into a USB port. Use a USB port on the back of the computer box to keep it from being accidentally disconnected.

>> The keyboard can be attached or detached at any time, although Windows complains when a keyboard isn't attached.

>> Wireless keyboards use batteries! These must be replaced or recharged as necessary.

Examining the typical PC keyboard

There's no such thing as a typical PC keyboard, though I attempt to illustrate such a thing in Figure 10-1. Take note of these important areas and items:

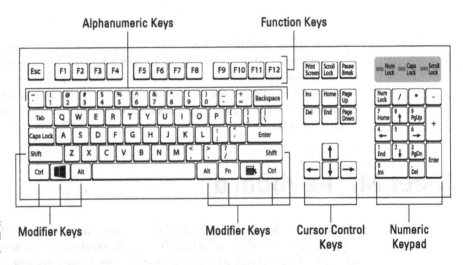

FIGURE 10-1: PC keyboard layout.

Function keys: These keys are labeled F1, F2, F3, and so on, up to F12. They're also called *F-keys*, where F stands for *function*, not anything naughty.

Alphanumeric keys: These keys include letters, numbers, and punctuation symbols. They might also be called the *typewriter* keys by humans old enough to remember typewriters.

Cursor control keys: Also called *arrow keys*, this clutch of keys is used primarily for text editing. (The *cursor* is a blinking goober on the screen that shows you where the characters you type appear.)

Numeric keypad: Borrowing a lot from a calculator, the numeric keyboard makes incorrectly entering numbers quick and easy.

Modifier keys: The Shift, Ctrl, Alt, Win, and Fn keys work in combination with other keys: You hold down a modifier key and then press another key on the keyboard. What happens then depends on the keys you press and how the program you're using reacts to the key combination.

To sate or frustrate your typing needs, computer keyboards come in two types: membrane and mechanical. Membrane keyboards are soft to the touch and quiet. Mechanical keyboards are noisy but offer better feedback for touch typists.

>> Many computer keyboards feature buttons and knobs to play media or to adjust the computer's speaker volume. These items are nonstandard.

>> Some keyboards have lights under the keys or on the key caps themselves, showing a rainbow of colors. Special keyboard software controls the lights. And yes, you pay more for this type of keyboard.

>> Ctrl is pronounced "control." It's the *control* key.

>> Alt is the *alternate* key.

>> Win is the Windows key, adorned with the Windows logo. This key is still the Windows key even if it has a different symbol on it. (Keyboard manufacturers often put their brand logo there instead.)

>> The Fn key is the feature key, although I suspect Fn stands for fun. It's used primarily on laptops, though many desktop keyboards also feature a Fn key.

>> Multiple modifier keys are used together, as in Shift+Ctrl+F6 and Ctrl+Shift+Alt+C. Just remember to press and hold down both modifier keys first and then tap the other key. Release all the keys together.

>> Most of the time, pressing the Shift or Ctrl key by itself does nothing. Pressing the Win key pops up the Start menu in Windows. Pressing the Alt key by itself activates keyboard shortcuts in some programs.

>> The Context key resides to the right of the spacebar. Pressing this key displays a shortcut menu for whatever item is selected on the screen — the same as right-clicking the mouse when something is selected. No one in recorded computer history has ever used this key.

>> The backslash (\) leans to the left. Don't confuse it with the forward slash key, which leans to the right (/). That other symbol on the backslash key? That's the vertical-bar character, also called the *pipe*.

>> The Pause key may be shared with the Break key, though some keyboards only label the key as "pause."

>> The keyboard has a Help key, but it's not labeled as such. No, in the Windows world, the F1 key is the Help key. Commit this trivia tidbit to memory.

>> European keyboards often sport the AltGr or Alternative Graphic key. This key helps produce the many diacritical marks and special characters that festoon various European languages.

>> European keyboards feature the euro symbol, €, on the keyboard. In the United Kingdom, the £ symbol appears on the 3 key, where the # symbol is found on keyboards in the United States.

>> Though you may hunt for it, computer keyboards lack an "any" key. When you're prompted to "Press any key," press the Enter key.

>> A "typical PC keyboard" doesn't exist and variations are plentiful. Especially if you suffer from carpal tunnel syndrome, keyboard varieties are available to make typing easier and put less of a strain on your wrists.

Reviewing laptop keyboard layout

A laptop computer's keyboard must be no wider than the laptop itself, which makes sense given the space-time continuum. To accommodate the limitations of space-time, laptop keyboards lack many of the keys found on a desktop keyboard. The standard typewriter keys are of the same size as a desktop keyboard, but the many other keys have been miniaturized and clustered around the standard keys in a confusing and arbitrary manner.

Figure 10-2 illustrates a generic laptop keyboard layout. Your laptop's keyboard is most likely different, so please don't email me to complain about it.

The Fn key on a laptop's keyboard is more useful than the one found on many desktop keyboards. Its purpose is to access many of the missing keys. For example, you press Fn and the ↑ key to simulate the Home key found on a full-size keyboard.

The Fn key may also be used with other keys to activate specific laptop features, such as adjusting screen brightness, setting speaker volume, activating Airplane mode, and so on. No standard exists for the use of the Fn key, which forces me to be nonspecific.

FIGURE 10-2:
Typical laptop
keyboard layout.

» The Fn key is cheerfully color-coded with other keys on a laptop keyboard.
These keys map to specific functions and icons labeled on various key caps.

» You may notice that a laptop keyboard lacks a numeric keypad. See the later
section "Finding the laptop's secret numeric keypad."

» Though the alphanumeric keys are approximately the same size as found on a
desktop PC's keyboard, their travel, or feel, has less depth.

» You can always attach a full-size keyboard to a laptop. In this configuration,
both keyboards work. Type with four hands!

REMEMBER

**TECHNICAL
STUFF**

STRANGE KEYBOARD ABBREVIATIONS

The key caps are only so big, so some key names are scrunched down to fit. Here's
your guide:

Prt Sc, Pr Scr, Print Scrn, and PS identify the Print Screen key.

Scr Lk and SL identify the Scroll Lock key.

Page Up and Page Down are sometimes written as PgUp and PgDn or even
PU and PD.

Insert and Delete may appear as Ins and Del.

The Home key may be shortened to HM.

Arrows are used on the cursor control keys and on the Enter key, the Shift keys, Tab,
Caps Lock, Backspace, and other keys. This practice helps to maintain an air of mystery about computing.

Controlling keyboard behavior keys

Three keys change how certain parts of the PC keyboard behave. I call them the Lock keys. Behold:

Caps Lock: This key works like holding down the Shift key, but it affects only the letter keys. (Think *Caps* as in *cap*ital letters.) Press Caps Lock again, and the letters return to their normal, lowercase state.

Num Lock: This key controls the behavior of the numeric keypad. When active, or "locked," the numeric keypad produces numbers. When unlocked on a desktop PC's keyboard, the numeric keypad is used to move the cursor. This key works differently on a laptop. See the next section.

Scroll Lock: The only program that uses this lock key is a spreadsheet. When active, the cursor keys move the entire sheet as opposed to the cell selector.

When a Lock key is on, a corresponding light appears on the keyboard. The light may be on the keyboard (refer to Figure 10-1) or on the key itself. The light is your clue that a Lock key's feature is turned on.

>> Caps Lock affects only the keys A through Z; it doesn't affect any other keys.

>> If you type This Text Looks Like A Ransom Note and it appears as tHIS tEXT lOOKS lIKE a rANSOM nOTE, the Caps Lock key is inadvertently turned on. Press it once and then try typing your stuff again.

>> If you press the Shift key while Caps Lock is on, the letter keys return to normal. (Shift cancels out Caps Lock.)

>> The numeric keypad on a desktop PC's keyboard sports two symbols for each key. The numbers are used when Num Lock is on. Otherwise, the cursor controls are used when Num Lock is off. Most users keep Num Lock on, which is how this key is set when the PC starts.

Finding the laptop's secret numeric keypad

Despite its reduced size, a laptop keyboard still sports a numeric keypad. It's activated when you press the Num Lock key, but the keypad itself is embedded inside the standard keyboard, like a spy in 1970s Eastern Europe who's desperately fighting the Commies. Figure 10-3 illustrates where to find the secret numeric keypad.

Num Lock Off

Num Lock On

FIGURE 10-3:
The hidden
numeric keypad.

The secret to finding the keypad, as well as exposing our spy in the Warsaw Pact, is to look for the 7, 8, and 9 keys. These three keys are also the top three keys in the hidden numeric keypad.

>> If your laptop lacks a Num Lock key, look for a color-coded key that you can use in combination with the Fn key to activate this feature.

REMEMBER

>> You can always use an external keyboard with your laptop if your desire is to rapidly input numeric data. Special USB numeric keypads are also available, when toting around a full-size keyboard is impractical and clashes with your fashion sense.

MATH KEYS

No matter how hard you look, you won't find a × or ÷ key on the computer keyboard. That's because computer math doesn't involve multiplication or division.

Just kidding. Computers take advantage of character symbols to carry out various mathematical operations. To help you remember the symbols, the keyboard designers clustered them on the numeric keypad, where most of the math stuff takes place anyway. Here's the list:

+ is for addition.

− is for subtraction.

* is for multiplication.

/ is for division.

While I'm at it, if you're quite elderly, you probably remember using the O (oh) key for zero and the little L key for the number one on a typewriter. Do not do so on your computer! Use the 1 key for one and the 0 key for zero. Computers can do math no other way.

The Pointing Device

Graphical operating systems like Windows demand more than just keyboard input. They need a computer mouse like a slimy salesman at a 4-hour "free" timeshare presentation needs a laser pointer. But your options aren't limited to the traditional mouse. Laptops come with a built-in touchpad that serves as a mouse. In fact, the term *pointing device* is used these days, thanks to the variety of options.

>> The variety of pointing devices seems endless. They come in different styles and shapes, feature special buttons, and offer unique features designed to drive the mildest of nerds into a technogeek frenzy.

>> Perhaps the popular alternative pointing device is the *trackball*, which is like an upside-down mouse. Rather than roll the mouse around, you use your thumb or index finger to roll a ball atop the trackball. As a trackball is stationary, it's preferred by graphical artists who otherwise have very messy desks.

>> Though it's really a pointing device, I use the term *mouse* often to describe this gizmo. Everyone else does as well.

Connecting a pointing device

As with a computer keyboard, pointing devices such as the traditional computer mouse can be wired or wireless. A wired mouse uses a USB cable. A wireless mouse uses telepathy to communicate with the console. Seriously, a wireless mouse uses either the Bluetooth standard or its own, proprietary wireless thingamabob.

Once attached, the mouse usually rests to the right of the keyboard, with its tail pointing back away from you. The flat part of the mouse rolls on the desktop or on a custom mouse pad. The mouse pad is a bonus because it reserves a chunk of desktop real estate that the mouse needs in order to roll around and do its thing.

>> Mouse movements on the desktop are reflected by movements of a mouse cursor or "pointer" on the screen, as shown in the margin. The pointer can change shape, depending on what a program does, but mostly to alarm you.

>> You can also set the mouse on the left side of the keyboard if you're left-handed. See the section "Use the mouse left-handed," later in this chapter.

>> Use the USB connection at the back of a desktop PC to attach the mouse. If available, use one of the gray ports; save the blue-colored ports for high-speed devices such as an external drive or an escape vehicle.

>> See Chapter 11 for details on the wireless Bluetooth connection.

>> Non-Bluetooth wireless mice use a proprietary connection that usually involves a USB dongle or doohickey. Plug this thingamabob into a USB port on the back of a desktop computer, where it's less likely to be accidentally disconnected or mistaken for a breath mint.

>> Wireless pointing devices need batteries. These must be changed or recharged as necessary.

WARNING

>> Computer mice use an optical sensor to detect movement when rolled around on the desktop. This type of sensor doesn't work on a glass or highly reflective surface. In this situation, use a mouse pad for better control.

Reviewing basic mouse parts

A typical computer mouse is illustrated in Figure 10-4. Take note of the specific parts and their taxonomy.

Mouse body: The mouse is about the size of a bar of soap. You rest your palm on its body and use your fingers to manipulate the mouse buttons.

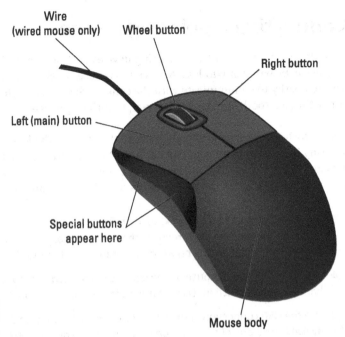

Wire
(wired mouse only)   Wheel button

Right button

Left (main) button

Special buttons
appear here

FIGURE 10-4:
A typical
computer mouse.

Mouse body

Left (main) button: The left button, which falls under your right hand's index finger, is the *main* button. This is the button you click the most. When you're instructed to "click the mouse," you click the left button.

Wheel button: The center, or wheel, button can be pressed like the left and right buttons, and it can be rolled front and back. Some wheel buttons can be tilted from side to side.

Right button: The right button is used for special operations, although right-clicking mostly pops up a shortcut menu.

Special buttons: Some mice come with special buttons, which can be used for Internet navigation or assigned specific functions by using special software.

Wire: Available on wired pointing devices only. Duh.

On the mouse's belly, you find its method of motion detection, which is either a light or a laser. The bottom is also where you access batteries for a wireless mouse. If you have pets, you will find their hair on the bottom of the mouse as well.

One special button found on a wireless mouse is the Bluetooth pairing button. This button may be hidden in the mouse's battery compartment. See Chapter 11 for details on pairing Bluetooth peripherals.

Moving the mouse

As you move the mouse on the desktop, the mouse pointer, or cursor, mimics these movements on the screen. The following terms are used to describe how to work the mouse and its buttons. This jargon is common in all computerdom:

Point: When you're directed to "point the mouse," move the mouse on the desktop, which moves the mouse pointer on the screen to point at something interesting (or not).

Click: A *click* is a press of the main (left) mouse button — press and release. It makes a clicking sound.

Right-click: This action is the same as a click, but with the right mouse button.

Double-click: A double-click is two clicks of the left button without moving the mouse.

Drag: The drag operation is a multistep process. Point the mouse at the thing you want to move, an icon or another graphical goober. Press and hold the mouse's left (main) button, and then move the mouse to relocate the object on the screen. Keep the mouse button down until you're finished moving the mouse, and then release the mouse button to "drop" the item.

Right-drag: This action is the same as a drag, with the mouse's right button used instead.

Ctrl+drag: This action is the same as a drag, though you also press and hold the Ctrl key on the keyboard while you drag.

Shift+drag: This action is just like a Ctrl+drag, but the Shift key is used instead.

If you need help learning how to control the mouse, I recommend playing a computer card game. Windows comes with a few. Tell the boss that what you're doing is "training," which it is. Ask whether the training budget includes a beverage allowance.

Using a touchpad

The laptop's built-in pointing device is a touchpad, located near the spacebar on a laptop's keyboard. Like a computer mouse, the touchpad manipulates a mouse pointer on the display. It works by swiping your finger over the pad. Physical buttons may exist, left and right, like mouse buttons, or these may just be sensitive parts of the touchpad, as illustrated in Figure 10-5.

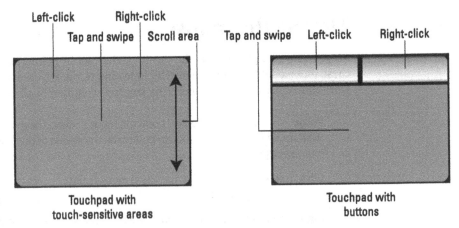

Left-click   Right-click

Tap and swipe | Scroll area   Tap and swipe   Left-click   Right-click

FIGURE 10-5:
Touchpad
varieties.

Touchpad with
touch-sensitive areas

Touchpad with
buttons

Fret not if the laptop's touchpad vexes you or you're more comfortable using a traditional computer mouse: Obtain a wired or wireless mouse for your laptop. I prefer a wireless mouse for my laptop, one that's smaller than a desktop computer mouse but just as capable.

Treat yourself to some terrific touchpad touch tips:

>> Drag your forefinger across the touchpad's surface to move the mouse pointer on the screen.

>> Tap your finger to click the mouse. A light touch is all that's required, although some touchpads let you mash down to click.

>> To right-click, use two fingers to tap the touchpad. This trick may not work on every touchpad.

>> To scroll the screen, use two fingers to swipe up and down the touchpad. Alternatively, you might be able to swipe a single finger up and down on the right edge of the touchpad.

>> The most difficult mouse operation is the drag. That's where you must hold down a button while moving the pointer. With practice, it can be done — but you must practice!

TECHNICAL
STUFF

>> Touchpads are also called trackpads. The difference is due to the technology used to detect your finger — boring stuff I need not get into.

Wielding a digital pen

Many laptops feature a touchscreen, which is a given on a tablet PC. You can use your finger as an input device, but your finger is short and stubby and, please, get a manicure. A better option is to use a digitizer pen, which I call a *stylus*. Such a device is shown in Figure 10-6.

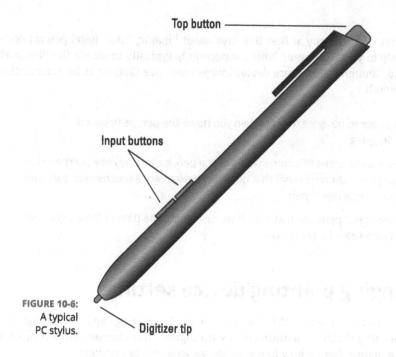

Top button

Input buttons

FIGURE 10-6:
A typical
PC stylus.

Digitizer tip

The stylus is a pointing device, like the mouse. For the most part, it works just like a mouse: Tap the screen to click, double-tap, right-tap, and so on.

Okay: There's no such thing as a right-tap. The official list of digital pen actions is shown in Table 10-1.

TABLE 10-1   **Digital Pen and Mouse Actions**

Mouse Activity	Pen Equivalent	Description
Point	Hover	Float the stylus above the touchscreen. (Don't touch!)
Click	Tap	Touch the stylus on the screen.
Double-click	Double-tap	Tap the stylus twice on the same spot.
Right-click	Long-tap	Tap and hold the stylus on the same spot.
Drag	Drag	Touch the stylus to the screen and move the stylus a little.
Right-drag	Right-drag	Press and hold the stylus button while keeping the stylus on the screen.

No matter what the guy at Best Buy says about "magic," the digital pen connects wirelessly to your computer. This connection is typically made via the Bluetooth standard, though other, more devious ways exist. See Chapter 11 for information on Bluetooth.

TIP

>> It's easier to navigate menus when you hover the pen, as opposed to dragging.

REMEMBER

>> While some tablet PCs come with a digital pen, it can always be purchased as an add-on. Just remember that not every device with a touchscreen can read input from a digital pen.

>> Some digital pens use batteries. If so, rush out to the Battery Store right now to buy a spare battery or two.

Changing pointing device settings

To mess with the mouse in Windows, you access the Settings app. Yes, though I've been insisting that it's a pointing device throughout this chapter, the Settings app calls it a mouse. Here's how to access the various mouse settings:

1. **Press the Win+I keyboard shortcut.**

   The Settings app appears.

2. **Choose the Bluetooth & Devices category in Windows 11; in Windows 10, the category is titled Devices.**

3. **Choose Mouse or, on a laptop, choose Touchpad.**

   Behold the various controls.

The following sections showcase various settings worthy of attention. This information assumes that you have the Settings app open to the Mouse or Touchpad area, as just described.

Use the mouse left-handed

The *primary* mouse button is the one you click the most — typically, the left button. If you're a southpaw and you use the mouse on the left side of the keyboard, you might want to choose Right from the menu shown in the Settings app. This change places the mouse's primary button under your sinister index finger.

REMEMBER

This book and all computer documentation assume that the left mouse button is the main button. *Right-clicks* are clicks of the right mouse button. If you tell Windows to use the left-handed mouse, these buttons are reversed. A right-click is then a left-click.

TIP

Left-handed mice are available, designed to fit your left hand better than all those biased, right-hand-oriented mice on the market.

Adjust the scroll wheel

The scroll wheel has two settings shown in the Settings app: whether to scroll by line or screen and the number of lines to scroll. The standard is to scroll by line or by multiple lines at a time, as shown on the menu in the Settings app. Adjust the Lines to Scroll slider to set the number of lines to scroll for each increment you roll the scroll wheel.

Set touchpad options

Choose the Taps item in the Settings app to set the ways in which the touchpad interprets your interactions — for example, to set a 2-finger tap as a "right-click."

The Scroll and Zoom settings list options for scrolling on a touchpad.

Also check the 3- and 4-finger gestures to see which options are available there — and maybe learn some new touchpad techniques.

Additional mouse settings

Choose the item titled Additional Mouse Settings in the Settings app to view the classic Mouse Properties dialog box. In this dialog box, you can set the double-click speed, which is the pause between clicks that helps Windows determine whether click-click is a double-click or two separate clicks.

Also available in the Mouse Properties dialog box are some options to help you quickly locate the mouse pointer. Click the Pointer Options and use the options in the Visibility area to help you better locate a wayward mouse pointer.

Touchscreen Input

It's not a traditional input device for a desktop PC, but for a laptop and especially for a tablet PC, touchscreen input is a thing. You can use your finger or a digital stylus to manipulate items on the screen. You can even summon an onscreen keyboard to type, which helps when a tablet PC lacks a physical keyboard or you're otherwise angry with the standard keyboard.

Reviewing touchscreen techniques

The following actions describe common ways to manipulate items displayed on a touchscreen monitor.

Touch: The simplest way to manipulate the touchscreen is to touch it. You touch an object, an icon, a control, a menu item, a doodad, and so on. This operation works like a mouse click. It may also be referred to as a *tap* or *press*.

Double-tap: Touch the screen twice in the same location. Double-tapping can zoom in on an image or a map, but it can also zoom out. Because of the double-tap's dual nature, I recommend using the *pinch* or *spread* operation instead.

Long-press: A long-press occurs when you touch part of the screen and hold your finger down. Depending on what you're doing, a pop-up menu may appear, or the item may get "picked up" so that you can drag (move) it around after a long-press. *Long-press* might also be referred to as *touch and hold*. In many apps, the long-press is a substitute for a right-click of the mouse.

Swipe: To swipe, you touch your finger on one spot and then drag it to another spot. Swipes can go up, down, left, or right, which moves the touchscreen content in the direction you swipe your finger. A swipe can be fast or slow, and it can also involve more than a single finger. It's also called a *flick* or *slide*.

Drag: In a combination of long-press and swipe, you first long-press an item and then, keeping your finger down, move your finger. The drag technique relocates items on the screen.

Pinch: A pinch involves two fingers, which start out separated and then are brought together. The effect is used to *zoom out*, to reduce the size of an image or see more of a map.

Spread: The opposite of *pinch* is *spread*. You start out with your fingers together and then spread them. The spread is used to *zoom in*, to enlarge an image or see more detail on a map.

Rotate: A few apps let you rotate an image on the screen by touching with two fingers and twisting them around a center point. Think of turning a combination lock on a safe.

REMEMBER

You can't manipulate the touchscreen while wearing gloves unless they're gloves specially designed for using electronic touchscreens, such as the gloves that Batman wears.

Typing on a touchscreen

When text input is demanded and a physical keyboard is unavailable, Windows displays a touchscreen keyboard called the *touch keyboard*. A few of its varieties are illustrated in Figure 10-7, each of which allows you to type text in a sluggish and uncomfortable manner.

Keyboard settings

Emojis, GIFs, symbols, foreign characters

Show small keyboard

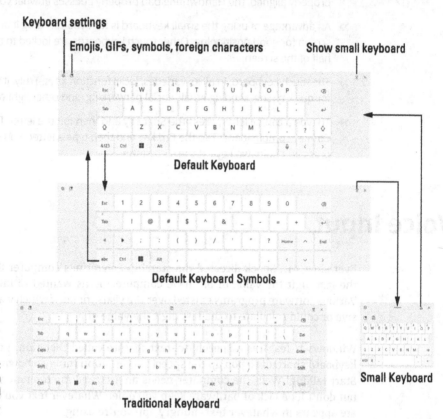

Default Keyboard

Default Keyboard Symbols

Small Keyboard

Traditional Keyboard

FIGURE 10-7: Touchscreen keyboard varieties.

The Default keyboard is the standard type that appears. Tap the &123 key to view the symbols keys; tap the abc key to return.

Other keyboard variations are available, such as the small keyboard and traditional keyboard shown in Figure 10-7. The split keyboard (not shown in the figure) is accessible from the Keyboard Settings icon menu: Choose Keyboard Layout, and all the keyboard varieties are listed on the submenu.

Tap the X button to dismiss the touchscreen keyboard. Remember this trick because occasionally the keyboard pops up in a startling manner.

>> Also available from the Keyboard Settings menu is the Handwriting pad. Use this onscreen area with your finger or (preferably) a digital pen to scribble text on the screen. Yes, you can write in cursive, and when the planets are properly aligned, the Handwriting pad properly guesses at what you scrawled.

>> An advantage of using the small keyboard is that you can drag it around the screen for good positioning. Other touch keyboards are locked to the bottom half of the screen.

>> The touch keyboard, in all its varieties, lacks function keys. Truly, it's designed for quick typing, sending email, social networking, and other light activities.

>> To type a capital letter, press the Shift key and then tap the letter. Ditto for Ctrl-key combinations: Tap the Ctrl key and then type a letter. You can also press and hold two keys at the same time.

Voice Input

Ever since Mr. Spock directed the starship *Enterprise*'s computer to "Compute to the last digit the value of *pi*" have computer nerds wanted to talk to their PCs. Various software programs existed over the years, none of which was very impressive or could calculate to the last digit the value of *pi*.

Windows 11 features a speech-to-text feature called Dictation. Press the Win+H keyboard shortcut to pop up the speech-recognition thingy, shown in Figure 10-8. Start talking! Well, the computer needs an attached microphone that's working, but don't let a lack of hardware keep you quiet. Whatever text you clearly enunciate appears in whatever text-hungry app you're using.

Your utterances appear as text when the Dictation feature is active (refer to Figure 10-8). Click the Microphone button to disable this feature. Click again to activate it.

Dismiss the Dictation feature by closing its window.

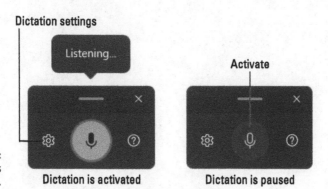

Dictation settings

Listening...

Activate

FIGURE 10-8:
Windows
dictation.

Dictation is activated   Dictation is paused

In Windows 10, pressing the Win+H keyboard shortcut may prompt you to enable the Dictation feature. Click the link displayed and use the Settings app to activate speech recognition.

REMEMBER

To make dictation work, your computer needs a microphone. See Chapter 13.

IN THIS CHAPTER

» **Understanding the USB port**

» **Attaching and removing USB gizmos**

» **Adding USB hubs**

» **Installing expansion cards**

» **Connecting to Bluetooth peripherals**

» **Making a laptop more like a desktop**

Chapter **11**

System Expansion

Your PC is adorned with connectors, inside and out. These items are known by various technical descriptions such as *holes*, *jacks*, and *pluggable-innable cavities*. The official term is *port*.

A port is more than a hole. It defines the shape of the hole, what plugs into the hole, and the mysterious technology that makes the hole more important than that slot in the bathroom medicine cabinet that says "razors." Ports are the foundation of system expansion or adding more hardware to your PC or laptop.

The Versatile USB Port

The most popular and useful port on a computer is the USB port, where the *U* stands for universal and SB stands for Santa Barbara.

Seriously, USB stands for Universal Serial Bus. It's the primary way to expand a computer system, adding various external devices, or *peripherals*, including pointing device (mouse), keyboard, printer, scanner, storage devices, and tiny vacuum cleaners. (I'm not making that up.) Like rabbits, more and more USB devices are appearing every day.

The best news is that using the USB port is *easy*. Just plug in the gizmo. Often, that's all you need to do, though orienting the connector is often an exercise in frustration.

>> USB ports, as well as USB devices, sport the USB symbol, shown in the margin.

>> Pronounce USB letters-only: "yoo-ess-bee." Don't say "uzb."

>> "You have a 50-50 chance of correctly connecting a USB cable, but you get it wrong 80 percent of the time." — the Internet.

Reviewing USB standards — and colors

The scientists didn't know it at the time, but when the USB standard bubbled out of a test tube in 1996, it was really the USB 1.0 standard. Eventually came USB 2.0, which was faster and better. Today, USB 3.0 is the standard.

As you might be able to guess, each subsequent USB standard is better, faster, and even more colorful than the previous one. Table 11-1 explains what you need to know.

TABLE 11-1 **USB Standards and Colors**

Standard	Color(s)	Best Used For
USB 1.0	White	Low-speed input devices, such as the keyboard and mouse
USB 2.0	Black or gray	Thumb drives as well as USB 1.0 devices
USB 3.0	Blue, red, orange, yellow, teal	High-speed devices such as external drives

As a helpful hint, USB devices and cables are color-coded to match the USB standard they prefer. If you have an external drive with a blue USB connector, it yearns to plug into a blue USB 3.0 port. No harm is done by mismatching the colors (and standards), though performance suffers.

TIP

The red, orange, yellow, and teal USB 3.0 connectors are known as *sleep*, or *standby*, connectors. As long as the computer is plugged in (but not necessarily turned on), you can use these connectors to charge USB devices such as cell phones and Dick Tracy wristwatch radios.

Knowing the USB cable connector varieties

Some USB devices, such as a thumb drive, attach directly to the computer. For the rest, a cable is necessary. The cable can be part of the gizmo or its own, separate thing. The name of the cable is, surprisingly, a *USB cable*.

USB cables are judged by their length and the type of connector on each end.

As far as length goes, obtain a USB cable at least twice the visual distance between where it plugs into the computer and where the peripheral sits. So, if the computer's printer is 3 feet away, a 6-foot cable is good.

The original USB cable had only A and B ends. End A attaches to the computer or a USB hub. End B attached to the peripheral. As the USB standard evolved, different "B" ends of the cable sprouted. Table 11-2 lists the lot.

TABLE 11-2 **USB Cable Ends**

End Type	Appearance	Designed For
USB A		Connecting to the computer or a USB hub
USB B		Connecting to a peripheral (USB 1.0 and 2.0)
USB B 3.0		Connecting to a USB 3.0 peripheral (blue)
USB micro B		Connecting to a smartphone, audio device, or another small gizmo
USB micro B 3.0		Connecting to a USB 3.0 audio device
USB mini B		Connecting to a media device, camera, or microphone
USB Type-C		Connecting to a newer device or external monitor, and used to charge devices

Most USB connectors plug in only one way. The USB A connector, however, is annoyingly easy to plug in upside-down. The USB Type-C connector was designed to address this complaint. Not only can it be plugged in any which way — it can also be used to drive an external monitor and even charge certain types of laptops. Yes, the USB Type-C connector is also a power cord.

The maximum cable range for a USB device is about 15 feet in the United States and 3 meters elsewhere on Planet Earth.

Adding and removing USB peripherals

One reason the USB port took over the world is that it's smart. Dumb things never take over the world. This is the reason why you don't see much cheese-flavored gelato.

To add a USB device to your computer, just plug it in. Windows instantly recognizes it and configures the device for you. For USB storage devices, you see an AutoPlay notice pestering you about what to do: Open the drive to view files, import images, play music, and so on.

To remove the USB device, unplug it. An exception is external storage, which must be properly unmounted before it's removed, lest Windows become cross with you. For a thumb drive or media card, follow these steps to remove the media:

1. **Press Win+E keyboard shortcut to summon a File Explorer window.**

2. **Choose This PC from the items listed on the left side of the window.**

3. **Right-click the external storage device's icon.**

   Which one is it? It's not drive C, I can tell you that. Otherwise, you play a guessing game.

4. **From the pop-up menu, choose the Eject command.**

   Windows displays a notification informing you that the device can be safely removed.

5. **Yank out the thumb drive or media card.**

The Eject command (refer to Step 4) doesn't appear for an external drive, like a hard drive or solid-state drive (SSD). To disconnect this type of USB gizmo, look for the Safely Remove icon in the taskbar's notification area, as shown in the margin. Click this icon to view a pop-up list of connected drives. Choose the USB drive to remove from the list. When Windows tells you it's safe to remove the drive, yank it out.

Using hubs to expand the USB universe

It seems like computers come with only a scant few USB ports. You will need more. To accommodate your lust for peripherals, you can attach a USB hub to your computer. The *USB hub* is a USB peripheral that allows you to add even more USB peripherals.

A typical USB expansion hub is shown in Figure 11-1. It connects to a USB port, just like any other USB gizmo, but it increases the number of available USB ports. And if one hub isn't enough, you can add more! The PC's USB universe can have a total of 127 USB devices attached. Collect them all!

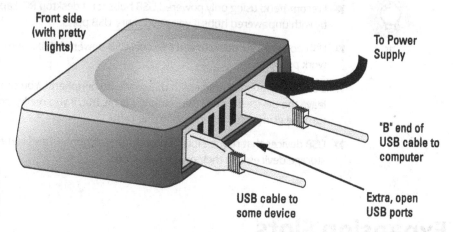

Front side
(with pretty
lights)

To Power
Supply

"B" end of
USB cable to
computer

USB cable to
some device

Extra, open
USB ports

FIGURE 11-1:
Use a USB hub to
add more
USB ports.

>> A desktop PC with internal expansion can add a USB expansion card for more hubs right on the box! See "Expansion Slots," later in this chapter.

>> Sometimes, you don't have to buy a separate USB hub. Some USB devices, such as external drives, act as their own hubs, providing connectors for adding more USB devices.

>> A hub that also plugs into the wall socket is known as a *powered* USB hub. This type of hub is necessary for some USB devices to operate. See the next section.

>> The computer itself serves as a powered USB hub.

>> An example of an unpowered hub is a keyboard with USB ports on it. Those ports are designed to connect non-USB-powered devices, such as a pointing device (mouse).

>> The first hub (your computer) is the *root* hub.

TECHNICAL
STUFF

Working with USB-powered gizmos

Quite a few USB gizmos don't require separate power cords. Instead, they use the power supplied by the USB port itself, making them *USB-powered* devices. The issue is that these devices must connect to USB-powered ports, such as those on the computer or on a powered USB hub.

WARNING

TIP

>> Yes, the USB cable not only provides a data connection but also supplies up to 5 volts of juice. Do not stick the cable in your mouth to test me on this fact.

>> A powered USB hub is one that's plugged into a power source, such as the wall socket. See the preceding section.

>> I recommend using only powered USB hubs for a desktop PC. Laptops can get by with unpowered hubs if you need more USB ports.

>> USB-powered gizmos plugged into non-USB-powered hubs won't work properly.

>> Don't worry about turning off a USB-powered peripheral. You can't! It's fine to leave the device on while the computer is on. But, if you really, *really* want to turn the gizmo off, just unplug its USB cable.

>> USB devices that require lots of power, such as printers and certain external storage devices, use their own power cords.

Expansion Slots

Desktop PCs can be expanded internally, not only by adding more storage but also by installing expansion cards. These plug directly into the motherboard, expanding your PC's hardware capabilities beyond that of a mere mortal computer.

>> Expansion cards plug into expansion slots. Tower PCs and minitowers feature expansion slots on the motherboard. Small-form-factor desktop PCs sadly lack this type of internal expansion.

>> Early-model PCs had four to six expansion slots. Some models boasted eight! Today, two or three expansion slots are the norm for a home or small-office computer. PC workstations offer more.

TECHNICAL STUFF

>> Laptops have no expansion slots, though some did ages ago. In fact, I recall one hulking laptop that could accommodate an internal expansion card. This feature was more of a "look what I can do" thing than anything practical.

Shopping for expansion cards

It's rare to install an expansion card these days because PCs come with all the hardware you normally need. When your needs are abnormal, you can obtain an expansion card, though the variety isn't as rich as it once was.

Typical expansion cards offer fancy video adapters, more USB ports, special audio capabilities, and other things I can't think of right now. The most popular of these are display adapters. In fact, your PC can sport multiple display adapters, one for each eyeball.

>> Expansion cards are available wherever nerd hardware is sold.

TECHNICAL STUFF

>> At one time, it was necessary to know which type of expansion slot dwelled inside your PC's bosom. Many standards existed and then went extinct. Today, the only standard is PCIe, which stands for Peripheral Component Interconnect Express.

>> Expansion cards come in varying lengths, so ensure that whatever you get fits inside the PC's case. The expansion card slots are also of a given length, which is something else you must check before you purchase.

>> Another important point to note is any power requirements for the card. For example, display adapters may require extra power, which means more power cords coming from the PC's power supply.

>> The backside of the expansion card contains ports or connectors to assist with what the card does: HDMI or DP ports for a display adapter, USB ports, audio jacks, and so on.

TECHNICAL STUFF

>> In the 1980s, installing expansion cards into your PC was a necessity. That's because those first models lacked enough memory, ports for the printer and modem, and even an internal clock battery. The computer mouse once needed its own expansion card. Ditto for the modem and network adapter. Today, all this technology is included on the motherboard. Refer to Chapter 6.

Installing an expansion card

Why pay someone else to install an expansion card when you can risk the certain death and destruction of your computer by doing it on your own? If you can wield a credit card to buy an expansion card, you can install it yourself! Follow these general steps:

1. **Turn off the PC and unplug it.**

In fact, put the power cord in another room, in case it gets any ideas.

2. **Remove the PC's case.**

   Stop here if this concept chills you into a catatonic state. Otherwise, locate the screws or latch that allows you to peer inside the box to witness the ugly mass of cables that obscure the computer's guts.

3. **Locate an unoccupied expansion slot.**

   If you thought I was using flowery language to describe the cables in Step 2, you will now see that I'm serious: You may need to move around — or even disconnect — various cables or other internal items to freely access an expansion slot.

4. **Remove the rear slot cover associated with the expansion slot that you desire to use.**

   If the expansion card is a double-wide, you must remove two slot covers.

5. **Gingerly cram the new expansion card into the available expansion slot.**

   The card's rump sticks out the back of the PC. A small clip on the motherboard anchors the card into place, producing a pleasing but barely audible click, which assures you that the card is snug. A latch or screw may be required to anchor the card's rear with the computer case.

6. **Connect any power cables.**

   Directions are provided with the card.

7. **Close 'er up.**

   Reattach any cables or other electronic detritus you moved. Affix the computer's lid or hatch. Plug it in. Turn it on. Pray.

TIP

If power cables aren't available inside the PC, it may need a new power supply. You can obtain and use power cord splitters in some cases. But while these tools provide access to power, the power supply itself may lack enough oomph to let the expansion card do its thing.

TECHNICAL
STUFF

Oomph is a technical term relating to electricity.

Wireless Connections with Bluetooth

Lots of proprietary wireless standards exist. For each, you must use a special USB dongle that provides communications with the detached peripheral. The Bluetooth standard, however, lets you connect with a wide variety of wireless peripherals without the need for each device to have its own custom USB dongle.

Laptops come equipped with a Bluetooth radio by default. Some desktop PCs come with Bluetooth, though you can easily add a Bluetooth USB adapter to any computer. Doing so opens the computer system up to a whole world of wireless peripheral connections.

>> *Bluetooth* refers to a wireless standard for connecting computer peripherals. The device that does the communicating is known as the *Bluetooth radio*.

>> Bluetooth peripherals include printers, keyboards, speakers, mice, monitors, robot butlers, and cell phones. You can even use Bluetooth for a crude form of wireless networking.

REMEMBER

>> Wireless peripherals use batteries. Specifically, wireless keyboards and mice need batteries to send and receive their signals.

>> To be certain that your desktop computer sports a Bluetooth wireless radio, look for the Bluetooth notification icon on the taskbar, as shown in the margin. If you see this icon, the computer features Bluetooth. This is the same icon found on Bluetooth peripherals.

>> A *dongle* is a stubby thingy that plugs into a USB port.

TECHNICAL STUFF

>> Bluetooth began its existence as a wireless replacement for the PC's serial or RS-232 port, which was common on PCs in the early days.

Accessing Bluetooth controls

You can use the Bluetooth notification on the taskbar to do Bluetooth things with your computer. A better option is to visit the Settings app and witness the full power of the Bluetooth battle station. To do so, follow these steps:

1. Open the Settings app: Press the Win+I keyboard shortcut.

2a. In Windows 11, choose the category Bluetooth & Devices from the left side of the window.

2b. In Windows 10, choose Devices and then ensure that Bluetooth & Other Devices is chosen on the left side of the window.

Figure 11-2 shows the Windows 11 version of this window. This location is best for adding, or *pairing*, new Bluetooth wireless peripherals as well as checking on the status of actively connected devices, as illustrated in the figure.

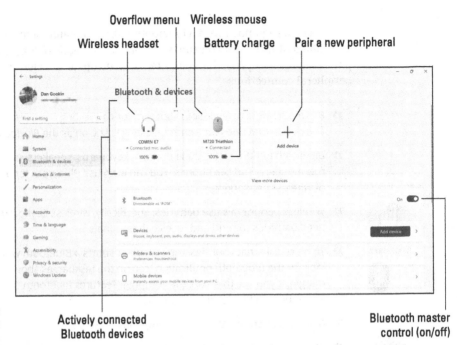

Overflow menu | Wireless mouse

Wireless headset | Battery charge | Pair a new peripheral

FIGURE 11-2:
Bluetooth
control center.

Actively connected
Bluetooth devices

Bluetooth master
control (on/off)

>> One item to note in the Settings app (and in Figure 11-2) is the Bluetooth master control. Ensure that this item is on so that the computer can access and use the wireless peripherals.

>> The list of Bluetooth devices shown in Figure 11-2 reveals which Bluetooth peripherals the computer is actively using. Paired devices appear only when they're turned on.

Pairing a Bluetooth peripheral

Beyond being a funny name, the point of Bluetooth is to wirelessly connect peripherals to your computer. Like matching a fine wine to your meal in a snooty restaurant, the process is called *pairing*.

For example, you pair a wireless mouse with your laptop. Once paired, the mouse is available anytime both it and the computer are turned on. Turn off the mouse, it's disconnected. Turn it on again, it's reconnected. Though the device is paired with the computer, it's available only when it's turned on.

Here are the general steps to pair a wireless Bluetooth peripheral with your PC or laptop:

1. **Turn on the Bluetooth gizmo.**

2. **On your computer, visit the Settings app, Bluetooth screen, and ensure that the Bluetooth radio is active.**

    Refer to the preceding section for directions.

3. **Make the Bluetooth peripheral discoverable.**

    Like the singles section of the local weekly, a Bluetooth device must broadcast its availability. This process differs for each peripheral. Typically, you press a special Bluetooth button on the device to activate its "I'm horny and desire to hook up" signal. The device's documentation offers the specifics.

4. **On the computer, in the Settings app, click the Add Device button.**

    Refer to Figure 11-2 as your guide. In Windows 10, the button is labeled Add Bluetooth or Other Device.

5. **In the Add a Device dialog box, choose Bluetooth.**

    A list appears of available Bluetooth devices. These peripherals are actively broadcasting that they're available to pair, like a line of scantily dressed women of questionable morals downtown.

6. **Choose the device from the list.**

    Devices are listed by brand name or model number, but may also show a description such as "keyboard" or "headset" or "Tesla Model 30."

7. **Obey the directions on the computer screen or on the Bluetooth device.**

    For example, you may be required to type a PIN on a wireless keyboard (and press Enter), click a button on the mouse, or match digits presented on the Tesla's dashboard display.

    Eventually, the device is paired and the computer can begin using it.

The good news is that after you initially pair the device, there's no need to pair it again. The computer and the Bluetooth peripheral are hitched.

REMEMBER

>> Pairing associates the Bluetooth peripheral with one computer. You cannot share a Bluetooth peripheral with another computer unless you pair the two. Likewise, another computer can't "steal" your Bluetooth peripheral.

>> All wireless devices have batteries.

>> You must turn on a Bluetooth device before you can use it.

WARNING

>> Unlike the long arm of the law, the Bluetooth wireless connection goes only so far. In the United States, the legal distance is about 20 feet. In Europe, the distance is far less, just over 6 meters.

Unpairing a Bluetooth device

If you want to stop using a wireless Bluetooth peripheral, turn it off. The connection is broken while the device is off. But if you suddenly come to loathe a Bluetooth device, you can unpair it and purge it from the Settings app's Bluetooth screen. Here are the steps:

1. **Visit the Bluetooth part of the Windows Settings app.**

   Refer to the earlier section "Accessing Bluetooth controls" for directions.

2. **In Windows 11, click the Overflow button on the Bluetooth device's tile in the Settings app. In Windows 10, click the tile itself.**

3. **Choose the Remove Device option.**

4. **If prompted, click the Yes button to confirm.**

   The device is no longer paired to your computer.

TIP

Unpairing really isn't ever necessary, though I'm required by the state of Wisconsin to write about it. You can always pair the peripheral with another computer without the need to unpair it first.

The Laptop Becomes a Desktop

If you plan to park your laptop in one place a lot, you can expand its system by replacing its keyboard, mouse, and monitor with more-robust desktop counterparts. Any of these desktop-size items can be added to, and used with, a laptop. As a bonus, you can disconnect them at any time and be once again free to roam the world wirelessly while you compute.

Using a full-size keyboard and mouse

The full-size action of a real PC keyboard and the free movement of a desktop mouse can easily be added to any laptop: Plug in the device's USB cable. You can start using the king-size peripherals the second they're plugged in.

WARNING

>> Adding an external keyboard doesn't disable the laptop's keyboard. Like a laptop with a desktop mouse attached, the computer now has two pointing devices. They both work. At the same time.

> » Some laptops have a limited number of USB ports. If so, obtain a USB hub and connect it to the laptop. You then connect the external keyboard and mouse to the USB hub. Refer to the section "Using hubs to expand the USB universe," earlier in this chapter.

Adding a monitor

Your laptop is ready to handle two monitors: the laptop's own screen and an external monitor. The reason for this eagerness is that many laptops are used to bore a roomful of unwilling people with a dreary PowerPoint presentation. The projector acts as a second monitor. Even if you're not making a presentation, the laptop is ready to handle a second monitor.

To add the external monitor, locate a monitor connector on your laptop's edge. This can be a mini-HDMI, mini-DP, or even a USB C port. Plug in the monitor. Turn on the monitor.

After a successful connection, you may be prompted to determine how the second monitor is used. Here are your options:

PC Screen Only: Use only the laptop's display; ignore the external monitor.

Duplicate: Echo the same image on each monitor. This option is ideal for running a slide show presentation.

Extend: This mode uses the second monitor to expand desktop real estate, combining both monitors into a single, larger desktop area. Desktop PCs with more than one monitor use this option.

Second Screen Only: Use only the external monitor; the laptop's screen is disabled until the external monitor is disconnected.

TIP

The keyboard shortcut to choose how to use a second monitor is Win+P. Think of P for projector.

The Microsoft Office PowerPoint program may override the four settings just shown, offering its own interactive display during the presentation. Don't let this jarring change alarm you.

TIP

When the monitor cable you have doesn't match any ports on the laptop, obtain an adapter. Many of these use the USB C port to connect to an HDMI or DP cable.

Monitor connections are also available on a laptop docking station.

Running the laptop with its lid closed

To fool everyone into thinking you have a desktop PC instead of a laptop, you can connect a keyboard, mouse, and monitor and then run your laptop with its lid closed. Yes, the laptop can stay on with its lid closed. No, it doesn't overheat or get angry.

Because the laptop may be preset to sleep or shut down when you close the lid, you must reconfigure the system. The goal is to direct the laptop to do nothing when the lid is closed. Follow these steps:

1. **Pop up the Start menu.**

   Tap the Windows key on the keyboard.

2. **Type the text** close the lid.

   Don't worry — the computer won't close the laptop's lid on you.

3. **From the Best Match list, choose the item Change What Closing the Lid Does.**

   The Control Panel opens, displaying a table of options for the power button and lid.

4. **Choose the second menu in the row titled When I Close the Lid, in the Plugged-In column.**

   The menu button may say Sleep or Shut Down.

5. **From the menu, choose Do Nothing.**

   You're directing the laptop to do nothing when it is plugged into a power source and you close the lid.

6. **Click the Save Changes button.**

7. **Close the System Settings window.**

Of course, you may have to open the laptop to turn it on, but after it's on, you can close the lid and use the external keyboard, monitor, and mouse just like you do on a desktop computer.

Do not choose the Do Nothing option for closing the lid while the laptop is on battery power. Doing so may cause you to think that the laptop is turned off, in which case its battery will drain itself in a most wasteful manner.

IN THIS CHAPTER

» **Understanding computer printers**

» **Locating printer features**

» **Feeding the printer ink and paper**

» **Connecting a printer**

» **Controlling the printer in Windows**

» **Printing documents and stuff**

» **Stopping a document from printing**

Chapter **12**

P Is for Printer

This chapter is brought to you by the letter *P*. *P* stands for *PC* and *peripheral*. One of the PC's preferred peripherals is a printer. *Printer* starts with *P*. PCs prefer printers, specifically for producing output on paper. Printing is possible and practical.

Step Aside, Gutenberg

As time marches onward from 1436, printing becomes less essential. In the digital age, most information is transferred electronically as opposed to printed on paper, the so-called *hard copy*. Even so, printing is still a necessary task. Therefore, a printer is considered a required peripheral for any computer system.

Surveying the printer landscape

Computer printers come in all shapes and sizes, some that just print and others that scan, fax, copy, and play the accordion. Even so, when you strip all that away, you find only two types of printers, categorized by how the ink gets thrown:

Inkjet: The inkjet printer creates an image by spitting tiny balls of ink directly on the paper. That jet-of-ink action gives this printer category its name. Inkjet is the most common type of computer printer.

Laser: Laser printers are found primarily in the office environment, where they deftly handle heavy workloads. The printer uses a laser beam to create the image, which somehow helps fuse toner powder (ink) onto the paper. The result is crisp and fast output, but at a premium price over inkjet printers.

All inkjet printers are color printers. Laser printers come in both monochrome and color varieties.

» Inkjet printers are by no means messy. The ink is dry on the paper by the time the paper comes flopping out of the printer.

» You can print a color image or document on a monochrome printer; the output will just be in black-and-white, like the entire world was before 1940.

» Black-and-white. Monochrome. Grayscale. It's all the same thing.

» For details on scanning documents, see Chapter 13.

Touring the typical printer

The doodads and knobs on a typical PC printer aren't called doodads and knobs. No, they have official names and functions, as presented in Figure 12-1. The printer shown is a basic inkjet model that lacks the scanner, copier, and accordion options.

Power button: Like other devices electronic, the printer features a power button. Press the power button to turn on the printer or to turn it off. Most people leave the printer on all the time, which is okay because today's printers are super energy efficient, practically ignoring electricity.

Control panel: Every printer has a control panel somewhere on its body. Basic printers feature only a few buttons and lights, including the all-important Cancel button. Advanced printers have touchscreen input, like a smartphone with controls for setting options, scanning documents, sending faxes, copying documents, playing Tetris, and canceling printing.

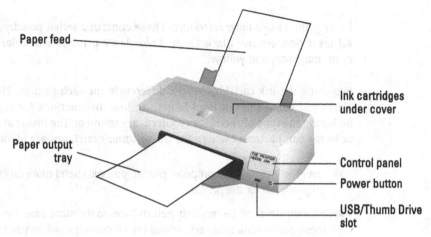

Paper feed

Ink cartridges under cover

Paper output tray

Control panel

Power button

THE PRINTER NEEDS JIM

FIGURE 12-1:
Notable places on
the printer.

USB/Thumb Drive slot

Paper feed: The paper feed is where paper is stored. This hopper supplies paper for the printer. See the section "Eating paper," later in this chapter.

Manual/envelope feeder: Not shown in Figure 12-1 because I'm too lazy to draw it, this location is where you can stick an envelope or special paper for printing. The manual feed opening may be hidden behind a panel. If it's unavailable, you must instead stock the regular paper feed with an envelope or special paper.

Ink/toner cartridges: Deep in the printer's bosom, you find one or more cartridges, the source from which the printer draws its ink. A hatch opens on the printer, revealing this secret location. See the next section.

USB port or media card slot: The USB port or media card slot is for reading images as well as for storing them. For example, if you plug in a thumb drive, the printer may urge you to print any photos stored there. For a printer that can scan or copy, you can save the documents to the thumb drive or media card. The availability of these features depends on the printer. Scanning and copying are manipulated from the control panel.

Paper output tray: The printed paper comes out and is stacked in the output tray.

Drinking ink

The Chinese invented ink over 3,000 years ago. Scholars remarked how ink gave a new purpose to the art of wiping brushes on blank sheets of paper. Even today, ink is important to a computer printer that would otherwise just be a paper warmer. Ink is a necessary part of printing.

Inkjet printers use *ink cartridges*. It's a single black cartridge plus three color cartridges: cyan, magenta, and yellow. Photo-printing inkjets use two additional ink cartridges: light cyan and light magenta.

Laser printers use *toner cartridges*. These contain a lethal powdery ink substance. All laser printers use black toner. Color laser printers add color ink cartridges: cyan, magenta, and yellow.

Replacing the ink cartridge works differently for each printer. The control panel alerts you when the ink level is getting low. Instructions for replacing the ink, including the type of cartridge required, are found on the inside of the printer's lid or in the compartment where the ink or toner cartridges are hidden.

>> Over the lifetime of a computer printer, you will spend more on ink than you originally did for the printer.

>> Ink cartridges can be recycled. Return them to the store where you purchased them. Some manufacturers include return envelopes when you buy ink online.

WARNING

>> Make sure you don't breathe in the dust from a laser toner cartridge or else you'll die.

>> Make a note of which type of inkjet cartridge your printer uses. Keep the catalog number somewhere handy, such as taped to your printer's case or as a note in your smartphone so that you can reorder the proper cartridge.

TIP

>> Carefully follow the instructions for changing ink cartridges. Old cartridges can leak. Use rubber gloves or simple household cleaning gloves when changing the ink or toner cartridge. I also suggest having an abundance of paper towels handy.

>> You can squeeze a few more pages from a laser jet toner cartridge by gently rocking it back and forth when the printer tells you the toner is low. This process helps redistribute the toner dust, but eventually, you need a new cartridge.

>> Never let your printer's ink run dry! You may think that squeezing every drop of ink saves you money, but it's not good for the printer.

WARNING

Eating paper

Next to drinking ink, printers eat paper. Fortunately, paper isn't as expensive as ink, not to mention that so few things need to be printed these days.

The paper goes into a feeder tray either near the printer's bottom or sticking out the top. For the feeder tray, ensure that you slide the cartridge all the way into the printer after it's loaded.

When printing on letterhead or a check, you must ensure that the paper is set in the right orientation: face down, face up, top, or bottom. Most printers feature Paper Feed icons telling you how the paper is oriented in the tray. Here's how these symbols translate into English:

>> The paper goes in face down, top side up.

>> The paper goes in face down, top side down.

>> The paper goes in face up, top side up.

>> The paper goes in face up, top side down.

If the printer doesn't tell you which way is up, write *Top* on a sheet of paper and run it through the printer. Then draw your own icon, similar to those just shown. Use it to help orient the paper in the printer's hopper.

Choosing the proper paper

According to the experts at Dunder-Mifflin, paper comes in different sizes, weights (degrees of thickness), colors, styles, textures, and flavors. Computer printers eat them all, save for some card stock that's too thick to wend its way through the printer's internal feeding mechanism.

The best general-purpose computer printer paper is standard photocopier paper. For better results from your inkjet printer, obtain specific inkjet paper, although you pay more for it. This higher-quality inkjet paper is good for printing colors because it's designed to absorb the ink.

At the high end of the spectrum are specialty papers, such as photographic papers that come in smooth or glossy finishes, transparencies, and iron-on T-shirt transfers. Just ensure that this special paper is made for your type of printer — inkjet or laser.

WARNING

>> Avoid using erasable bond and other fancy papers in a printer. The powder coating on these papers gums up the works.

>> High-end printers are capable of handling larger-size paper, such as legal or tabloid size. If so, make sure you load the paper properly and tell your application it's printing on a different paper size. See the later section "Printer Operation" for more information.

TIP

>> When paper gets stuck inside a printer, the result is a printer jam. The goal is to remove the paper, and often instructions are offered on the printer's control panel display.

>> Printer jam is different from printer jelly, which comes in more flavors.

>> Stocked and restocked with paper, the printer can go all night long.

>> That's what she said.

The Union of Printer and PC

A printer is a necessary part of a computer system, but not vital — like the human appendix. It's also not necessary that every computer have its own printer, just as several humans can share a single appendix.

I might have my anatomy wrong. Regardless, like all computer peripherals, a computer and printer share a connection, wired or wireless. This connection is maintained, even though the printer may sit around bored more often than other computer peripherals.

» A printer is really its own separate computer, but one that's designed with a specific purpose.

» Keep the printer manual with the printer. I hide mine underneath the printer, which I do right away because I know I'll eventually need to read it later.

» Windows knows about and can connect with hundreds of different printers. You don't need to hunt for a "Windows compatible" printer.

Connecting the printer

Printers can be attached directly to the computer, but most often they are connected to the local-area network.

To directly connect a printer to your computer, you use a standard USB cable, just like the cable that doesn't come with the printer. That's right: Printers don't come with cables. It's a computer industry tradition.

The network connection can be wired or wireless. For a wired connection, attach the network cable to the proper network orifice on the printer. Use the printer's control panel to configure the wireless network connection. This step involves knowing the wireless network's name and password.

» A printer connected to a single computer can still be shared on the network. Even so, if you want to share the printer on the network, just connect it (wired or wirelessly) to the network directly.

» See Part 3 of this book for details on networking.

TIP

» Portable printers are available for use with a laptop when you're on the road. While this type of printer is one more item to carry, if you really need to print, this option is available. Oh! And don't forget that the portable printer needs paper. That's one more thing to carry. Did I mention batteries for the portable printer? Better see the later section "Printing when you don't have a printer" and call it good.

TECHNICAL STUFF

>> Once Windows recognizes the printer, it installs special software to control the printer. This step is done automatically.

>> The software required to run the printer is called the *printer driver*.

>> You can use the Bluetooth wireless standard to connect to a Bluetooth printer, though I recommend using wireless networking instead. Refer to Chapter 11 for information on Bluetooth if you really want to torture yourself by connecting a Bluetooth printer.

>> Some printers demand that you install custom software provided by the printer's manufacturer, though this step isn't necessary to use the printer. The software often lets you perform special printer functions from Windows, such as scanning or copying. I find such software annoying.

>> A single computer can use multiple printers, providing they're all available on the same network or — if you're crazy — connected to a single computer.

Finding printers in Windows

Windows is good at finding available printers, but are you good at finding where Windows lists available printers?

I thought so!

Once a printer is connected, Windows introduces itself right away and sets up things just so. Network printers may require a bit of effort, but they can also be added easily. To confirm that a printer is available, use the Settings app. Heed these directions:

1. **Press the Win+I keyboard shortcut to conjure the Settings app.**

2. **In Windows 11, choose Bluetooth & Devices; in Windows 10, choose Devices.**

3. **Choose Printers & Scanners.**

   A list of available printers appears, as illustrated in Figure 12-2.

The list of printers includes real printers, either directly connected or found on the network, plus non-printers such as the Microsoft Print to PDF printer, shown in the figure.

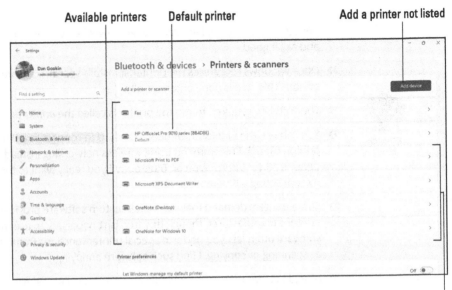

Available printers   Default printer   Add a printer not listed

Non-printers

FIGURE 12-2:
Available printers
in Windows 11.

One of the printers in the list is known as the *default* printer (refer to Figure 12-2). This is the printer the computer desires to use most often, though this choice can be changed. See the later section "Setting the default printer."

REMEMBER

A printer is available only when it's turned on and broadcasting its presence on the network. If a printer is off, it won't show up in the list.

Adding a printer manually

When a printer doesn't appear in the list, you can force Windows to add it. This situation arises primarily with network printers that Windows doesn't particularly like or older printers that do nothing but complain. To set Windows on a printer hunt, follow these steps:

1. **Bring forth the Settings app screen that shows available printers.**

    Refer to the preceding section for specific steps.

2. **Click the Add Device button in Windows 11; choose Add a Printer or Scanner in Windows 10.**

    Windows tries in vain to find the printer. It can't.

3. **Click the Add Manually link in Windows 11; in Windows 10, click the link The Printer That I Want Isn't Listed.**

   An Add Printer Wizard appears.

4. **Choose an option to force Windows to locate the wayward printer.**

For example, choose the option to find an older printer, click the Next button, and follow the onscreen directions. For an older network printer, you must obtain its IP address. This information can be obtained from the printer's control panel. Use the deets to direct Windows to locate and use the printer.

Deets = details.

Setting the default printer

Though Windows can access multiple printers, it's also easily confused. To help out your computer's operating system, you can choose one printer as your favorite. You tell Windows to use the specific printer as the default. This printer is always chosen for you any time you print something, meaning you don't waste time choosing a printer when several are available.

Another option is to let Windows choose the default printer for you. This decision is based on the last printer you use, which causes the default printer to change. Because of this inconsistency, I detest this option. Ensure that it's unchecked in the Printers & Scanners window: Follow the steps from the earlier section "Finding printers in Windows" and remove the check mark by the option Let Windows Manage My Default Printer.

When the option to let Windows manage your default printer is unchecked, you set a default printer by following these instructions:

1. **Display the Printers & Scanners part of the Settings app.**

   Refer to the earlier section "Finding printers in Windows."

2. **Choose the printer you want to make the default.**

3. **In Windows 10, choose Manage.**

4. **Click the button Set As Default.**

   The selected printer is now the default, chosen automatically when you need to quickly print something.

Only one printer is set to the default.

Printer Operation

When you're done creating that wonderful whatever, you can keep it in the computer or you can export it. Just obtain the proper tariffs or bribe the correct customs officials, and you're good.

Oh. I'm being informed that computers do a different type of exporting. In this manner, *exporting* means to send or share the wonderful whatever in a realm outside of the computer. One of these options is to print the wonderful whatever on paper. This job falls to the printer. In fact, *job* is the official name for printing a wonderful whatever.

Printing a wonderful whatever

Not all Windows programs can print, but those that do have a Print command. This command is very consistent: It's found on the File menu. The keyboard shortcut is Ctrl+P. I could go on about the term *Ctrl+P*, but I'm not being paid by the word.

The Print command summons the Print screen or Print dialog box, as illustrated in Figure 12-3.

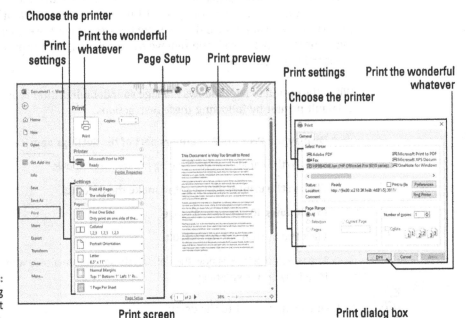

FIGURE 12-3:
The Print dialog box and Print screen.

Here are some common printing tasks:

Print to a specific printer. If you want to use a printer other than the default, such as that nice color laser printer that Edward hogs in his office, choose it from the list of printers.

Print only a specific page or range of pages. To print only pages 1 through 5, choose the page range option and type **1-5** in the text box. To print pages 4 and 8, type **8,4**. Or, to print only select text, choose Selection.

Print multiple copies. Set a value other than 1 by the Copies or Number of Copies field to print more than one copy of your wonderful whatever.

Click the Print button after making your choices to print your document. Click Cancel or press the Esc key to not print anything.

» Printing something creates a printer job. It's possible to send multiple jobs to a printer, in which case they're queued and print one after the other.

» You do not need to wait for one printing job to quit before you print again.

» Printers don't print when they're out of ink or out of paper.

» Many programs feature a "quick print" command or icon. When you choose this command, the entire document prints on the default printer. The print screen or dialog box doesn't appear.

» Some printer options, such as paper size and orientation, are found in the Page Setup dialog box. To get there, choose the Page Setup command from the File menu. You might also find a Page Setup or Preferences button in the Print dialog box or screen.

TIP

» Preview before you print. Use the print preview window (refer to Figure 12-3) to see how the document looks when printed. A Print Preview command might also be available on the File menu. It's better to see ugliness in the Print Preview window than to waste paper.

» Some programs lack a Print Preview command. If so, waste paper — but recycle it.

Printing when you don't have a printer

It's difficult to lug a printer with your laptop, not to mention that sometimes the thing you want to print must be sent as an email attachment. One solution for these predicaments is to print the document as a PDF (Portable Document File).

To "print" a PDF, choose the Microsoft Print to PDF printer, as shown earlier, in Figure 12-3. After clicking the Print button, you're presented with a Save As dialog box, where you can save the "printed" document in the PDF format. From there, you can email the PDF or do whatever with it.

>> If you have Adobe Acrobat installed, a second PDF option appears: Adobe PDF. Either choice produces a PDF, though I've had better success with the Microsoft Print to PDF "printer."

>> The PDF file is one of the most universal and common file formats available. Though it can be opened by a variety of programs (including most web browsers), the Acrobat Reader program is the original. This program can be obtained free from https://acrobat.adobe.com.

TECHNICAL STUFF

Stopping a printer run amok

The fastest, bestest way to stop printing is to mash the Cancel button on the printer's control panel. Press the button and printing stops, though it may not stop immediately if a page is already spewing out the printer's maw.

It's also possible to stop a printer from within Windows, though this method doesn't often meet with success. The reason is that printers today come with oodles of memory, so the printing job is most likely already in the printer when you go to cancel in Windows.

TECHNICAL STUFF

To view printing jobs queued for a given printer, follow these steps:

1. **Visit the Printers & Scanners part of the Settings app.**

   Refer to the earlier section "Finding printers in Windows" for directions.

2. **Choose the printer in question.**

3. **In Windows 11, choose the option Open Print Queue; in Windows 10, click the Open Queue button.**

   You see the list of current and pending print jobs.

The printer queue is empty most of the time, unless you're printing a lot of jobs. Options are available for each job, including Stop, Pause, and Resume.

For example, if you were silly and tried to print the same job several times because you were frustrated or had too much coffee, you can select a job and cancel it. This method works *before* the job gets to the printer. Otherwise, you can click the Cancel button on the printer's control panel as the job prints.

Chapter 13

Webcams, Scanners, and Audio

As silly as it sounds, having a speaker on a computer was once considered a luxury. Supposedly, some C-suite muckamuck insisted that not having a speaker in the TRS-80 Model I microcomputer would save the company five dollars a unit. That was real money back then.

Thankfully, that muckamuck is dead now. If not, he would be dead anyhow because computers require speakers as well as webcams for online meetings, voice commands, and being silly. These once obscure and derided computer peripherals are today considered a vital part of your digital life.

The Computer Is Watching You

Somewhere lurking near your laptop's screen is a webcam, a combination still camera and video camera. A desktop computer monitor may also have a webcam, though it's often added as a peripheral. You can use the webcam to record yourself for attending online meetings, and with video chat.

>> It would make sense for the laptop's webcam to be located at the top center above the screen, but don't count on it. My laptop's webcam is in the lower left corner of the screen. I'm sure some C-suite muckamuck thought it was an ideal location.

>> Many programs are available to let you use the webcam, including the popular Zoom online meeting app. In Windows, you can use the Camera app to take pictures or record videos.

>> Some PC tablet models have a second camera on the back of the tablet.

>> See the later section "Securing the webcam" if you're concerned about the computer watching you.

>> A webcam is not a scanner. Don't use the webcam to take pictures of documents, like your computer-illiterate great aunt does. See the later section "The Document Scanner."

Obtaining a webcam

Desperate desktop PC owners can add a webcam peripheral, blessing their computer systems with the same gizmo that laptops have included already. Webcam prices range from embarrassingly cheap to obnoxiously expensive, depending on the quality and features desired. Base your decision on what you plan on doing with the webcam, not just to one–up your laptop pals.

>> If you plan on using the webcam primarily for online meetings, go cheap. You don't need a high-end, high-quality camera to attend boring meetings.

>> For budding YouTube stars and other online "performers," I recommend getting a webcam capable of 4K resolution. Additional features include autofocus, auto-follow, and remote control pan, tilt, and zoom.

>> Most webcams come with a microphone, which is one less thing to buy. Even so, if you desire quality audio, see the later section "Exploring microphone options and connections."

Attaching the webcam

Webcams not built into a monitor use the USB interface to connect with the computer system. In fact, many computer monitors have a USB hub included, which makes attaching the webcam easier. Just ensure that the monitor has a USB cable connected to the computer.

Perch the webcam top center on the monitor. Use whatever mechanism is included to pinch the camera to the monitor's case. It needs to be only snug, and not clenching the monitor like an eagle grabbing a fish.

TIP

>> Refer to Chapter 11 for details on the USB interface.

>> The reason you want the webcam atop the monitor is to avoid the dreaded Nostril Cam you've probably seen in online meetings. The human face appears more pleasant when viewed head-on or even slightly higher. The lower you put the webcam, the more distorted and gross you look. No one wants to look up your nose during a meeting.

Securing the webcam

Having a webcam's eye gazing away on your computer means that — theoretically — anyone on the Internet can use it to look at you. The good news is that such unwanted peeping doesn't happen unless *you* allow it. Even so, it's best to be cautious.

All webcams have a lamp that illuminates when the camera is active. This lamp is a hardware feature and cannot be disabled by some creep on the Internet. When the lamp is on, the camera is on.

Many webcams feature a privacy screen, a flap that folds down over the lens. This screen ensures that even if the camera is somehow on while its activity lamp is disabled, no one can see you. I always close the privacy screen when I'm not using my webcam.

TIP

If your laptop's webcam lacks a privacy screen, I recommend using a Band-Aid to cover the webcam: Ensure that the padded part of the bandage covers the camera's lens so as not to damage it. Avoid using a sticky note to obscure the webcam as the gummy stuff can damage the lens surface.

Windows offers security settings for webcam hardware, allowing you to choose which apps have permission to access the camera. To view these settings, follow these steps:

1. **Press the Win+I keyboard shortcut.**

   Behold the Settings app.

2. **Choose the Privacy item, titled Privacy & Security in Windows 11.**

   One section on the Privacy and Security screen is labeled App Permissions. This section is on the left in Windows 10.

3. **Choose Camera.**

   You see a master control for Camera Access, plus master controls for each app or program that can use the camera.

4. **Set the master control items off for those apps you do not want to access the camera.**

If you disable an app from using the camera or you disable all camera access, you may still be prompted whenever a program wants to use the camera. At this point, you can grant or deny permission.

REMEMBER

No app can use the camera when you deny permission. It's not possible.

Even denying permission cannot prevent the Bad Guys from accessing the camera if *you let them in*. Do not disable security settings unless you are being directed to do so by legitimate tech support or from someone you trust.

WARNING

The Document Scanner

Where a webcam is more like a digital camera, a scanner is more like a photo-copier. In fact, most computer scanners these days are built into printers. If not, the scanner dwells in its own box, looking like Figure 13-1.

Whether it's part of the printer or its own gizmo, the scanner is used in the same manner: You place something flat on the scanner glass, like a photograph, docu-ment, or daguerreotype. Press a button on the device to scan the image, or use the software that came with the scanner/printer to do the same. The scanner trans-lates the flat item into a digital image, which is beamed to the computer via a USB cable where the image is stored as a file for further examination, manipulation, or exploitation.

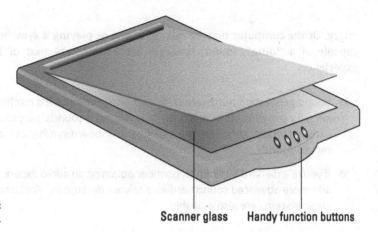

FIGURE 13-1:
A typical scanner.

Scanner glass   Handy function buttons

- » Windows comes with the Scan program, which provides basic scanning capabilities. If you can't find this app on the Start menu's All Apps screen, obtain a free copy from the Windows Store. (The Windows Store is yet another app that comes with Windows.)

- » Handy function buttons may adorn the scanner's control panel (refer to Figure 13-1). Use them to quickly scan, copy, fax, email, or read text from whatever item is placed on the scanner glass.

- » Scanners can also read slides and film negatives, providing they have something called a *transparency adapter*.

- » When you scan a document, the scanner converts it into a picture file. To read the document's contents and create a text file, you need optical character recognition (OCR) software. This program examines the image and uses tiny digital tweezers to extract the text. The process is fairly accurate, though reviewing the results is always a requirement.

- » Yes, you could use a webcam to snap a photo of a document, just like your computer-illiterate great aunt I wrote about earlier. And, you can smash your face in a scanner to take a self-portrait. It's best, however, to use the proper tool for the job: webcams for three-dimensional things and scanners for flat things.

Computer Goes Beep

It was once true that every time a teletype bell rang, a computer nerd salivated. Computers lost their bells years back, though nerds still salivate. Instead of a bell, however, today's computers have speakers. One is built into the computer case. The sound it makes is important. It means, "Pay attention!" The computer is angry. Or the computer may be talking to you or playing a symphony. More than capable of a "ding" sound, speakers are a necessary part of the computing experience.

>> Sound-generation hardware is located on the computer's motherboard. This circuitry can process and play digitally recorded sounds, play music from external media, generate music using the onboard synthesizer, and record sounds.

>> If you're a diehard audiophile, consider obtaining an audio expansion card to add more advanced sound hardware to your desktop PC. For laptops, USB audio systems are also available.

TIP

Setting up speakers

Both laptops and desktops come with a teensy, tiny internal speaker. It works, but it's not the best way to hear computer sound.

For a desktop, or a laptop docked at a workstation, stereo speakers can be added. They connect to the computer's audio output jack (color-coded green) or to a USB port. Position them to either side of the monitor: The left speaker goes on the monitor's left as you face it; the right speaker goes on the right.

To get fancy, you can add more speakers to the computer's audio system. The first step is to add a *subwoofer*. It's a speaker box designed for low-frequency sounds, which gives oomph to the bass in music, adds emphasis to the sounds in games, and truly frightens the neighbors.

Even more fancy is to add surround sound speakers, like the sound setup for a home theater. Figure 13-2 illustrates potential locations for speakers in a surround sound setup. You'd be nuts to have *all* those speakers connected at one time, but it's possible.

Table 13-1 describes how the surround sound numbering system works. The .x part of a surround sound specification refers to the presence of a subwoofer: .0 means no subwoofer; .1 means one subwoofer; .2 means two subwoofers.

>> Some computer monitors have built-in speakers, though they're generally terrible — if you can get them to work.

>> I recommend getting speakers that feature a volume control knob. A bonus is a Mute button.

TIP

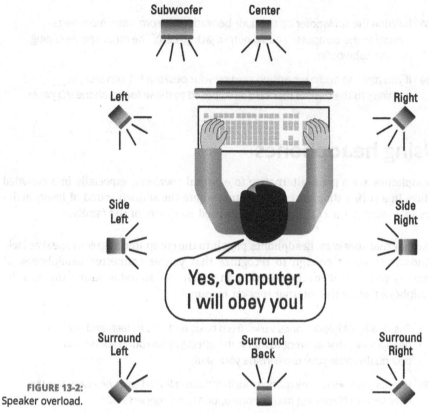

FIGURE 13-2:
Speaker overload.

TABLE 13-1 **Surround Sound Speaker Options**

Surround Sound Version	Speakers Used
3.0	Left, right, surround back
4.0	Left, right, surround left, surround right
4.1	Left, right, surround left, surround right, subwoofer
5.1	Left, right, center, surround left, surround right, subwoofer
6.1	Left, right, center, side left, side right, back surround, subwoofer
7.1	Left, right, center, side left, side right, surround left, surround right, subwoofer

>> Position the subwoofer on the floor beneath your computer. It connects directly to the computer's audio output jack (green). The other speakers plug into the subwoofer.

REMEMBER

>> If you have an audio expansion card on your desktop PC, connect the speakers to the back of that card as opposed to those found on the I/O panel.

Using headphones

Headphones are a great alternative to external speakers, especially in a crowded office, in a coffee shop, or even at home, where the sudden sound of heavy artillery in a video game can upset easily startled members of the family.

Like external speakers, headphones plug into the computer's (green) speaker jack. Windows is smart enough to recognize that you've connected headphones. It prompts you to confirm the selection, in which case sound is output through the headphones while the internal speaker is muted.

>> The quality of headphones varies from basic earbuds to high-end gaming headphones that attempt to mimic the effects of surround sound and can potentially rattle your brain inside your skull.

REMEMBER

>> Headphones with a microphone included are referred to as *headsets*. See the later section "Exploring microphone options and connections."

>> Quality headphones come with a volume control and maybe even a Mute button.

>> The audio jacks on the front of a desktop PC are designed for headphones.

REMEMBER

>> Headphones can also be wireless, either connecting to their own USB dongle or using the Bluetooth standard. Remember that wireless headphones require batteries or must otherwise be recharged regularly. Refer to Chapter 11 for more information on Bluetooth.

>> Look for headphones that are comfy on your ears, with big, puffy "cans."

TIP

>> Inevitably, you will drop the headphones and break them. To avoid this disaster, consider getting a headphone stand or bracket for storing the headphones when they're not pinching your head.

Configuring the speakers in Windows

Windows lets you control two aspects of the computer's capability to go "beep:" setting the sound volume and choosing which sound device to use for output. The second aspect is necessary because most computers have more than one sound-output thingy.

Controls for setting the volume as well as choosing the output device are found in the Settings app, but most of the cool kids use the audio shortcut icon on the taskbar, shown in the margin and traditionally found in the lower right corner of the display. Click this icon to see a pop-up, as shown in Figure 13-3.

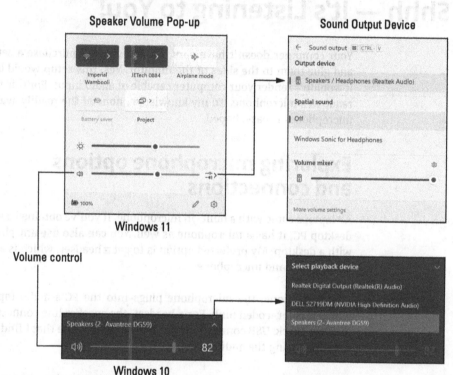

Speaker Volume Pop-up

Sound Output Device

Imperial Wambooli   JETech 0884   Airplane mode

Battery saver   Project

100%

Windows 11

← Sound output ▣ CTRL V

Output device

Speakers / Headphones (Realtek Audio)

Spatial sound

Off

Windows Sonic for Headphones

Volume mixer

More volume settings

Volume control

Select playback device

Realtek Digital Output (Realtek(R) Audio)

DELL S2719DM (NVIDIA High Definition Audio)

Speakers (2- Avantree DG59)

Speakers (2- Avantree DG59)   82

FIGURE 13-3: Adjusting sounds in Windows.

Windows 10

Use the slider to adjust the speaker volume. When you click the slider, you hear Windows beep. This tone clues you in to the actual volume level.

To change the sound output device, choose the appropriate item for Windows 10 or Windows 11 (refer to Figure 13-3) to see a list of available hardware. Choose the desired sound output device from the list.

» Before you don your Master of Sound robes and don that nifty hat, know that individual apps can override the Windows volume setting as well as the preferred sound output device. Games, YouTube, and other apps feature their own volume controls. The Zoom app lets you choose both sound output and input devices. Even so:

» If you mute the sound in Windows, all sounds are muted.

» Volume controls are everywhere! Apps, external speakers, and even key-boards have a volume knob or gizmo. Despite this variety — and confusion — I recommend adjusting the Windows volume control first.

Shhh — It's Listening to You!

Your computer doesn't have ears, though you can purchase a set of rubber ears and glue them to the sides of the monitor. Yes, this setup would be hilarious, but it wouldn't render your computer capable of audio input. For this task, the system requires a microphone. To my knowledge, none of the readily available computer microphones is ear-shaped.

Exploring microphone options and connections

All laptops come with a built-in microphone. If you've obtained a webcam for your desktop PC, it has a microphone as well. You can also use any cheap microphone with a desktop. My preferred option is to get a headset, which is a combination of headphones and microphone.

For connections, the microphone plugs into the PC's audio input or mic jack, which is color-coded pink. For a headset, the speaker line connects to the (green) line input jack. USB connections are also an option, one that I find to be more reli-able than using the audio jacks.

» Headsets are ideal for both laptops and desktops. Using a headset not only makes playing games easier but is also best for online meetings as well as dictation.

» Headsets also avoid the weird (and annoying) audio echo you hear when you use external speakers and an external microphone.

» Refer to Chapter 10 for more information on dictation and voice input.

» The speaker jack is color-coded lime green.

» The microphone jack is color-coded pink.

» If you're colorblind, both jacks are color-coded gray.

» It's possible to use a professional microphone with your computer, though you need an audio-to-USB adapter. This gizmo accepts a ¼-inch mic jack or XLR connector and then translates the analog signal into digital for the computer. Several models are available, including the popular Scarlett Solo brand.

Configuring the microphone

The most important part of configuring a microphone is setting the sound input level. To perform this task, obey these steps:

1. **Press the Win+I keyboard shortcut to bring up the Settings app.**

2. **Choose the System category.**

3. **Choose Sound.**

   The Input area lists available microphones in Windows 11. In Windows 10, choose a microphone from the menu. The microphone you select becomes the default audio input device.

4. **In Windows 10, choose the Device Properties link.**

5. **Use the Volume slider to set the microphone's input level.**

Though you can use the Settings app to set the default microphone (see Step 3), most apps that consume audio input also feature controls that let you choose which microphone to use. For example, the Zoom app lets you select which microphone to use for input at the start of every meeting.

TIP

If you use a headset for an online meeting, ensure that the meeting app uses the headset's speakers and microphone, not the microphone on the webcam.

Securing the microphone

Just as you don't want any weirdo on the Internet peeking at you from your computer's webcam, you probably don't want unknown or unwanted programs to access your computer's microphone. To ensure that the microphone is secure, and to control which apps have access, follow these steps:

1. **Open the Settings app.**

   Press the Win+I keyboard shortcut.

2. **Choose the Privacy & Security item.**

   This item is titled just Privacy in Windows 10.

3. **Choose Microphone from the App Permissions list.**

4. **Set the main master control to the On position to allow apps and programs to access the microphone.**

   Or, you can leave this item off to disable all microphone access.

5. **Review the list of apps that can request microphone access, using the master control to allow or deny (on or off) access for each one.**

When access is granted — say, for a voice recorder program — you can use the microphone right away. Otherwise, when access is denied, the program begs you to give it permission to access the microphone. If you deny access, the program goes on and assumes that your computer lacks a microphone.

Older Windows programs, such as a few computer games, may not obey the permissions you set for the microphone. That's okay. These programs are dumb and won't use the microphone surreptitiously.

3

Network and Internet Stuff

Chapter **14**

The Networking Thing

s the network a peripheral for the computer, or is the computer a peripheral for the network? Don't bother climbing a mountain to ask a guru. The only point you need to remember is that the network is a necessary part of computing. Even by yourself in a cabin in the woods, your computer needs a network. One may not be available, but you need it.

The Big Networking Picture

Like kindergarten, computer networking is about communication and sharing. Various electronic gizmos connect and chat with each other, sending and receiving information. They share resources, including storage, printers, and modems. And they learn the ABCs: ARP, BGP, DHCP, DNS, FTP, HTTP, IP, SMTP, POP, TCP, and UDP.

Figure 14-1 illustrates a typical computer network, such as one you may desire for your home or that's already configured in the office. This type of network is known as a *local-area network*, or *LAN*, which I forgot to list in the preceding paragraph.

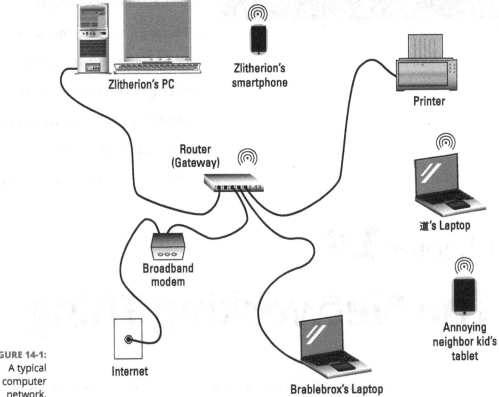

FIGURE 14-1:
A typical
computer
network.

Ignoring the network's overall octopus-like layout, a single computer's network connection looks more like this:

PC (or device) ⇨ Router or Gateway ⇨ Modem ⇨ Internet

Device: Anything connected to the network is a device: a desktop, laptop, smartphone, tablet, printer — anything with networking hardware. This hardware connects the device to a central location, wired or wirelessly.

Router or gateway: The central location in a network is commonly called a *router*, though technically it's a *gateway*. (Routers are far more sophisticated.) All network devices connect to this location. The gateway manages local network traffic between the devices. For example, your laptop can use a network printer, or your desktop can steal files from Zlitherion's PC.

Modem: Internet traffic is forwarded by the gateway to a modem. It also receives Internet traffic from the modem and distributes it to those devices requesting the information.

Internet: The *Internet* is the immense collection of all computers in the world that send, receive, store, and share information, most of which is not pornography.

When special software magic is applied, all these network hardware components merrily work together. They help your desktop PC or laptop communicate with other computers, share information, and access the Internet.

>> In some network configurations, the gateway and modem are the same device.

>> A wireless gateway can also be referred to as a *base station*.

>> Not shown in Figure 14-1 are extensions to the wireless network. Called a *mesh*, this type of network has several secondary gateways or base stations that extend the wireless signal across a larger area than a single base station can handle. Only one of these locations serves as the main gateway.

>> All laptops feature wireless networking. Some desktops have wireless networking included but also wired networking. Smartphones and tablets use wireless networking exclusively.

>> Network software magic is supplied by Windows in conjunction with mythical pagan beasts and deities. See the nearby sidebar "Network terms to ignore."

TECHNICAL STUFF

>> Setting up your own network isn't that difficult, especially if you use an all-wireless configuration. I do strongly recommend that your first network action is to apply an administrator password to the gateway (router) and create a complex, difficult-to-type, and impossible-to-remember password for the Wi-Fi network.

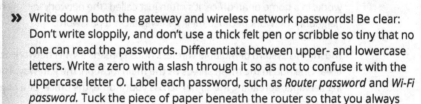

TIP

>> Write down both the gateway and wireless network passwords! Be clear: Don't write sloppily, and don't use a thick felt pen or scribble so tiny that no one can read the passwords. Differentiate between upper- and lowercase letters. Write a zero with a slash through it so as not to confuse it with the uppercase letter O. Label each password, such as *Router password* and *Wi-Fi password*. Tuck the piece of paper beneath the router so that you always know where to find it.

NETWORK TERMS TO IGNORE

Computer scientists have concluded that the basic networking concepts of communications and sharing are too easy to grasp. Therefore, they've invented some interesting terms and acronyms to describe computer networking in a complex and irritating manner. Here are a few:

802.11: This number refers to the current wireless networking standard. It's followed by various letters of the alphabet. As long as you get the "802.11" part correct (say "eight-oh-two-eleven"), the letters that follow are of concern only to the nerds.

Base Star: This is the bad guys' spaceship in *Battlestar Galactica*. This term has nothing to do with computer networking.

base station: This generic term applies to a wireless hub or gateway used as a central connection point in wireless networking.

Ethernet cable: This cable connects computers with networking equipment. The term *CAT* also refers to this type of cable, where *CAT* is followed by a famous number, such as 5 or 6.

gateway: The correct name for what's commonly called a router, this item organizes and manages information on a local network. The gateway also serves as the interface between a local network and the Internet.

hub: A central location to which networked computers are connected, either wired or wirelessly, is called a hub. It allows the connected devices to communicate with each other. Unlike a gateway, a hub doesn't manage network traffic.

LAN: This acronym stands for *local-area network*, which is how computer networking works in a home or an office. It's often just called "the network" or "my network" or "the neighbor's network because their gateway lacks a password."

mesh: This system of multiple wireless hubs spreads a Wi-Fi network across a large area. One hub in the mesh serves as the main location, the gateway. The rest act as willing servants, spreading the signal across your home, the office, or a huge building filled with sleepy government workers.

modem: Originally a portmanteau of *modulator/dem*odulator, today's broadband modems provide high-speed Internet access to your home or office network.

NIC: This acronym stands for *network interface card* (or *controller*). It's the computer hardware that provides the network connection — wired and wireless.

router: This is the common name for a gateway. Technically, a router is a sophisticated and expensive device used only in large, intimidating networks.

switch: Another term for a hub, though specifically for wired networking. You use a switch to add more wired network connections to a gateway.

Wi-Fi: This term refers to wireless networking. Supposedly, it stands for *wireless fidelity*, but various Internet nerds will argue this point with you. And it's written with a hyphen. If you see *WiFi*, feel free to point and laugh.

Make the Network Connection

According to some nerds, wired networking is faster and more secure than wireless. But why should you listen to someone who bathes only once a week? Truly, as long as your computer has networking hardware installed (and it does), you can connect to a network and use all its glorious resources.

Connecting to a wired network

To make the wired connection, locate the Ethernet port. It looks like an old telephone jack and is found on the rear of a desktop PC or on the edges of a laptop. Plug the Ethernet cable into the port. It makes a pleasing clicking noise when fully connected.

The other end of the Ethernet cable plugs into a wall socket or directly into a hub or gateway. This plug-in arrangement is the extent of the physical, wired connection.

The software side of the connection is handled by Windows, though you must assert whether the network is public or private. See the later section "Checking and setting the network type."

>> Perhaps you're too young to remember what a phone jack looks like. Kids. The Ethernet jack is rectangular in shape with a notch on one of its long sides.

>> Ethernet cables can be obtained at any office supply or computer store. Even Home Depot has them. Just ask a Home Depot employee. And if you can't find a Home Depot employee, you're in the right place.

TECHNICAL STUFF

>> The technical name for an Ethernet port is RJ-45. It's okay to call it an R2-D2 port if you want to annoy a nerd.

>> It doesn't matter which end of the Ethernet cable you use for the connection. It cannot plug in backward, not in this dimension.

Accessing a Wi-Fi network

A wireless network connection is possible anywhere a Wi-Fi signal is available. You need to know the network's name and perhaps a password. Upon success, your computer can use the network and access the Internet without the burden and embarrassment of wires.

To connect with a Wi-Fi network, wirelessly follow these steps:

1. **Press the Win+A keyboard shortcut to bring up the Windows Action Center.**

2. **Choose the Network tile.**

If you don't see the Network tile in Windows 10, click the Expand link.

In Windows 11, the Network tile says "Available" when a wireless network is within range. Click the chevron, as illustrated in Figure 14-2, to see a list of networks.

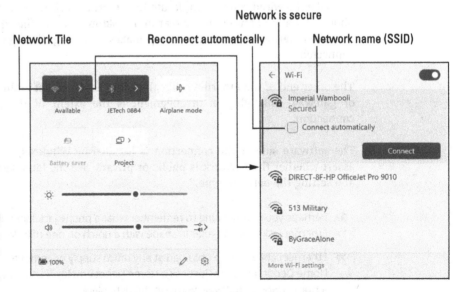

FIGURE 14-2: Selecting a Wi-Fi network in the Windows 11 Action Center.

3. **Choose a Wi-Fi network from the list.**

4. **Place a check mark by the Connect Automatically option.**

   This option ensures that your computer automatically reconnects to the network whenever it's in range. For a desktop that seldom moves, this is a good choice. For a laptop, choose to reconnect automatically if you plan on frequenting the Wi-Fi network's location.

5. **Click the Connect button.**

6. **If prompted, type the network password and click the Next button.**

   Networks without passwords, such as those in airports and public libraries, may have you visit a website to complete the sign-in process.

Your computer is now connected to the wireless network. The networking notification on the taskbar changes to reflect the wireless connection, as shown in the margin.

>> After connecting, ensure that Windows is using the proper network security. See the later section "Checking and setting the network type."

TIP

>> By choosing the Connect Automatically option (refer to Step 4), you ensure that whenever your laptop is in range, it connects to, signs in to, and accesses the specific network. This way, you need to configure the network and type its password only once.

>> Some Wi-Fi networks are metered. This type of connection measures the amount of data transferred over the network, which limits what you can do. Be aware of metered connections. Try to avoid streaming or downloading as too much data transferred may disconnect you.

![warning icon]

WARNING

>> Avoid connecting to unknown networks in a public location. For example, if you're at an airport and you see both the Airport Free Wi-Fi and Julie's iPhone networks, you probably want to connect to the airport's network, not Julie's. You take a security risk when you don't know which network you're using.

Connecting to a hidden Wi-Fi network

For security reasons, or perhaps out of embarrassment, some wireless networks don't broadcast their network names. Obviously, you cannot connect to a network when you don't know its name, mostly because the unnamed network doesn't show up in the list of available Wi-Fi networks.

To discover the network name, you must ask someone, such as the network manager or perhaps the indifferent young person who served you coffee and a stale pastry of questionable vintage. After you obtain the network name, plus details such as the password, follow these steps to establish the connection:

1. **Open the Settings app.**

   Press the Win+I keyboard shortcut.

2. **Choose Network & Internet.**

3. **Choose Wi-Fi.**

4. **Choose Manage Known Networks.**

   You see a list of every Wi-Fi network the computer has ever connected to. Yes, your laptop is promiscuous.

5. **Click the Add Network button (Windows 11) or Add a New Network (Windows 10).**

6. **Type the network's name or SSID.**

   The network name is referred to as the SSID, where *SSID* stands for *service set identifier.*

7. **Set the Security Type.**

   This detail should be given to you by that same indifferent barista. If not, try the WEP2 Personal option.

8. **Put a check mark by Connect Automatically.**

9. **Click the Save button.**

   Because you directed Windows to connect automatically with the hidden network, the connection is made.

You may need to type a password and choose other options to complete the connection, each of which is delightfully explained in the preceding section.

Checking and setting the network type

When it comes to betting on the network type, Windows chooses public over private every time. The difference between the two is security: A public network is more secure, which is what you want at the airport or library where lurking hordes of hackers desire your data, possibly.

A private network is one you trust, such as the one at your home or office. This setting doesn't mean the network lacks security, but rather that you can do more with the network. For example, you can share files and access network printers and other network resources.

To review the currently connected network type, heed these steps in Windows 11:

1. **Press the Win+I keyboard shortcut to summon the Settings app.**

2. **Choose Network & Internet.**

3. **For a wired connection, choose Ethernet; for a Wi-Fi connection, choose Wi-Fi.**

4. **For a Wi-Fi connection, choose the currently connected network on the next screen.**

5. **Set the Network Profile Type option to Public Network or Private Network.**

In Windows 10, obey these steps to check the network type:

1. **Bring forth the Settings app: Press the Win+I keyboard shortcut.**

2. **Choose Network & Internet.**

3. **For a wired connection, choose Status; for a Wi-Fi connection, select the currently connected Wi-Fi network.**

4. **For a wired connection, click the Properties button below the current network icon.**

5. **Set the Network Profile option to Public or Private.**

Windows initially classifies all new networks as public. If you're sitting snugly at home or in your office, you can choose Private. This setting allows you access to more network goodies, which is often necessary in a home or a home office or another professional situation.

REMEMBER

Always choose a public network type when you're using your PC or laptop in a public location. This choice is the most secure.

Break the Network Connection

The question may not seem necessary, but that doesn't stop people from asking: How do you direct the computer to break a network connection in a friendly manner that won't incur the wrath of the network gods? Unlike in human relationships, breaking the connection between a PC or laptop and a network doesn't require counseling or a lawyer or a cryptic social networking post.

Disconnecting from a wired network

To stop using the wired connection, unplug the Ethernet cable. That's it.

>> You can unplug the cable whether the computer is on or off.

>> If an established Wi-Fi connection is available, the computer instantly switches to using this connection as soon as the wired connection is terminated.

WARNING

>> Don't break the connection while you're using the network to access files. If you're in doubt about whether files are accessed over the network, first close any applications and then unplug the cable.

Releasing the Wi-Fi connection

You don't need to take formal action to disconnect from a Wi-Fi network. For a laptop, simply moving out of range does the trick. The typical wireless network has a range of about 50 or so feet, which is only 15 or so meters in Europe. So, pick up your laptop or desktop PC and run 50 feet in any direction. Knowledgeable onlookers will recognize that you're trying to break the Wi-Fi connection and not assume that you're on fire.

Turning off the computer or putting it to sleep also disconnects the wireless network. These actions seem less frantic to concerned onlookers.

It's possible to manually disconnect a Wi-Fi network. For Windows 11, follow these directions:

1. **Press the Win+A keyboard shortcut to pop up the Action Center.**
2. **Click the right-pointing chevron by the Internet icon.**

   Refer to Figure 14-2, earlier in this chapter.

3. **Click the Disconnect button.**

   The Disconnect button replaces the Connect button shown in Figure 14-2.

Heed these steps in Windows 10:

1. **Press the Win+A keyboard shortcut to pop up the Action Center.**
2. **Choose the currently connected wireless network.**
3. **Click the Disconnect button.**

With a heavy sigh, the network releases your computer, letting go with an extended, open hand and a tiny lump in its throat.

REMEMBER

The network stays disconnected. If you move out of range and then move back into range, the wireless network is reconnected if you've configured it to automatically connect. Or, you can reconnect by choosing the same network again, as described earlier in this chapter.

Forgetting a Wi-Fi connection

Windows remembers every Wi-Fi network your laptop has ever accessed. This memory is how the laptop easily reconnects to an established network instantly — unless you direct Windows to forget a network.

To forget a Wi-Fi network connection, or to review and be appalled at the list of saved networks, follow these steps:

1. **Open the Settings app.**

   The keyboard shortcut is Win+I.

2. **Choose Network & Internet.**

3. **Choose Wi-Fi.**

4. **Choose Manage Known Networks.**

   Behold! It's your laptop's Little Black Book.

5. **In Windows 10, choose the network you want to un-remember.**

6. **Click the Forget button.**

   The network you deem unworthy of reconnection is off the list.

Of course, you can always reconnect to any wireless network. You must type in the password again as well as set the network type, as described elsewhere in this chapter. Upon establishing a connection, the network will cheerfully greet you and never hold a grudge.

IN THIS CHAPTER

» **Understanding the Internet**

» **Gaining Internet access**

» **Using other web browsers**

» **Opening undercover browser windows**

» **Searching the web**

» **Saving a web page image**

» **Exploring email options**

Chapter **15**

The Internet

N etworking is important to your computer because of the Internet. Windows updates itself over the Internet. You obtain new software from the Internet. You read the news, watch movies, listen to music, and make fun of losers on social media all on the Internet. It's a big deal.

What Is the Internet?

Beyond accelerating the downfall of human civilization, it's important to understand that the Internet isn't a single thing. No, it exists as billions of things.

The *Internet* consists of all the devices connected to the Internet, the software they run, and the wires and signals that connect them. This definition may seem weird, mostly because people think of the Internet as a single computer or a program. It's not. Whenever your PC or laptop is *on* the Internet, it's part of the Internet.

» The computers on the Internet send information, they receive information, and — most important — they store information. This interaction is the

Internet in a nutshell. There. I just saved you $35 on an old O'Reilly Publishing book.

>> No one owns the Internet, just as no one owns the oceans. But like the oceans, lots of people pollute the Internet.

>> The company you pay for Internet access is merely providing you with the access, not with the Internet's content.

>> When you get something for "free" on the Internet, it still costs you. That's because *you* are what's being sold.

REMEMBER

Internet Access

The Internet comes pouring in from a hole in the wall, but you can't see the Internet if you peer into the hole. Likewise, the Internet may flow across the air, which you can't see either. The Internet appears when you pay a company for access. The Internet may also be provided free of charge at locations such as an airport, a library, a coffee shop, a prison, and so on.

For home or office Internet access, you pay an outfit called an *Internet service provider*, or ISP. The fee you pay determines the Internet access speed, which is how quickly the Internet comes flowing in through that hole in the wall. The ISP determines the type of access, whether it's wireless or using fiber optic, cable, DSL, satellite, or the mobile data (cellular) network.

>> Internet access is described as *broadband*, meaning that the signal is on all the time. Unlike the old telephone dialup service, you don't need to sign in to the Internet every time you need access.

REMEMBER

>> The *S* in *ISP* stands for service. You pay a fee, and the ISP provides you with Internet access *and* service. Service means technical support. Keep the ISP's support number handy for the next time you experience an Internet outage.

>> When the Internet does go down, you can use your smartphone to access the Internet. Two methods are available: You can have the smartphone act as a Wi-Fi hotspot, or you can tether the smartphone to your computer, having it act as a modem. The availability of these features depends on your mobile data plan.

TIP

It's a World Wide Web We Weave

I'm certain that you've been on the World Wide Web, browsed a few pages, looked up an old friend, and scammed that recipe for peanut butter cookies from a celebrity chef. Therefore, I have nothing to offer you. Feel free to avoid reading this entire section.

Finding another web browser

The software you use to access the web is called a *web browser*. You need this software to surf the Wide World of Web. Windows comes with the Edge browser, which isn't that bad, though it has only a 13 percent market share. Other, alternative web browsers are available.

The most popular web browser is Google's Chrome, with a whopping 65 percent market share. Other, alternative web browsers include Firefox (7 percent) and Opera (a pitiful 3 percent). You can easily install and use these alternative browsers if you don't want to be stuck with Microsoft Edge. To do so, heed these directions:

1. **Open the Edge browser.**

    Yes, you must use a web browser to obtain a web browser. This step is like driving a car to purchase a new car.

2. **Visit the website of the alternative browser.**

    Chrome: www.google.com/chrome

    Firefox: www.mozilla.org/firefox

    Opera: www.opera.com

    Type the web page address into the browser's address bar, and then whack the Enter key.

3. **Click the link to download the browser.**

    The link is titled Download or Download Now.

    Avoid clicking a "download" link on an advertisement.

WARNING

4. **Follow the directions on the website to open the download and install the alternative web browser.**

When you first run the new web browser, it asks whether you want to make it the default browser. You do. Click Yes.

You can have as many web browsers as you like on your computer. One demands to be the default, which opens links in email messages and elsewhere. You can run the other web browsers, though each time you do, the software begs you to make it the default. Deny the temptation.

Browsing tips

Here are my web-browsing tips, collected, honed and polished over the past two centuries:

>> The keyboard shortcut to enter an address into a web browser's address bar is Ctrl+L.

>> To make web pages with small text more visible, zoom in: Press the Ctrl++ (plus, or Shift+=) key. To zoom out, press the Ctrl+– (minus) key. Remember: Plus to zoom in and minus to zoom out.

>> If a web page doesn't load, try again! The web can be busy, and often when it is, you see an error message. Reload a web page by pressing Ctrl+R on the keyboard. Think R for refresh.

TIP

>> Refreshing a web page is one quick way to fix the missing-picture problem. Refreshing also works when a page doesn't render properly or otherwise looks wacky.

>> When a web page isn't found, you probably didn't type its address properly. Try again. But do recognize that some web pages go offline to observe various pagan holidays.

Most web links are text, but quite a few are graphical. The way to know for certain is to aim the mouse pointer at what you believe may be a link. If the pointer changes to a pointing hand, as shown in the margin, you know that it's a link you can click.

>> When you accidentally click a link and change your mind, click the Stop button, which appears on the address bar with an X symbol.

>> Press Ctrl+D to add any web page you're viewing as a bookmark or to add it to your favorites. Don't be shy about it! It's better to add it now and delete it later than to regret not adding it in the first place.

Going undercover on the web

Efforts are made to track your path as you meander through the Wonderful World Wide Web. This tracking can be benevolent, such as remembering the contents of your online shopping cart, or less benevolent, such as discovering that you have a dire need to obtain dog food. Once it's revealed, you find yourself bombarded with dog food advertising.

When you prefer not to be tracked, you open an undercover tab in the web browser. The various web browsers refer to the undercover tab by different names, but the result is the same: As you browse undercover, your history isn't tracked, and evidence that you've visited certain sites ("cookies") isn't saved.

>> In the Edge web browser, going undercover is referred to as *InPrivate* browsing. Press Ctrl+Shift+P to create a new InPrivate browsing window.

>> In Google Chrome, it's referred to as *Incognito*. The keyboard shortcut is Ctrl+Shift+N.

>> Firefox uses the term *Private window*. To bring up a Private window, press Ctrl+Shift+P.

With these browsers, the first undercover window you see after pressing the shortcut keys displays a summary of how the browser behaves in this mode. You also see some tips and suggestions on how to use undercover browsing. Be aware that this feature doesn't stop all snooping, but it's good for a modicum of anonymity.

To exit your secretive adventures, close the undercover window or tab.

TIP

>> If you find yourself frequently deleting your web history, consider going undercover instead.

>> Items such as usernames and passwords are not automatically filled in when you use an undercover window.

>> An example of going undercover is shopping. I do my pre-shopping and browsing in an undercover window. With this approach, I'm not bombarded with advertising for the items I've just browsed.

>> Yes, you can use an undercover window to look at naughty things on the web. Do keep in mind that other information about you, such as your computer's IP address, can still be tracked when you browse undercover.

TECHNICAL STUFF

>> A *cookie* is a small tidbit of text saved from the website to your computer. Its contents are typically numeric, a code relevant only to the website or advertising on the website, which identifies you as an individual user.

Searching-the-web tips

The web is full of information, most of it accurate. The issue is locating the information you want. Here are my web-page-searching tips:

>> My main search engine these days is Google, at www.google.com, but I can also recommend the Microsoft search engine, Bing, at www.bing.com. This recommendation has nothing to do with the fact that I own Microsoft stock.

>> You can also type the information you want to search for in the web browser's address bar.

>> Web search engines ignore the smaller words in the English language. Words such as *is, to, the, for, are,* and others aren't included in the search. Therefore:

>> Use only keywords when searching. For example, to look for *The Declaration of Independence,* typing *declaration independence* is good enough.

>> Word order matters. If you want to find out the name of that red bug with six legs, try all combinations: *bug red six legs, red bug six legs,* or even *six legs red bug.* Each variation yields different results.

>> When words *must* be found together, enclose them in double quotes, such as *"electric chair" configuration.* A quoted search finds only web pages that list the words *electric chair* together and in that order.

Stealing an image from a web page

Most images you see on the web are yours for the taking — if you know the secret trick. That is, to use the image for yourself and not for your business or to make money. Many images are copyrighted. So be aware of what you purloin.

The secret to stealing an image is to right-click on it and choose the Save Picture As command from the pop-up menu. Use the dialog box that appears to find a happy home for the picture on your computer's mass storage device.

>> The Save Picture As command may be titled differently, such as Save Image As.

>> Not every website allows you to save an image.

>> Some images are saved in unusual file formats, which your computer may be unable to read. If so, bummer.

Copying text from a web page

You can copy text from a web page and paste it into another app or an email message. Here's how:

1. **Drag to select the text you want to copy.**

2. **Press Ctrl+C to copy.**

3. **Start or switch to an app that accepts text, such as your word processor, email program, or what-have-you.**

4. **Paste the text into a document or an email message.**

   Press Ctrl+V on the keyboard or choose Edit ⇨ Paste from the menu. Then use the proper commands to save or print or edit the text.

Text can be pasted only into a program that accepts text input. If you can't paste the text, it means the program doesn't consume text or you need to choose the proper item into which text can be pasted.

Printing web pages

Printing a web page isn't easy. The problem is that a web page is formatted for a computer screen, not a sheet of paper. Unless the page is laid out like a document, generating a printed copy is an ordeal.

Here are my suggestions for getting a web page to print properly:

>> The print command is Ctrl+P for all web browsers. You might also find a Print button on the toolbar or hidden on a menu. Press Ctrl+P to summon the Print dialog box or screen. It contains settings for controlling the printer.

>> Change the page orientation from portrait (tall) to landscape (wide). This setting can be found in the Print dialog box.

>> Use the Shrink to Fit or Shrink to Page command in the Print dialog box to reset the web page's size to match the paper size.

>> Consider saving the web page; press the Ctrl+S keyboard shortcut. After the page is saved, you can open the web page file in Microsoft Word or Excel or any web page editing program and then edit or print it from there.

Sharing a web page

When you love a web page so much that you must share it with everyone you know, follow my friendly yet threatening words of advice: Share only the web page address.

Please do not copy and paste the entire web page into an email message or on Facebook. Instead, just copy the web page's address from the address text box. Follow these steps:

1. **Click the mouse in the web browser's address bar.**

2. **Select the entire text — all of it.**

   The keyboard shortcut to instantly select the current web page address is Ctrl+L. Pressing the F4 key might also work.

3. **Press Ctrl+C to copy the text.**

4. **Switch to whichever program you're using to share that address.**

   For example, switch to your email program.

5. **Press Ctrl+V to paste the web page address.**

Some web browsers may feature a Share button. Click this button to bring up a list of places to share the web page address. This trick may not work in all browsers, because the command called Share might do something else, such as purchase Microsoft stock.

Email Messages

A long time ago, humans sent letters — real mail. It was an art form. People bought envelopes and stamps. They wrote in cursive, pages of personal information spelled correctly. Times were easier then. You could buy a house for $240 or a bushel of apples. Those were the days.

Modern humans turned from real mail to the newfangled email. It was once the number-one reason for using the Internet, way in front of porn and arguing with strangers on social media.

Today, the kids send text messages. Even so, email is still a thing old people like to use, especially business humans and online stores that want to scream their latest bargains at you. Yes, email is a small part of the Internet.

Using an email program

Windows comes with an email app called Mail. It provides basic email services, allowing you to access your various email accounts in a single location. This feature is perhaps the Mail program's greatest benefit.

Most email today is offered on the web. You can visit your email service's website to check your messages, compose new messages, manage that bloated inbox, and do other fun email-ish things. But because you most likely have several email websites — including work — using an email program makes sense, as opposed to repeatedly visiting multiple websites several times a day.

>> Odds are good that that large, intimidating organization you work for uses Microsoft Outlook as its email program. If so, you can use Outlook on the web, but you can also obtain the Outlook program. It's part of the Microsoft Office or Microsoft 365 suite of programs.

>> Outlook is not the easiest program to use.

>> The Mail app that comes with Windows isn't the only email app available. For example, you can try Mozilla Thunderbird as an alternative. If I can think of any other email apps, they'll magically appear here in the future. Try opening this book again in a few weeks to check.

Configuring email

For each email account, you have an account name and a password. The *account name* is some name you made up or were assigned when the account was created, followed by an at sign (@) and then the webmail service's domain name, such as gmail.com or ymail.com. These three tidbits are all you need to know to configure an email account:

>> Your account name

>> Your password

>> The service name

In the olden days, more details were required — and they may still be, for some email services. For example, the Microsoft Exchange Server (which provides the smarts for Outlook) has settings for a domain name and other gobbledygook that no one but the nerds know or care about.

If you're curious, here are some common email acronyms and terms used to describe the various email formats. Please do not memorize any of these items:

POP or POP3: This acronym represents the traditional type of Internet email, the kind supplied by an Internet service provider (ISP) in the olden days. POP stands for Post Office Protocol. It has nothing to do with the government mail service.

IMAP: This is the most common type of email, also known as webmail. IMAP stands for Internet Message Access Protocol.

SMTP: This service is used in combination with POP and provided by a traditional ISP. POP picks up the email, but SMTP sends it. It stands for Simple Mail Transfer Protocol.

Some ISPs may still offer POP and SMTP for their email service. If so, you need to know the specific server addresses (numbers) and configuration to set up email in a program like Microsoft Mail or Outlook. Fortunately, these requirements are no longer needed for most email services offered today. And for this fact, everyone is most grateful.

IN THIS CHAPTER

» **Exploring files on the network**

» **Using mapped drives**

» **Sharing a folder to the network**

» **Accessing cloud storage**

» **Adding cloud storage files**

» **Sharing files from the cloud**

Chapter **16**

Files from Elsewhere

ass storage is the home for your computer's files, boosted by media cards, thumb drives, and external drives. All these gizmos are local to your computer, within arm range or otherwise easily visible for you to admire or sneer at. Beyond these gizmos, files are also available over the network. These files from elsewhere can dwell on other network computers, a network server, or even the Internet, in the lofty form of cloud storage.

Files Lurking on the Local Network

The big kumbaya of networking is that resources are shared. It's like communism, but without guns. One of the network resources that can be shared is files. These include regular boring files, but also media resources, such as music and video. To see what kind of goodies lurk on the network, open the Network window. Heed these directions:

1. **Press Win+E to conjure up a File Explorer window.**

2. **From the items on the left side of the window, choose Network.**

   The Network window appears, as shown in Figure 16-1, showing available network resources.

Network item

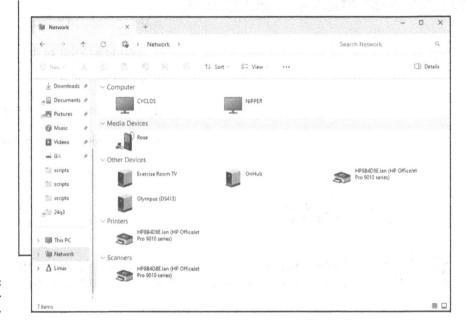

FIGURE 16-1:
The Net-
work window.

The Network window organizes network goodies by category, as illustrated in Figure 16-1. Icons appear for other computers on the network, media devices, smart TVs, network servers, network printers, scanners, robots, and so on.

>> Not all computers on the network show up in the Network window. Only when they have Network Discovery active on a private network type are the computers available. See the next section.

>> When your computer is connected to a public network, the Network window looks rather sparse. The reason is that Windows automatically cranks up network security and restricts access on public networks.

>> Available network printers are accessed automatically. Refer to Chapter 12 for details on printing.

Activating Network Discovery

To surrender your computer to the network, plus any resources on your computer you desire to share, you activate Network Discovery. This choice is optional, but if you wonder why others on the network can't access your computer, Network Discovery is the reason.

Heed these directions to activate Network Discovery in Windows 11:

1. **Press the Win+I keyboard shortcut to summon the Settings app.**
2. **Choose the Network & Internet category.**
3. **Choose Advanced Network Settings.**
4. **Choose Advanced Sharing Settings.**

   Three areas are available for sharing: Private Networks, Public Networks, and All Networks.

5. **Ensure that Network Discovery is on for your private network.**
6. **If you want to share folders from your computer to others on the network, ensure that File and Printer Sharing is active.**
7. **For laptop computers, expand the Public Networks item to ensure that both items presented are deactivated.**

In Windows 10, follow these ancient steps:

1. **Bring up the Settings app.**

   Press the Win+I keyboard shortcut.

2. **Choose the Network & Internet tile.**
3. **Choose Network and Sharing Center.**

   The Control Panel appears, presenting the Network and Sharing Center.

4. **From the left side of the Networking and Sharing Center window, click the Change Advanced Sharing Settings link.**
5. **Expand the Private (current profile) area.**
6. **Choose the item Turn On Network Discovery.**
7. **Choose the item Turn On File and Printer Sharing.**
8. **Expand the Guest or Public area.**
9. **For a laptop, turn off Network Discovery and File and Printer Sharing for Public Networks.**

If you choose not to use file and printer sharing, you can disable the items shown in these steps. But to access file sharing on the local network, activating these features is necessary.

WARNING

Never use Network Discovery on a public network, such as a coffee shop, airport, library, or bordello. Doing so is a security risk. Refer to Chapter 14 for information on determining the network type, public or private.

Accessing a network folder

Someone on the network (probably Ed) is foolish enough to surrender a folder for everyone else to use! Perhaps Ed wants others on the network to access files stored there, such as media files, graphics such as the company logo, a database, or something else Ed has deemed important. To take advantage of Ed's digital generosity and access the shared folder, you follow these steps:

1. **Open the Network window.**

   Press the Win+E keyboard shortcut, and in the File Explorer window, choose Network from the list of fun locations on the left side of the window. You see a window festooned with computer icons (refer to Figure 16-1), one of which represents Ed's computer (not shown in Figure 16-1).

2. **Open a computer icon.**

   The computer owner must have shared a folder for it to appear in the computer's window. If not, tell them to buy a copy of this book and read the later section "Sharing a folder."

3. **Open a folder to access its contents.**

   Folders with security — which is all of them — require a user account and password for access.

4. **Type your username and password as assigned on the network computer.**

   These credentials may be different from your own computer. For a local network at home or in a small office, you must either have an account on the network computer to gain access or know the computer's owner's account name and password.

5. **Peruse files in the shared folder.**

   At this point, using the folder works like using any other folder on your PC.

TIP

A better way to share files is to use cloud storage. This topic is covered later in this chapter.

Mapping a shared folder

The steps for accessing a shared folder on the network are arduous, specifically requiring that you type your username and password. A better solution is to map the shared network folder to a drive letter on your own computer. This trick allows you to always access the network folder without any overdramatic acting, intense wailing, or feigning death.

Figure 16-2 shows mapped network folders in the This PC window. These are called *mapped network drives* in Windows slang, though they're secretly just folders.

This PC item   Overflow icon

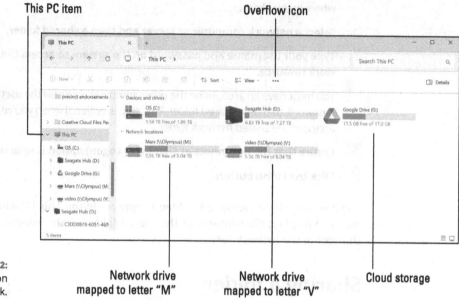

Network drive
mapped to letter "M"

Network drive
mapped to letter "V"

Cloud storage

Follow these steps to map a shared folder (network drive, whatever) on the network:

1. **Open the Network window in File Explorer.**

   Specific directions are hidden earlier in this chapter.

2. **Choose This PC from the list of locations on the left side of the window.**

3. **In Windows 11, click the Overflow icon (the three dots) and choose Map Network Drive; in Windows 10, click the button titled Map Network Drive.**

   Refer to Figure 16-2 for the location of the three dots in Windows 11.

   In Windows 10, the Map Network Drive button is found on the File Explorer window's Computer tab.

4. **Choose a drive letter.**

   A drop-down list of available drive letters appears in the Map Network Drive dialog box, negating the need for you to sing the Alphabet Song. I recommend using a letter more toward the Z end of the alphabet so that the mapped network drive won't interfere with any removable storage you add to your PC. For example, I map drive letter V to my network file server.

5. **Click the Browse button.**

A mini-network window appears, listing available storage devices on the network. These are locations flagged for shared folders, as described elsewhere in this chapter.

6. **Select a network computer or server and then a shared folder.**

7. **Type your username and password on the system to access the network resource.**

You must have an account on the other computer, or know the username and password, to map a shared folder. This step is optional when you've already accessed the shared network folder.

8. **Ensure that the Reconnect at Sign-in (or Logon) option is selected.**

9. **Click the Finish button.**

The new drive letter, assigned in Step 4, appears in the This PC window. Opening this icon displays the contents of the shared folder on the network, giving you a shortcut to the network resource.

Sharing a folder

Say you're one of those people who wants to share your files with everyone on the network, like your computer has herpes or something. If so, you can sacrifice one of your computer's folders, making it available to other users on the network. Here's how to make it happen:

1. **Right-click the folder you want to share.**

The folder shouldn't be on cloud storage, because such a folder is shared differently. See the section "Sharing a file from cloud storage," later in this chapter.

2. **Choose Properties from the folder's pop-up menu.**

3. **Click the Sharing tab.**

4. **Click the Advanced Sharing button.**

5. **Put a check mark by the option labeled Share This Folder.**

You can set a share name, which helps to better identify the folder on the network if the folder is currently named something stupid.

TIP

If you want others to have full access — to add as well as delete files — click the Permissions button and place a check mark in the Allow column by the Full Control item. Otherwise, the shared folder is read-only.

6. **Click OK.**

The folder is now shared.

7. **Click the Close button to dismiss the folder's Properties dialog box.**

Other PCs can now access the folder on the network, as described in the earlier section "Accessing a network folder."

REMEMBER

>> To unshare a folder, repeat the steps in this section, but in Step 5 remove the check mark.

>> Shared folders are available only when the network resource is available.

>> A better way to share information is to use cloud storage. See the next section.

>> Other network denizens can access the shared folder only if they have an account on your computer or know your username and password.

WARNING

>> Don't share an entire storage device, such as drive C. Don't share your entire user profile or Home folder. Doing so is a security risk. Share only specific folders, such as a project folder.

Cloud Storage Synchronization

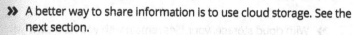

A computer network does a bang-up job when sharing resources such as printers and modems (for Internet access). Where the process becomes frustrating is with sharing files.

If you can map network storage to local storage, as discussed elsewhere in this chapter, things work better. But the ideal solution is to use cloud storage to share files. Don't look outside. Don't check the local weather forecast. *Cloud storage* is just a flowery way to describe storing files on the Internet.

The cloud storage solution not only easily gives different users access to the files you store there but also allows you to access your own files on different computers. For example, your desktop at the office and your laptop on the road both have access to files stored on the cloud.

Understanding cloud storage

Beyond bows and flows of angel hair, the cloud is a digital realm where you can keep all your files, contacts, appointments — your digital life. The goal is to sign in to any Internet-connected gizmo and have all your stuff available. You don't need to transfer files, grant access, manage a series of thumb drives, memorize incantations, or perform other encumbrances.

Just two things are needed to make the cloud thing happen: a broadband Internet connection and access to a cloud service.

The Internet connection is provided by your desktop PC, a laptop, a computer at the library, a smartphone, a tablet, and so on.

The cloud services are offered by an online provider. These services are abundant. I've listed a few in the next section.

>> With cloud storage, your files remain with you no matter where you are. Update a file in another city on your laptop, and when you get home, the same file is available on the cloud via your desktop computer. Anywhere you can get on the Internet, you can grab your cloud information.

>> Some cloud services are files-only. Others offer shared information on your calendar, email, contacts, photos, and so on.

>> Another advantage of cloud storage is that everything is backed up automatically. In fact, cloud backup is an alternative to the traditional form of backup. See Chapter 22.

>> You don't need to use cloud storage. You especially don't have to understand why the word *cloud* was chosen. Obviously, humidity isn't an issue.

Exploring cloud storage options

Surprising no one, Microsoft has a cloud storage service that is fully integrated into Windows. As a Microsoft stockholder, it's my duty to inform you that this service works well with Windows, serves as a backup for your files, and is fully integrated into the Microsoft Office suite of productivity apps. But OneDrive is not your only choice.

Here are your cloud storage options:

OneDrive: Microsoft's cloud storage, as just described. Its home on the Internet is onedrive.live.com, though it can also be accessed from the Windows Settings app on the main Home screen.

Google Drive: If you use Android mobile devices or have a Gmail account, you most likely already have Google Drive cloud storage. It synchronizes well with your phone or tablet and lets you share files with your computer. Visit `drive.google.com`.

iCloud: This service is used by Apple fanatics, those who have Macintosh computers, iPhones, Apple Watches, and whatever other expensive toys they offer. Visit `icloud.com/#iclouddrive` and follow the directions to download and install the cloud storage. Yes, this app works under Windows.

Other cloud storage services are available as well, such as Dropbox at `dropbox.com`. You can explore the lot online, but if the large, intimidating organization to which you've sworn fealty (your workplace) uses a specific service, I recommend adding that service to your personal computer as well.

> >> Basic access for cloud services is free. You must pay, however, when your storage requirements exceed the free allocation or when more features are desired.

WARNING

> >> Windows truly wants you to use OneDrive as your computer's backup. Be mindful of this choice! If you activate OneDrive's backup features, all files on your computer are saved to OneDrive by default. Depending on the quantity of files you store, such a move can quickly fill your allowed quota for cloud storage.

> >> Yes, it's possible to use multiple cloud storage systems. You can use these services in addition to storing files on local media.

TIP

> >> I use both local storage and cloud storage. For my work files, I store projects on the cloud. This choice makes it possible for me to access my work at home or on the road. Once I complete a project, I move its files to local storage for archiving.

TECHNICAL STUFF

> >> Microsoft's cloud storage service was originally called SkyDrive. Then they found out someone else owned the name SkyDrive or that it was a popular street name. Oops. So Microsoft changed the name.

Integrating cloud storage

Cloud storage isn't an atmospheric phenomenon and involves no precipitation. It exists on the Internet, but it need not be found only there. Files you store on the cloud can also be available on your computer, appearing as part of the mass storage system. You can work on them there even when an Internet connection isn't available.

To make local copies of cloud storage available, you must install cloud storage software on your computer. This program synchronizes files between the computer's mass storage system and the Internet.

Cloud storage software is obtained from the cloud service's website. You need an account with the service, such as your Microsoft account with OneDrive. Create an account, if you haven't already. Then follow the directions to install and configure the program. Once it's installed, your cloud storage is duplicated to local storage, as shown in Figure 16-2 with the Google Drive icon.

TIP

>> Obtain the cloud storage app for your mobile device as well as your computer. You can quickly access cloud files from your phone or tablet; plus, you can share files — and photographs — between your mobile device and your computer.

>> Files saved to the cloud are always available from the cloud service's website. You can manage them there or on your computer.

>> On your PC or laptop, you can choose whether to have the cloud files downloaded when accessed or always available. Having them stored on the cloud is beneficial in that they occupy less local storage space. Storing the files locally, however, ensures that they're available even when the Internet is down.

REMEMBER

>> Anytime a file is added to your cloud storage, it's added everywhere; other devices see the new file right away. With cloud storage, you don't have to synchronize anything; it's done automatically.

>> Cloud storage files are updated instantly or, when the Internet is down, they're updated the moment access is restored. When a conflict exists, you're alerted and given the opportunity to resolve the conflicted files, though the cloud storage software may just create two files in an effort to confuse you.

WARNING

>> Although creating a shortcut to a file works on your desktop or laptop computer, file shortcuts referencing cloud storage don't work. Always copy the entire file to share it from cloud storage. See the next section.

>> When you delete a file from cloud storage, it's removed from all cloud storage devices. Cloud storage has a recycle bin or "trash," though files are permanently removed after a given amount of time.

Sharing a file from cloud storage

Yet another advantage of cloud storage is that you can share links to your files. These links work like any web page link, allowing others to access the file. Full folders can be shared as well, which is a great way to collaborate and share the blame with others.

Each cloud storage service has its own specific steps to share a file or folder. The following steps work with OneDrive, which is integrated into Windows. Other cloud storage services work similarly:

1. **Browse to the folder containing the file or folder you want to share.**

2. **Right-click the file or folder icon.**

3. **Choose the Share item from the pop-up menu.**

    Two options present themselves in the Share dialog box. The first lets you send an email message to one or several people. The cloud file/folder's link is shared in the message.

    The second option just copies the link, which you can then paste into an email message or wherever pasting is allowed by law.

4. **Choose the permissions for the link.**

    For OneDrive, the options are that anyone with the link can edit the file, or they can just view the file. You can also add an expiration date for the link. Set these options before you share the link.

5. **Click the Send or Copy button.**

When you choose to send the link, the recipient(s) can click it from the email message to visit the document on the web, doing whatever with it.

TIP

>> Other cloud storage services share files in a similar manner. Some even have shortcut items on the file/folder's pop-up menu when the files are saved locally.

>> Alternatively, you can visit the cloud storage service's website and share files from there.

>> Often a Public folder is available specifically for sharing files. Consider copying your files to this folder and then sharing them. Doing so makes managing the shared files easier as they're all in one location.

REMEMBER

>> Always set the file's permissions — especially when sharing a full folder.

>> Remember that if you share a link, anyone with the link can access the file. If possible, set an expiration date.

>> Managing shared files is done on the cloud storage service's website. Look for an item that shows which files are currently shared. For example, on the OneDrive home page on the web, choose the Shared item from the list of categories on the left side of the window. You can then view files shared with you or by you.

Chapter **17**

Internet Safety

magine it's the 1970s and you're a scientist using the Internet, called the ARPANET back then. You receive an email message from someone purporting to be another scientist who has sent you a program that he claims solves a mutual problem. You open the email. You save the attachment. You run the program. Lo, it does solve your problem! Technology is truly a godsend.

Now imagine the same scenario today, but the email message is from a foreign prince who claims that you've won an international lottery. All you must do is save and run the attached program and provide your bank account number, and then millions of dollars are yours. Hopefully, you're a bit less trusting than that 1970s computer scientist. Welcome to the world of Internet safety.

» Being safe on the Internet comes down to two words: Be smart. Don't be too quick to click a link or open an unknown email attachment. Think! Software tools can help you, but — and I don't mean this as an insult — you are the weakest link in the security chain.

» Also see Chapter 21 for information on how to access the Windows Security Center.

Behind the Firewall

In the real world, a *firewall* is a specially constructed part of a building designed to impede the progress of a blazing inferno. The firewall acts as protection for whatever lies on the other side. It takes hours to burn through, whereas a regular wall bursts into flames quicker than a wino sitting too close to a campfire.

A digital firewall works the same way, protecting your computer from flaming winos.

Seriously, the purpose of a firewall is to supervise network traffic. The firewall ensures that information received has been asked for and that information sent has permission to leave. When something unknown wants in or out of the network, the firewall stops the action and generates a warning. You then choose whether to allow or deny access.

>> Windows comes with a firewall called Windows Defender Firewall. This utility is automatically activated and always running.

>> The gateway, or router, on your local network may also come with a firewall, called a *hardware firewall*. This doubling up of protection is perfectly fine.

>> A firewall cannot protect your computer from a virus. The reason is that viruses arrive as programs — usually, an email attachment or something you choose to download from the Internet. If you initiate the action on your own, the firewall assumes it's okay.

>> Use antivirus software to protect from viruses. In fact, you should use *both* antivirus software and a firewall. See Chapter 21 for more information on fighting the viral plague.

TECHNICAL STUFF

>> Firewalls monitor ports. A *port* is an individual Internet connection. At any time, your computer may have dozens of ports in use or open for a connection. When a network program knocks on a port's door, the firewall perks up and confirms that the program has permission to enter or leave. If not, a prompt appears, and you can decide for yourself whether to allow or deny access.

Finding the firewall

The Windows Firewall is configured to be on and working all the time. To confirm the firewall's status, obey these steps:

1. **Open the Windows Security Center app.**

   Click the Start button on the taskbar and type **Windows Security**. Choose the Windows Security app item from the search results.

2. **Choose Firewall & Network Protection.**

The Windows Firewall interface is rather plain, almost boring. Each item — Domain network, Private network, and Public network — should show that the firewall is on. That's it.

If any firewall item is off, choose it and click the master control icon to the On position.

You need not worry about setting firewall permissions for specific programs. If a program triggers the firewall, a warning appears. See the next section.

>> Refer to Chapter 14 for information on the network type, public or private.

>> For a private network, firewall protection is set to the lowest setting, which is fine. On public networks, the firewall is on full-bore.

Dealing with a firewall warning

When Windows Firewall freaks out, a pop-up message appears, like the one shown in Figure 17-1. The message alerts you that either a program is attempting to access your computer from the Internet or a program on your computer is trying to flee to the Internet.

When the warning appears, *read it*. The name of the program is listed. In Figure 17-1, the game *Red Dead Redemption 2* is attempting to connect with the Internet. In this instance, I started the program myself. It's requesting Internet access. Therefore, the warning is expected: Click the Allow Access button for private networks when you recognize why a program has triggered the firewall warning. Otherwise, click the Cancel button. You're safe.

REMEMBER

>> Take firewall warnings seriously! Don't panic, because nothing bad has happened. Yet! Still, don't let yourself develop the habit of automatically clicking the Allow Access button every time you see a firewall warning.

>> The purpose of the warnings is to train the firewall. It remembers your choices. The more you use the computer, the fewer warnings you see. Hopefully.

>> New software triggers a firewall warning. As long as you recognize the program and you're currently running it, allow access.

Program name and details

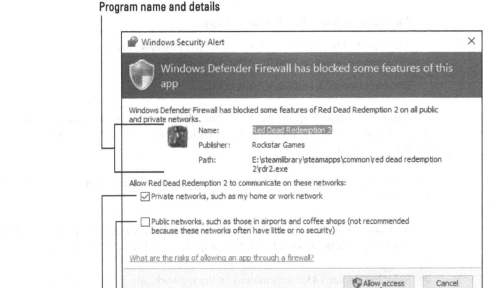

FIGURE 17-1:
Is it okay for
this program
to access
the Internet?

Choose for a public network

Choose for a private network

The program has permission
to go through the firewall

Beware the Bogus Website

It's easy to spot the Evil Captain Kirk in the old *Star Trek* TV show: He had black eyeliner. Well, and he was evil. On the Internet, bad and phony websites don't put on black eyeliner. But you do have a few tricks and tools to use that help you identify when one website pretends to be something else.

Checking the website's security

TIP

Always look at the web browser's address bar when you visit an important website, such as for banking or shopping or any website where you provide sensitive information. You need to ensure two things: The site is what you want, and it's secure. Figure 17-2 shows what to look for.

The website's address should match what you think it is, such as the name of your bank or a shopping site. If the web address looks "off" or has a spelling error or contains extra words, raise your suspicion flag. It may not be the site you think it is.

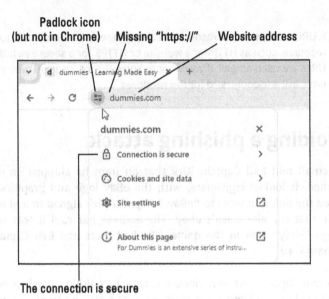

Padlock icon
(but not in Chrome)   Missing "https://"   Website address

FIGURE 17-2:
Checking a
website's security.

The connection is secure

Another item to look for is the website's security status. At the top of the web browser window, to the left of the website's address, many browsers show a padlock icon for a secure website. For some reason, in Chrome (shown in Figure 17-2), you instead see the cuneiform word for *padlock*. Regardless, click the icon, and then the drop-down menu indicates that the site is secure — a good sign.

A secure website uses the https URL. This URL is like the standard http but with an *s* added. The *s* stands for *secure*. Modern web browsers hide the URL for most websites, as can't be seen in Figure 17-2. If you click on the address bar, however, the full URL shows up. From Figure 17-2, it would be https://www.dummies.com/. The https means that the site is secure.

>> Just because a website lacks the padlock icon (graphically or in cuneiform) doesn't mean the website is unsafe. Lots of older websites lack such security. Even so, I recommend being wary on such sites.

>> Sometimes, visiting a site prompts the web browser to inform you that the site is unsafe. This situation can happen when the site's security certificate is out-of-date. If so, wait for a day to revisit the site. By then, the security certificate should be updated. Otherwise, do not visit the site!

>> HTTP stands for the HyperText Transfer Protocol. It's the method the Internet uses to cough up a web page. This initialism is different from HTML, which is the HyperText Markup Language used to format a web page. Evil Captain Kirk wouldn't know these terms, but Mr. Spock would.

TECHNICAL STUFF

>> A URL is the *universal resource locator*. It directs Internet traffic to a specific resource, such as HTTP for a website or HTTPS for a secure website. Other URLs are used as well. If you want to know the lot, and you have plenty of time, ask a friendly nerd for the rundown.

Avoiding a phishing attack

The email told Evil Captain Kirk that an item he shipped on eBay was being returned. It looked legitimate, with the eBay logo and graphics. Therefore, he clicked the link and went to "eBay." Captain Kirk signed in and only then did he notice that the site wasn't eBay. The address bar said it was some other site, though "ebay" was in the name. The bad guys had Evil Captain Kirk's login and password.

What Evil Captain Kirk experienced is called a *phishing attack*. It usually comes as an email cleverly disguised as legitimate. The attack can also come from another website or a pop-up window that looks like an official Windows error message.

If Evil Captain Kirk quickly visits the legitimate eBay site and changes his password, he might be okay. But most of the time people don't notice a bogus website until it's too late. Even checking the address bar may not help, because not everyone is keen on deciphering a web page address. Therefore, Windows has a tool to assist you: SmartScreen.

To ensure that SmartScreen is active, obey these steps:

1. **Whip out the Settings app.**

    Press the Win+I keyboard shortcut.

2. **Choose the App & Browser Control tile.**

3. **Click the link Reputation-Based Protection Settings.**

4. **Ensure that SmartScreen for Microsoft Edge is active.**

    Set the master control to the On position.

    SmartScreen is specific to the Microsoft Edge web browser. Google Chrome uses the Safe Browsing feature, which is always active.

5. **Ensure that the master control below the Phishing Protection heading is on.**

    Two check mark items are selected by default: Warn Me About Malicious Apps and Sites and Automatically Collect Website or App Content.

6. **Ensure that the master control below the heading SmartScreen for Windows Store Apps is set to the On position.**

These settings ensure that any known malicious website, one that pretends to be your bank, an online store, or some government entity, is flagged as dangerous. When you attempt to visit the site, the web browser displays a terrifying warning. Heed it.

REMEMBER

» The useful tools that detect phony websites may not catch all the Bad Guys. It's up to you to be vigilant, just as Mr. Spock knew in Episode 79 that Evil Captain Kirk was acting irrational and so he shot him with a phaser.

» The best way to confirm a bad website is to check the address bar. For example, eBay's website says ebay . com. It contains no other words, and *ebay* appears right before the dot-com.

» To test an email message, check the sender's address. If the address doesn't match the purported source, such as your bank, the message is illegitimate.

TIP

» The number-one way people are fooled into visiting a malicious website is to click a link in an email message. My advice is to always visit the site directly. For example, when I receive an email from my bank — even a legitimate one — I never click the link. I always visit my bank's bookmarked site in my web browser.

» Yes, I know that Mr. Spock didn't shoot Evil Captain Kirk with a phaser at the end of Episode 79. I just wrote that to see whether any nerds would send me an email correction.

4

On the Go with Your Laptop

Chapter **18**

Portable Power

The desire for portable computers started in the 1950s when scientists put the monstrous ENIAC on castors and wheeled it outside on a sunny day. Since then, portable computers have dramatically decreased in size and weight, and have shed nearly every wire. The culmination is today's laptop. You can easily and proudly tote it everywhere, from a cozy coffee shop to a cramped airliner soaring high in the sky.

Though laptop manufacturers have solved the issues of size and weight, one issue that remains is battery power: How long can you use the thing without having to scramble desperately for a wall socket? Given other advances in science, today's laptop batteries should last for days, not hours. Managing a laptop's battery life is an art form.

» If a laptop's processor is the muscle, and software the brain, the battery is its heart. As long as that battery keeps beating, you can use your laptop anywhere.

» Thanks to the ganglia of wires and cables, desktop computers are tethered to one location. I mean, you could theoretically take a desktop computer with you. But it's not light, and it's hardly portable, and it needs a wall socket to operate.

» The first laptop I used on a plane was a Dell 360. It weighed 16 pounds and came with a 20-minute battery. It had no Internet access. I used it on the plane ride just to prove that it could be done. We've come so far.

>> Desktop computers connected to a UPS also feature battery settings. Though the UPS isn't designed to run a desktop for extended periods, many of the settings covered in this chapter also apply to a desktop with a UPS. See the later section "Reviewing the power management plan."

TIP

The Battery Will Get a Charge Out of This!

Look at that wall socket! It seethes with jealousy, eyes hollow and mouth agape. How it longs for a plug to hide its needy face. A desktop PC makes it happy. But a laptop, with its fleeting connection, has the freedom to leave the wanting wall socket behind.

Using the battery (or not)

Your laptop is indifferent when it comes to a power source. When the power cord is connected to an AC power source, the laptop gladly drinks up the electricity — plus, it charges its battery, if need be. When the laptop is unplugged, the battery takes over. Either way, it works.

>> The laptop's battery is always ready to take over. You can plug in or unplug the laptop with the power on. The device runs uninterrupted the entire time.

>> Here's a shocker: Battery power drains as you use the laptop. See the later section "When the Power Gets Low."

>> The battery type determines how long it lasts and how to recharge it. Today's laptops use a lithium-ion battery. These beefy batteries can run for a long time, though as they age the battery life shortens. Don't refer to the nearby sidebar, "Trivial Information on Battery Types."

>> Feel free to use and charge the laptop's battery at any time. You need not wait for the battery to drain completely before recharging.

>> Older laptops featured easily removable batteries, primarily because their lifespan was so short. After one or two hours, you could physically swap batteries. Today's laptop batteries can last up to ten hours when they're new. Swapping laptop batteries is no longer a thing.

>> Over time, battery performance suffers. An older laptop can survive three to five hours on a single charge, and less as the battery ages.

TRIVIAL INFORMATION ON BATTERY TYPES

Batteries store electricity like squirrels store nuts. How the electricity is stored depends on the chemicals used and other magic going on inside the battery. Those chemicals determine the battery type and how the battery smells. Here are some popular battery types:

Alkaline: This type of battery is the most common. It's used in flashlights, remote controls, and kids' toys. It's standard, but not rechargeable. These batteries are okay for wireless mice, but not for the laptop itself.

Lead acid: If ever two words could make an environmentalist blanch, they're *lead* and *acid*. Yet those two chemicals supply the robust power of a car battery. The batteries are durable, long -lasting, and rechargeable, but they're too heavy and caustic for use in a laptop.

NiCad: Nickel-cadmium batteries were some of the first consumer batteries that could be recharged. Sadly, they suffered from a malady known as the *memory effect*, which makes them impractical for laptops. Unless you fully drain a NiCad before recharging, battery life shortens dramatically.

NiMH: The nickel-metal-hydride battery proved to be longer lasting than the NiCad, but it too suffers from the dreaded memory effect.

Lithium-ion: This type of battery is the one you most likely have in your laptop. Lithium-ion, or *Li-ion*, batteries are lightweight and perform better than other types of batteries. Plus, they don't suffer from the dreaded memory effect. Their power is managed by the computer, and they can be rapidly recharged.

TECHNICAL STUFF

>> Batteries were developed in the 1700s, originally from a Leyden jar, which was a device used to store static electricity. Benjamin Franklin used Leyden jars arranged in a series, like an artillery battery, which is where the term *battery* comes from.

>> By the way, those cylinder batteries used in your laptop's wireless mouse were developed in the 1890s.

Monitoring the battery

Your suspicions are confirmed: The laptop's battery drains as you use it. You should plan for at least two or three hours of active computer use with the battery fully charged. For a newer laptop, the active computer time can be much longer.

The rate of drain varies, depending on what you're doing with the laptop and your proximity to large magnets or the planet Jupiter.

 The best way to check the laptop battery status is to gander at the tiny battery icon in the taskbar's notification area, shown in the margin. This icon graphically shows how much power remains — but it's way too tiny!

To see more battery details, click the teeny-tiny battery icon on the taskbar to view a larger report. Figure 18-1 shows this larger view in Windows 11, which also serves as the Action Center, but it's still disappointingly tiny. The Windows 10 version is much larger and more detailed.

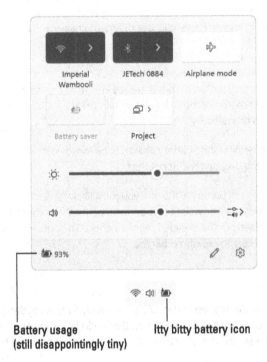

FIGURE 18-1:
Battery
notification and
Action Center.

Battery usage
(still disappointingly tiny)

Itty bitty battery icon

To view more details about the battery in Windows 11, click the still-too-small battery icon (refer to Figure 18-1) to see the Power & Battery part of the Settings app, shown in Figure 18-2. This screen is far more detailed, offering a pleasingly large battery percentage indicator, charge time info, and a history of the battery levels. To view a similar screen in Windows 10, open the Settings app (press Win+I) and choose the System category and then the Battery category.

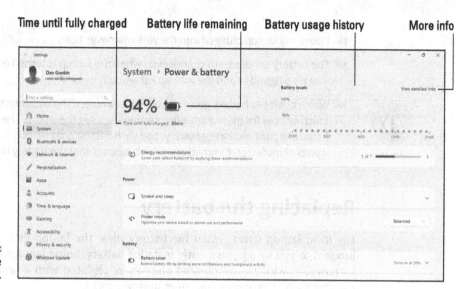

Time until fully charged   Battery life remaining   Battery usage history   More info

FIGURE 18-2:
Battery HQ in the
Settings app.

>> The tiny battery-notification icon appears differently when the laptop is plugged into AC power, as shown in the margin. Windows 11 features a lightning bolt on the icon (see the margin). In Windows 10, an AC power plug appears.

>> Use the tiny battery-notification icon to confirm that the AC power is available. If the icon doesn't appear as shown nearby, the laptop is using battery power and isn't being charged.

>> Your laptop may feature a battery light on its case. The light may change color as the laptop drains or otherwise indicate the battery charge.

>> The battery percentage doesn't decrease in a linear fashion as power drains. A battery meter at 50 percent after using the laptop for two hours doesn't guarantee that you have two more hours of battery life left. The charge remaining is a best guess, most likely based on the current moon phase.

Charging the battery

This task is easy to do: Plug the laptop into a wall socket, and the battery begins to charge. Yes, you can continue to use the laptop while it's charging. Use it to the extreme! The charging rate is unaffected by whatever you're doing on the laptop.

REMEMBER

>> You can recharge your laptop's battery whether the battery is fully drained or not. There's no need to fully drain your laptop's lithium-ion battery every time you use it.

>> I leave my laptop plugged into the wall whenever I can.

>> The battery continues to charge even when the laptop is turned off (providing that it's plugged in and the wall socket works).

WARNING

>> Watch out if the battery gets too hot! For example, if the battery is too hot to touch or hold for more than a few seconds, unplug the laptop. The heat can be a sign of a malfunctioning battery, and such a thing is *dangerous*. Contact the laptop manufacturer immediately if you suspect that the battery is running hot.

Replacing the battery

For most laptop users, when the battery dies, the laptop dies. This funeral is brought to you by a permanently installed battery. Some laptops have removable batteries, in which case the dead one can be replaced with a new one, and your carefree mobile existence continues uninterrupted.

>> Some laptops continue to work on AC power only, even without a battery installed. Just plug in the laptop and you're good to go.

>> If your laptop features a removable battery, you can replace it. Use only approved replacement batteries and ensure that the replacement comes with a warranty.

WARNING

>> Using unapproved batteries in your laptop may lead to hazardous situations, such as, oh, the laptop catching fire and exploding. If you doubt me, search for *exploding laptop* on YouTube.

When the Power Gets Low

Nothing turns a casual afternoon of café computing into an urgent panic like a low-battery warning. Experienced laptop owners don't wait that long. They constantly monitor the battery's condition and take necessary action before the claxons sound. The idea is to be proactive, not reactive, before the power runs low.

Setting low-battery warnings

Windows must recognize that you can't see the annoyingly small battery icon on the taskbar. When the battery gets low, a warning pops up. Recognizing that you don't take the computer seriously, a more serious warning appears just before the computer itself has had enough and shuts itself down. Heed these warnings!

The best strategy is to save your stuff when you see the first low-battery warning and then go hunting for a wall socket. The good news is that you have control over the initial warning as well as the later, sterner warning. These are called Low Battery and Critical Battery levels. Follow these steps to set each level and determine which actions are taken:

1. **Press the Win+E keyboard shortcut.**

   A File Explorer window appears.

2. **At the left end of the address bar, click the chevron and choose Control Panel from the menu.**

   The creaky ol' Windows Control Panel appears.

3. **Choose Hardware and Sound.**

4. **Choose Power Options.**

   You see the laptop's power plans, which are covered later, in the section "Reviewing the power management plan." The battery warning levels are set for a specific plan.

5. **Next to the active power plan, click the Change Plan Settings link.**

6. **In the Edit Plan Settings window, click the Change Advanced Power Settings link.**

   Finally, the Power Options dialog box shows up. It's *the* happening place for all things having to do with power management in Windows.

7. **Scroll the list and locate the item labeled Battery.**

   As you would expect, it's the last item on the list.

8. **Click the plus sign (+) by Battery to display various battery notification and action options.**

   Each item has two subitems: one for settings when the laptop is on battery power and a second for when the laptop is plugged in.

9. **Set the battery level warnings.**

   The warnings are illustrated in Figure 18-3.

   In chronological order, here are the items you can set:

   (a) *Low-battery notification:* Sets a warning for a low-battery level, before the situation becomes critical. Values are set to On to set the low warning and set to Off to ignore it.

   (b) *Low-battery level:* Determines the battery percentage for the low-battery-level warning. This value should be generous, well above the critical level.

Click to expand

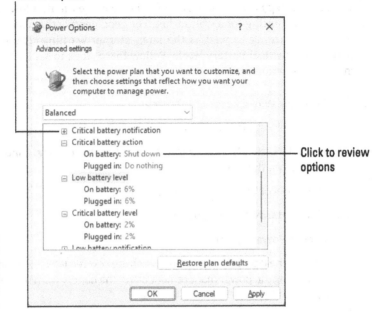

FIGURE 18-3:
Power options
for setting
low-battery
warnings
and actions.

Power Options   ?   ✕

Advanced settings

Select the power plan that you want to customize, and
then choose settings that reflect how you want your
computer to manage power.

Balanced   ∨

⊞ Critical battery notification
⊟ Critical battery action
   On battery: Shut down ————————————— **Click to review**
   Plugged in: Do nothing   **options**
⊟ Low battery level
   On battery: 6%
   Plugged in: 6%
⊟ Critical battery level
   On battery: 2%
   Plugged in: 2%
⊞ Low battery notification

Restore plan defaults

OK   Cancel   Apply

(c) *Low-battery action:* Directs the laptop in what to do when the battery charge reaches the low-battery level. I recommend the Do Nothing setting. Other options are Sleep, Hibernate, and Shut Down.

(d) *Critical battery level:* Sets the battery power level (percentage) for the crucial battery-level action.

(e) *Critical battery action:* Directs the laptop to sleep, hibernate, or shut down when the critical battery level is reached. I recommend choosing the Hibernate option.

10. **Click OK to confirm your choices.**

You can close any open dialog boxes and windows.

Setting the warnings is only one part of good power management. Hopefully, you never see the low-battery notification and, most definitely, you never have the laptop automatically shut down on you (for the critical-level action).

» The low-battery warnings are independent of the Battery Saver setting. See the next section.

» That critical-battery notice is serious. Laptop time is over! You see no warning; the laptop simply turns itself off or obeys whatever setting you've made.

TIP

>> The best thing to do when power gets low: Plug in! This is the reason you should take the laptop's power cable with you wherever you go, as uncool as that sounds.

Using the Battery Saver

This section is brought to you by the word *parsimonious*. It's a polite word for *stingy*, which is an excellent adjective to describe how the Windows Battery Saver feature works.

The Battery Saver kicks in automatically when your laptop's power percentage drops below a certain threshold — typically, 20 percent. You can, however, bolster the battery's life by activating the Battery Saver at any time. Follow these steps:

1. **Display the Action Center.**

Press the Win+A keyboard shortcut.

2. **Click or tap the Battery Saver button.**

If the button is disabled, the laptop is AC-powered, which means nothing needs saving.

When Battery Saver mode is active, the screen instantly dims. Laptop activity is curtailed, including Internet access. The idea is to power the laptop by using just a trickle of power. So don't be surprised if some of your favorite laptop features or programs don't work while Battery Saver is active.

Repeat the preceding set of steps to disable the Battery Saver.

To control the Battery Saver's features, visit the Settings app. Follow these steps:

1. **Open the Settings app.**

Press the Win+I keyboard shortcut.

2. **Choose System.**

3. **On the left side of the window, choose Power & Battery, or just Battery.**

4. **Choose the Battery Saver item.**

5. **Set the percentage at which the battery saver activates.**

On my laptop, the battery saver kicks in when the battery level drops to 20 percent. This setting is in addition to the warnings set in the Control Panel, covered in the preceding section.

Reviewing the power management plan

To help you squeeze every electron from the battery, Windows offers a power management plan. Key to the plan's success are disabling various battery-hungry laptop features — specifically, when the power starts to wane. To review or modify your laptop's power management plan, obey these steps:

1. **Press the Win+I keyboard shortcut to conjure the Settings app.**

2. **Choose System.**

3. **In Windows 11, expand the Screen and Sleep area; in Windows 10, choose Power & Sleep.**

   Two items are presented: Screen and Sleep. Options to turn off the display or sleep the computer are presented for both battery and AC (plugged-in) power.

4. **Choose timeout values.**

   For example, on battery power, I turn off my laptop's screen after 3 minutes; the device is put to sleep after 5 minutes. When the laptop is plugged in, I have the timeouts set to "never."

The laptop's power manager can afford longer timeout durations when the device is plugged in. My advice is to choose shorter timeouts when the laptop is on battery power.

TIP

For a desktop PC connected to a UPS, set all battery-powered options to Shut Down. When the UPS is activated, you want to shut down the computer right away. I set my timeouts to 2 minutes maximum, which gives me enough time to save my stuff and manually shut down the PC. Otherwise, the power management plan should turn off any desktop computer running from a UPS.

REMEMBER

» Adjust these settings if you find the laptop screen going blank or the thing shifting into Sleep mode too quickly.

» Windows is smart enough to know when you're using the laptop to watch a video. Especially when the video is enlarged to a full-screen presentation, the laptop may ignore the Display and Sleep power settings. Even so, be mindful that the battery is draining while you're entertaining yourself. A quick check of the battery status during intermission may be warranted.

» No, they no longer have intermissions in movies. I'm just old.

Chapter **19**

O, the Places You'll Go

Take your laptop to the park. Use the laptop after dark.

Bring your laptop on a plane. Stroll with laptop down the lane.

Laptop with your cousin Ned. Sleep with laptop in a bed.

Charge your laptop from the wall. Waltz with laptop at the ball.

Take your laptop where you please. Wi-Fi access overseas.

Use your laptop from afar. Drink with laptop in a bar.

Laptop with a cup of joe. Laptop, laptop, on the go.

Laptop here! Laptop there! Laptop, laptop, everywhere!

In the Bag

CELINE. Gucci. Louis Vuitton. CHLOÉ. They got nuthin' when it comes to the number-one fashion accessory for the chic laptop-toting world traveler: a decent laptop bag. Never mind the four- (or five-) digit price tag. You need something practical and accommodating for your laptop and all its glorious accessories. Style and luxury must take a back seat.

Features to look for

It's possible to walk around and carry only your laptop. You see happy workers do so on corporate campuses across the world. Then again, it's a good idea to also carry that power cord. Oh, and don't forget the wireless mouse. Maybe a laser pointer, pen and paper, a snack, your eyeglasses, and other items are necessary to have. Yeah, you need a laptop bag.

REMEMBER

The idea behind a good laptop bag is to safely carry and protect the laptop while you wander from point A to point B. Here are some thoughts regarding selecting a useful fashion accessory in which to place your laptop:

Size

The bag must close over the laptop without bursting at the seams. For some people, a small bag that contains only the laptop is all they need. When you need more room inside the bag, you get something larger — but not too large.

REMEMBER

Keep in mind that when flying, your laptop bag must fit beneath the seat in front of you. Don't buy a bag so big that it must be stashed in the overhead bin.

Style

If you desire the briefcase style, get a soft-case laptop bag, not a hard model. If the case has a shoulder strap, use it.

TIP

My preference is a backpack. The bonus here is that shouldering the backpack keeps both arms and hands free. This way, I can hold my phone with a boarding pass in one hand and my beverage in the other while still carrying my laptop and other necessary goodies in my backpack.

If your laptop has bulky accessories, such as a video projector, consider getting a laptop case with wheels and a retractable handle.

Zippers are preferred over snaps, buckles, or latches. For me, it's easier to work a zipper when I'm in a cramped space, like an airline seat, or sitting in a crowded café.

WARNING

Avoid laptop cases and bags that have the word *Laptop* on them or that feature a brand name. Such text advertises to thieves that valuable items lie within.

Pouches and places

Does the bag feature plenty of pouches? You need them for storing accessories, office supplies, thumb drives, manuals, Altoids, year-old receipts, and other items you plan to carry around with you. The pouches can also be used for smuggling.

Having an easy-access pouch on the outside of the bag or case helps with storing important documents and other information that you need to grab quickly.

Things to pack in your laptop bag

REMEMBER

A good laptop bag is useful for holding more than the laptop. Otherwise, it would be called a laptop *cozy* and not a bag. When you're at a loss about what to put into your laptop bag, consider this list for inspiration:

>> Pack the power cord and AC adapter!

>> Bring headphones if you plan to listen to music or watch a movie. Noise-canceling headphones are worth the extra price. Wearing a headphone is more polite than sharing your laptop's noise with people sitting next to you. Many airlines require you to use headphones during the flight.

>> Pack any necessary peripherals, such as a wireless mouse, thumb drives, a laser pointer (for slide shows), and so on.

>> Two words: office supplies. Pens. Paper. Sticky notes. Paper clips. Rubber bands. Highlighter. And so on.

REMEMBER

>> When you're traveling overseas, remember to bring along a power conversion kit or an overseas power adapter.

>> Ensure that you have some screen wipes.

>> Bring a deck of cards. That way, you'll have something to play with after the battery dies.

See Chapter 27 for more goodies you may want to stuff into your laptop bag.

Flying with Your Laptop

Taking a laptop onboard a commercial airliner today is about as normal as bringing onboard a sack lunch or a crying infant. That's good news, unlike in the old days, when having a laptop was cause for concern by airport security. Today, you most likely won't be the only person in your row with a laptop on the tray table during the flight.

WARNING

>> The airlines view your laptop bag as a personal item. Your laptop bag and your suitcase that barely fits into the overhead bin are counted as two items.

>> Do not check your laptop as luggage! You don't want to subject the laptop to the kind of torture that checked bags endure. You don't want your laptop to be stored in the subzero cargo hold. You do not want your laptop to visit Albania when you're flying to Japan. Do not check your laptop!

Things to do before you leave

Unlike your car keys or an electric blender, you can't just grab your laptop and head out on the road. Especially for a planned trip, and not necessarily for flying, here are some things you should consider doing before you toddle off with your laptop:

TIP

WARNING

>> Charge the battery! In fact, this task is probably something you want to do well before you leave.

>> If you haven't used the laptop in a while, check for Windows updates. You want to ensure that the update installation doesn't delay your work — or prevent it. See Chapter 21 for information about Windows updates.

>> Ensure that your work files are on the laptop or that they're available on the cloud. See Chapter 16 for more information.

>> Though most cloud applications help you resolve synchronization issues, you can avoid them in the first place by ensuring that you don't work on files on a system when it's not connected to the Internet.

Laptop inspection

Once upon a time, airport security had me remove my laptop from its bag and turn it on to demonstrate that it wasn't a bomb. Today things are easier, as fewer bombs are laptop-shaped. Still, the airport security rules seem to change all the time.

The bottom line is to always follow directions given at a security checkpoint. It doesn't matter what the other airport did or what happened on your last trip. Just follow what you're told: Keep the laptop in the bag, take out the laptop, balance the laptop atop your head, whatever.

Yes, your laptop can take a ride through the X-ray machine. X-rays don't harm laptops, though I believe that they secretly want to.

No matter what, when you've escaped security, put the laptop back in its bag, put your pants back on, and be on your way.

All aboard!

After taking your seat, store the laptop bag under the seat in front of you. This location is easier to get to. Use the overhead bins only as a last resort; otherwise, you run the risk of having latecomers jamming their steamer trunks and body bags into the overhead bins and crushing your laptop.

Keep the laptop in its bag! Wait until you hear the announcement that you can turn on your electronic devices before you whip out your laptop.

>> If you want easy access to your laptop, avoid bulkhead seats that lack under-seat storage.

>> When the airline offers an extended legroom class, such as the exit row, take it! More room for legs means more room on the tray table for your laptop.

>> Be aware that the jerk in front of you will lower his seat back. Until he does, keep the laptop far enough away that the lid won't break.

>> Return the laptop to its bag when you're done. Do not stick the laptop into that pitiful seat-back pouch where you stuff candy wrappers and your water bottle.

>> I prefer window seats for computing aloft. This way, I can control the window blind to shield my laptop's screen from the sun. Plus, I can more easily angle the laptop toward me and away from prying eyes in other seats.

TIP

>> 3M makes a special laptop display cover, the 3M Laptop Privacy Filter. It prevents peering eyes from seeing the information on your laptop screen, which is a problem on airplanes. The filter can be found at office supply and computer stores all over the place.

Air power

Many airlines offer seat power, where you can plug in your laptop just like you're back at the office. The only drawback is that you're tangled in a cable. This situation is yet another reason I like window seats, because I don't need to unplug my laptop when another passenger needs to pee.

REMEMBER

>> If the standard power socket isn't available, you can use USB to charge certain laptops. If the laptop features a USB C port, connect a USB cable to see whether it charges the laptop.

>> In-flight power is useful, but without it, your laptop runs just fine on its own battery — just not as long.

>> You're required to disconnect your mobile devices from seat power during takeoff and landing. Always obey instructions from the flight crew.

Airplane mode

Like other wireless mobile devices, laptops feature Airplane mode. The goal is to disable Wi-Fi and Bluetooth, which can cause the plane to lose its mind and tumble toward the ground in a great fireball of death.

To avoid the great fireball of death, activate Airplane mode before you use your laptop aloft. Heed these steps:

1. **Press Win+A to summon the Action Center.**

2. **Click or tap the Airplane Mode tile.**

   When Airplane mode is active, an airplane icon appears in the notification area on the taskbar, as shown in the margin.

Here's the stupid part: Once you're in Airplane mode, you can reactivate Wi-Fi and Bluetooth: Press Win+A again to view the Action Center and choose the Network tile. Activate Wi-Fi to access the airline's in-flight Internet service. You can also activate Bluetooth to use your wireless headset. Aren't you happy that the laptop is in Airplane mode? So much for that great fireball of death.

TIP

Some laptops feature an Airplane mode shortcut key. It's usually one of those Fn-key combinations, so look for a color-coded airplane icon on the keyboard to see whether your laptop features this shortcut.

In-flight Wi-Fi

Many airlines offer in-flight Wi-Fi service. It might be free, primarily for airline-offered services such as flight information or video entertainment. Accessing the Internet, however, may come at a cost. Either way, your laptop can use the in-flight wireless network just as it does at the local coffeehouse.

To activate Wi-Fi, open the laptop's web browser to visit the in-flight sign-up page. This location is where you either accept the terms or fork over a credit card number to access the service. Some airlines require that you sign in by using your frequent flyer number.

TIP

>> If Airplane mode is active (and it should be, according to the preceding section), you must manually enable Wi-Fi. Do so from the Action Center: Press the Win+A keyboard shortcut.

>> Specific directions for accessing in-flight Wi-Fi are usually found in the seat pocket in front of you, right next to the barf bag.

>> The in-flight Wi-Fi providers don't like you using Zoom, Skype, or similar programs to make phone calls. Your seatmates won't like it, either.

>> In-flight Wi-Fi may drop off for long-distance flights — specifically, those over this planet's vast oceans. Don't be duped into paying for in-flight Internet access unless you can be assured that the signal is consistent throughout the flight.

Arriving at your destination

As you roam the planet with your trusty laptop, you'll encounter something strange from your home location: a new time zone. Your laptop won't understand this time zone and prefers to show the hours of the day relative to your home location's time zone. If such a discrepancy bugs you, reset the time zone by following these instructions:

1. **Press the Win+I keyboard shortcut to launch the Settings app.**

2. **Choose Time & Language.**

3. **Choose Date & Time.**

4. **Activate the option to set the time zone automatically.**

The option to set the time zone automatically isn't available in all versions of Windows. If you don't see it, choose the current time zone from the Time Zone drop-down menu. The system clock is updated to reflect the local time.

>> When you manually set the time zone, you must manually reset it back to home or whatever time zone matches up with your next stop.

>> Setting the time zone automatically depends on factors such as your location and Internet connection. When these items don't provide accurate information, the automatic time zone setting doesn't work.

>> Though computers use the Internet to keep accurate track of the time, they don't care about time zones. The computer uses Coordinated Universal Time (UTC) as its internal clock but outputs a time value based on the time zone you set. So, while it may be high noon in Singapore, your laptop may show 3:00 A.M., which is the time back home.

Café Computing

It used to be that you'd walk into a coffeehouse, order a cappuccino, sit around with artsy folks dressed in black turtlenecks, and discuss the plight of the common man. Today, you go to the coffeehouse, order your double-tall decaf macchiato two-pump soy, and discuss the plight of the common man over the Internet.

Find a good seat

The unofficial rules of café computing require that you stake out a seat *before* walking to the counter to order a beverage or food. Finding a good place to sit in a café is an art form. Not only that, you're competing with plenty of others. Fortunately, you have this book.

The most important item with regard to seat selection is a wall socket. If you can use the café's power, great! Those seats next to the wall socket are best, and they usually go first.

You want a table, a flat surface upon which to set up the laptop. The alternative is balancing the laptop on your knees while you sit on a sofa or an old sack of Columbian coffee beans. If that's your thing, great!

Grab a location that's either away from the windows or facing the windows. You want to avoid having that bright light from the windows reflecting on your laptop screen and washing out the display.

When you really and truly want to get work done, find a spot away from the door and away from the sales counter. Do the opposite if you prefer to be social.

>> Along with avoiding windows, keep an eye out for skylights or windows high up on the wall. As a sunny day grows long, the sun sweeps a slow swath of bright light across some tables, which can thwart your laptopping efforts.

>> After successfully finding a wall socket, plug in your laptop. Ensure that it's drawing power, as described in Chapter 18.

Other tips 'n' stuff

Don't be a moocher. If you've planted yourself in a café, order something to drink. Buy a snack. Tip the kind-but-underpaid employee who gave you the Wi-Fi password.

The management at some places enjoys having laptop and mobile users because they add to the location's trendy atmosphere. Keep in mind that the place is a business and that free Wi-Fi is a perk for supporting the business. Also, the courts have established that you can be thrown out for using the wireless networking if you don't buy something, so buy something!

Though you should avoid placing beverages near a computer, it's not an easy task to manage while using a laptop in a café. Therefore, ask for your beverage in a cup with a saucer. Grab several napkins, just in case.

WARNING

Never leave your laptop unattended! Though it might not be stolen, it's a distinct possibility. See Chapter 20 for more information on laptop security.

Sometimes, you may be asked to leave or relocate, especially when you're taking up an entire booth all by yourself. Be knowledgeable about this situation in advance. If you see the place filling up, move to a smaller table, or just pack up and leave.

In a Hotel Room

The hotel industry expects you to need Wi-Fi service in the room, just like you want fresh towels and an ice bucket. The desk in the room most likely has power sockets that are easily accessible and even a few USB connectors for phones and tablets. Welcome to the 21st century.

You obtain the Wi-Fi password from the front desk. It's probably on one of those bits of paper they gave you along with the room card key. If not, you'll find the password in the room on the desk or you use your room number and last name to sign in. Be aware that some cheap motels make you pay separately for Wi-Fi services.

REMEMBER

TIP

>> When you first connect to the hotel's wireless network, you're prompted to set its security level. Choose the Public type of network. See Chapter 14.

>> If the room features an Ethernet port, try it out. The Ethernet connection is more reliable than the Wi-Fi connection, which can slow down from an abundance of mobile devices vying for the service. (This is the reason I recommend tossing an Ethernet cable into your laptop bag.)

>> Some hotels provide an Ethernet cable; look for it either in the desk drawer or (oddly) hanging in the closet.

>> When you have no choice but to pay for the hotel's Wi-Fi connection, buy as large a block of time as you can for your stay. If 24 hours is the largest block, start your 24-hour session at 6 P.M. This way, you can use the connection that evening and then the following morning and throughout the next day's afternoon.

Mind the Laptop's Temperature

One reason that your laptop lacks the latest, fastest microprocessor is heat. Even in a desktop PC, cutting-edge technology generates lots of heat. Managing this heat in a desktop is a huge chore, so you can imagine the things your laptop has to do to keep cool, especially when you're on the road.

TIP

>> Your laptop comes with a wee li'l cooling fan. It may even have two speeds — one for normal operation and a faster speed to cool down the laptop quickly. Even so, don't let your laptop get too hot to touch. If so, turn it off at once.

>> Avoid putting your laptop in direct sunlight.

>> Do not store the laptop in your car's trunk.

>> Don't let the laptop run in a closet or in any closed environment where air cannot circulate.

>> Do not block the little vents on the laptop that help it inhale cool air and expel hot air.

>> Consider buying your laptop a cooling pad. Chapter 26 covers this and other useful laptop gizmos.

IN THIS CHAPTER

» **Preventing a theft ahead of time**

» **Attaching a security cable**

» **Identifying your laptop**

» **Watching for crooks**

» **Using effective passwords**

» **Resetting your laptop**

Chapter **20**

A More Secure Laptop

The convenience of portability leads to a common problem with laptop computers: theft. It's the laptop's size that's the issue. For example, it's easier to purloin a battery-operated drill gun than a standing drill press. Someone may steal a miniature Eiffel Tower from a souvenir shop, but the real thing is too big to swipe. And the French would notice.

Thieves are out for your laptop. You need to protect the device itself, protect your data, and try to get the thing back, should it ever be liberated by one of society's lesser individuals.

The Hot Laptop

Sure, your laptop can get hot. Managing heat is one of the laptop hardware's primary duties. This section's title does not, however, deal with this kind of "hot." No, the topic here is hot as in stolen, pilfered, purloined. Bad Guys out there want your laptop more than you do. The lighter and more portable, the better.

Well, a thief doesn't desire to run a quick what-if scenario in Excel. No, he wants to steal your laptop and sell it for drug money. Some thieves want the data inside your laptop, stored on the mass storage system. They want to look for passwords and get into your online banking and investments.

The Bad Guys get what they want, mostly because the typical laptop owner doesn't think like a thief. In addition to being good-looking, laptop users are a rather trusting lot. This trust is, sadly, what makes laptops easy to steal.

First, the good news: Most laptops are forgotten and not stolen. As silly as it sounds, people leave their expensive laptops sitting around unattended more often than someone sneaks off with them. Don't let this trivial tidbit lull you into a false sense of security; many laptops are stolen right out from under the eyes of their owners.

TIP

Think of the laptop as a sack of cash sitting around. To a crook, this description is exactly what it is. Treat the laptop as a bag full o' money, and chances are good that you'll never forget it or have it stolen.

The best way to protect your laptop is to label it. Specific instructions are offered later in this chapter. Keep in mind this statistic: Ninety-seven percent of unmarked computers are never recovered. Mark your laptop.

Here are some troublesome statistics:

>> The chance of your laptop being stolen is 1 in 10.

>> Most laptop theft occurs in the office. The culprits include both coworkers and Well-Dressed Intruders (thieves in business suits — and not just bankers).

>> Laptop theft on college campuses (from dorm rooms) is up 37 percent.

>> A thief who steals a $1,000 laptop typically gets about $50 for it on the street.

>> According to law enforcement, 90 percent of laptop thefts are easily avoidable by using common sense.

Before Your Laptop Is Stolen

Like any shopper, a thief enjoys convenience: If your laptop is more difficult to pinch than the next guy's, it's the next guy who loses.

Attaching the laptop to something sturdy

Some laptops feature a special "belt loop" through which you can snake a security cable. Another option is the Kensington Security Slot, or K-Slot. The slot looks like a tiny oval labeled with the padlock icon and sporting a *K* in the middle.

Of course, this security feature means nothing unless the security cable is attached to something solid and immovable, like a heavy desk or a pipe organ. The idea is to prevent the laptop from being stolen, not to add a cool chain to your portable PC.

>> The best place to find a security cable for your laptop is in a computer store or office supply store.

>> Some cables come with alarms. You can find alarms that sound when the cable is cut, plus alarms that sound when the laptop is moved.

>> Many desktop PCs — specifically, small-footprint models — also feature a USS or K-Slot.

Marking your laptop

You can help in the recovery of a stolen laptop if it's marked. I recommend either engraving it or affixing to it a tamper-resistant asset tag. After all, the best proof that something is yours is your name on the item in question, though I advise against tattooing your children.

>> You can use an engraving tool to literally carve your name and contact information on your laptop.

>> Asset tags are available from most print shops. The tags peel and stick but cannot be easily removed or damaged. For an investment of about $100, you can buy a few hundred custom asset tags, for not only your computers but also other valuable items (cameras, mobile devices, bicycles, TVs, pet fish, and so on).

TIP

>> The STOP program offers a barcode asset tag that leaves a special tattoo if it's removed. The program also offers a recovery system that automatically returns stolen (or lost) property directly to your door. STOP stands for Security Tracking of *Office* Property, although home users and (especially) college students can take advantage of the service. Visit www.stoptheft.com for more information.

Registering the laptop and its software

Be sure to register your laptop. Visit the manufacturer's website to register your laptop online or fill in the registration card if one was provided. Do the same for any software you're using. If the laptop is stolen, alert the manufacturer and software vendors. When someone using your stolen laptop ever tries to get the system fixed or upgraded, the company cares enough (you hope) to help you locate the purloined laptop.

REMEMBER

Keep with you a copy of the laptop's serial number and other vital statistics — specifically, in a place other than in the laptop's carrying case. That way, you know which number to report to law enforcement as well as to the manufacturer.

Paying attention to your environment

They say that a casino is a purse snatcher's paradise. The reason is that people with purses or backpacks are too wrapped up in gambling to notice that their property is being pilfered. Your personal stuff can be on the floor, at your feet, or even in your lap. Thieves know the power of distraction.

When you're out and about with your laptop, you must always pay attention to where it is and who can have access to it. Watch your laptop!

For example, when you're dining out, place the laptop in its case beneath the table. If you need to leave the table, either take the laptop with you or ask your friends to keep an eye on it for you. You have friends, right?

Take your laptop with you when you leave to talk on your cell phone. And, yes, leave the restaurant dining area to talk on your phone, thank you.

WARNING

Be especially mindful of distractions! A commotion in front of you means that the thief about to take your laptop is behind you. A commotion behind you means that the thief is in front of you. Thieves work in pairs or groups this way, using the commotion to distract you while your stuff is being stolen.

Pay special attention at the airport screening station. Just one raised voice or "the woman in the red dress" can divert your attention long enough for your laptop to disappear. Also be aware of distractions on crowded escalators, where the movement of the crowd can knock you down and someone can easily grab your laptop bag and take off.

Protect Your Data with a Strong Password

Passwords protect only your laptop's data, not the laptop itself. Most thieves looking to make a quick buck don't care about the contents of your laptop — they just want the cash it brings. But a data thief wants more.

Data thieves feast on information. They want your passwords. They want credit card numbers, which are valuable to sell. Furthermore, they can use your own computer to order stuff on the Internet or to make transfers from your online bank account to their own.

A *strong password* is long. It contains letters, numbers, and symbols. The letters must be in different cases. Yes, it's a pain in the rear to type, though it's possible to be clever. For example, consider a password as a collection of two or more regular words with a symbol separating the words: like^this-54321

WARNING

TIP

>> Have a strong password or PIN for your Windows account on the laptop. Only with the password or PIN can the data thief access your computer.

>> Computer security nabobs say that you should change your password every few months or so, and more often in high-security areas. In fact, if you use your laptop with a corporate account, you'll probably be pestered to change your password on a regular schedule.

>> If you forget your password, you're screwed. It's possible to recover Windows, but all your account information may be utterly lost and not retrievable. Keep this warning in mind when you're choosing a password.

>> When you have trouble remembering your password, write it down! Just don't keep the password list near your computer. I know folks who write their passwords on their kitchen calendars or in their recipe books. Random words and numbers there may not mean anything to a casual onlooker, but they're helpful when you forget the password.

SILLY PASSWORDS

Data thieves steal passwords all the time. What they find isn't interesting. The reason is that people tend to use the same passwords over and over — and simple, predictable passwords as well.

After an online database was hacked, security experts examined the stolen data. What they discovered was that far too many people were using insecure passwords. In fact, most of the passwords were downright silly.

Here's a sampling of real passwords used by folks who should know better — no matter what, never use any of these passwords!

- 111111
- 1234567
- 2000

- 654321
- 696969
- abc123

- baseball
- dragon
- football

(continued)

(continued)

- iloveyou
- letmein
- master
- monkey
- mustang
- passw0rd
- password
- qwerty
- rockyou
- shadow
- sunshine
- superman
- trustno1

The Laptop Reset

The ultimate form of laptop security is to erase everything on your laptop, effectively returning it to the same (or similar) state when it first popped out of the box to greet you. I call this process the *factory data reset*, and it's a pretty drastic security step.

About the only time you'll want to perform a factory reset is when you sell or dispose of your laptop. The process erases all your files and restores the laptop to a bare minimum machine. Obviously, this isn't a task to be taken lightly, nor is it considered routine.

When it's time to reset your laptop, follow these steps:

1. **Open the Settings app.**

   Press the Win+I keyboard shortcut.

2. **In Windows 11, choose System; for Windows 10, choose Update & Security.**

3. **Choose Recovery.**

4. **In Windows 11, click the Reset PC button; in Windows 10, below the Reset This PC heading, click the Get Started button.**

   An ominous window appears. Two options are available:

   Keep My Files: Apps are removed and programs uninstalled, but choosing this option doesn't erase your files. Windows settings are reset to the factory default.

Remove Everything: Apps, programs, and all your data are removed from the laptop when you choose this option. Windows remains, but in its raw, as-yet-to-be-configured state.

5. **Choose an option — and be careful.**

   You eventually see a Reset button and confirmation. Even so, do not choose any option casually!

WARNING

This move is desperate. I don't know what happens after you click an option, because it appears to me that Windows plows ahead and does whatever deed you requested — with no confirmation!

>> These steps also apply to desktop computers. If you plan on selling your PC, reset it before you finally bid it adieu.

TECHNICAL STUFF

>> A third reset option may appear if you've upgraded from an older version of Windows. This option, Restore Factory Settings, restores the previously installed version of Windows.

5

Security and Maintenance

Chapter **21**

System Security

They say that the Internet was designed to withstand a nuclear attack, but apparently it easily folds under pressure from a socially awkward teenager holding a grudge. Still, not all "hackers" are teenagers, nor are they all malicious. A few bad actors do exist. They weave their tapestry of mayhem across the Internet, seeking to extort money, disrupt society, or lob chaos bombs into what is an otherwise vital part of modern culture.

Fret not, gentle reader. Windows comes with plenty of Internet safety and security tools. These provide a defense against the malcontents and Bad Guys who, sadly, are an unwelcome part of our digital lives.

The Windows Security Center

When it comes to online security, you have two choices:

First, you can smear your body with honey and walk naked through the bear cage at the zoo. This is not a good choice.

Second, you can visit the Windows Security Center.

I don't like telling other people what to do, but I strongly recommend the second option when it comes to online security. It involves less driving and isn't as messy.

To visit the Windows Security Center, follow these steps:

1. **Pop up the Start menu.**

   Tap the Windows key on the keyboard.

2. **Type** Windows Security.

   You don't need to type all the text — just enough until you see the Windows Security app appear in the list.

3. **Choose the Windows Security app to open it.**

Figure 21-1 illustrates the Windows Security Center as it appears in Windows 11 (Windows 10 is similar). Each of the tiles found there represents some aspect of security or protection offered for your computer.

Redundant list of categories   Green check mark   Tiles

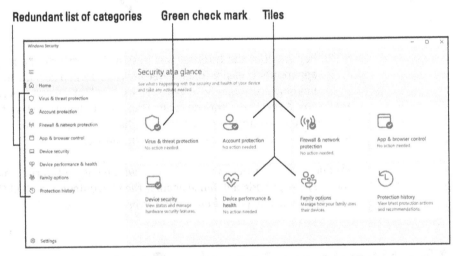

FIGURE 21-1:
The Windows
Security Center.

The key to using the Security Center is to look for the green check mark icons (refer to Figure 21-1). These indicate that the category, such as Virus & Threat Protection, is properly defended. You can click a tile to examine more options, but in the big picture, you're okay.

When you see a yellow warning icon in the Windows Security Center, as shown in the margin, it means that an item demands your attention. If a button appears on the tile, such as Scan Now for the Virus & Threat Protection title, click it. Otherwise, click the tile to follow the directions for what to do next.

>> Don't panic like a vegan at the butcher's shop when you see a yellow warning icon. It means that Windows has spotted an issue or prevented something horrible from happening.

>> Some yellow warnings don't go away. For example, the Device Security tile may show a yellow warning because a security feature isn't enabled. But with some computer hardware, this security feature cannot be enabled. When this situation occurs, you can ignore the yellow warning — but only after you've confirmed the reason.

>> The Windows Security yellow warning also appears in the notification area on the taskbar. If you see a shield icon there with a yellow warning icon superimposed, click it to visit the Windows Security Center, and dutifully obey the directions offered.

WARNING

BEWARE OF SOCIAL ENGINEERING

Social engineering is the art of getting you to do something you wouldn't do if you were sober, like remarrying an ex-wife. This technique is the primary way that most malware infects computers.

For example, you receive an unsolicited email message. A friend urges you to open the attachment or visit a link to see some politician in a compromising position or perhaps to ogle a celebrity doing something obnoxious. You follow through and — ta-da! — your computer is infected.

Another common infection vector takes advantage of your impatience. You download a legitimate program, but on the confirmation web page, you neglect to uncheck the option to install "bonus" software, some of which may be malware or just unwanted programs.

Some antivirus software can thwart this type of human engineering, but don't count on it. The only way to truly be careful is to never be casual. Always pay attention to what you click. Mind the warnings. Avoid the temptation to do something quickly, even when the recommendation to do so appears to have come from someone you trust.

The Malware Scourge

Is your computer vulnerable to a virus? Did that email spy on you? How do you know that your computer is infected? Will the virus spread to you? Should you wear a mask or set up a plexiglass screen while you compute? These are all vital questions deserving of an answer.

Before I answer the questions, primarily just to keep you in suspense, know that the possibility of nasty things happening to your computer is real. But at the same time, understand that the Windows Security Center is working every nanosecond to ensure that bad things don't happen.

>> Here are the answers: Yes. Maybe. Windows Security Center tells you when your computer is infected. No. And definitely no.

>> *Malware* is a generic term that covers all different types of deliberately inflicted PC maladies. See the nearby sidebar, "Computer supervillain roundup."

>> Rather than worry, be cautious. Computer security mustn't be taken lightly, even when using an anti-malware program like the Windows Security Center.

COMPUTER SUPERVILLAIN ROUNDUP

As with most computer jargon, malicious software — or *malware* — is named in either a highly technical or extremely silly manner. Neither type of name helps: Technical names are confusing. The silly names are clever only for people who would otherwise understand the technical names. Here's your handy guide:

phishing: Pronounced "fishing," this term applies to a web page or an email message designed to fool you into thinking that it's something else. For example, a fake email from your bank has a link that displays a fake website looking like your bank's. The idea is to *fish* for information, such as account numbers and passwords. The web page or email tricks you into providing that information because it looks legitimate. It isn't.

hijacking: You want to visit one web page, but you're taken to another. Or, you discover that the home page you see when you start the web browser is something unexpected, an advertisement-filled monstrosity. This redirection is known as hijacking.

ransomware: This is a specific type of virus that infects your computer, copies all your data to the Internet, and then encrypts the computer's mass storage. You cannot access your data unless you pay the ransom, usually in the form of Bitcoin. If you pay, the Bad Guys provide you with the decryption key. Otherwise, your data is sold on the Internet.

spyware: A rather broad category, spyware refers to a program that monitors, or spies on, what you do on the Internet. The reasoning is advertising: By knowing where you go and what you do on the Internet, information obtained about you can be sold to advertisers who then target ads your way. Most spyware exists as shopping helpers or special search bars installed in the web browser.

Trojan: A program is labeled a Trojan (horse) whenever it claims to do one thing but does another. For example, a common Trojan is a special screen saver that saves the screen but also uses your computer to relay pornographic images on the Internet.

virus: A virus is a nasty program that resides in your PC without your knowledge. The program may be triggered at any time, taking over the computer, redirecting Internet traffic, sending a flood of spam messages, or doing any of several nasty and inconvenient things.

worm: A worm is a virus that replicates itself, by sending out copies to other folks on your email list, to other computers on the network, and so on.

Doing a virus scan

The Windows Security Center constantly checks memory and files for signs of malware. You need not do a thing, though occasionally you may be prompted to run a quick scan. If so, obey these steps:

1. **Pop up the Start menu.**

   Press the Windows key on the keyboard.

2. **Type** Security **to find and open the Windows Security app.**

3. **Click the Virus & Threat Protection tile.**

   The tile may sport a Quick Scan button, especially if you've been prompted. For example, the security icon in the taskbar's notification area may have a yellow flag on it.

4. **Click the Quick Scan button.**

   Windows performs a quick scan of memory and files to ensure that no infections lurk undetected.

Most of the time, the scan comes back informing you that everything is okey-doke. If not, a suspicious file is located and placed into quarantine. See the next section, "Dealing with a quarantined file," for what to do next.

>> All items on the Virus & Threat Protection screen are configured automatically. You can review them at your leisure to understand and appreciate the protection Windows offers.

>> I often get asked whether it's necessary to run an additional antivirus program, such as Norton or McAfee. If it makes you feel better, do so. Running a computer security program beyond Windows Security Center doesn't harm a thing, though these other programs require subscriptions and will pester you about paying.

WARNING

>> Some legitimate antivirus programs are available for free on the Internet. The problem is that many of these "free" programs are, in fact, illegitimate and may be viruses themselves. Therefore, I advise that you either pay for the third-party antivirus software or obtain it from a reputable source.

Dealing with a quarantined file

When the Windows Security Center locates a suspect file, it places it into quarantine. This placement doesn't delete the file, but it does prevent the malware from doing its nasty deed. It also allows you to rescue falsely accused files from imminent peril.

To review quarantined files, follow these steps:

1. **View the Virus & Threat Protection screen.**

   Refer to Steps 1 through 3 in the preceding section to visit the Windows Security Center, Virus & Threat Protection area.

2. **Click the Protection History link.**

3. **Ensure that Quarantined Items is selected.**

4. **Click the View Details button.**

   You see a list of any suspect files.

It's okay to keep the files in the list; they can do no harm.

To rescue an incorrectly identified file, select it from the list and then click the Restore button. Please be extra certain that the file isn't infected! Do an Internet search on the filename to see what others have discovered. (This approach is how I once rescued a wrongly accused file.)

To remove actual infected files, select them in the list and then click the Remove All or Remove button. The infected files are obliterated.

Paying attention to the UAC warnings

Depending upon your user account security level, you may see plenty of User Account Control warnings, or UACs. These annoying messages pop up for a purpose, which is system security and protection. Your choice is to approve or disapprove whatever action is being requested.

A typical UAC is shown in Figure 21-2. This message appears atop everything else on the screen, which may dim to help focus your attention on the message's importance. Do you want to proceed?

FIGURE 21-2:
A typical UAC.

You choose Yes or No in a UAC, depending on what you've just done. These warnings appear whenever you alter your account or make a system-wide change to Windows, such as installing new software. If you initialized the action, click Yes. Otherwise, click No.

>> You can expect to see a UAC's warning pop up when you click or select an item flagged with the UAC shield icon, shown in the margin.

>> If see an unexpected UAC warning, click No. For example, when you're on the Internet and you see a UAC warning about installing software or changing your home page, click No or Cancel.

>> The quantity of UAC warnings you see depends upon your account's security level. A system administrator account, which is the first or only account on a Windows computer, sees fewer warnings than a standard user account.

>> The frequency of UAC warnings is adjusted from the Control Panel app in the User Accounts area. I don't recommend that you adjust this setting, so I won't tell you where it's hidden.

Keep Windows Up-to-Date

One key to your computer's security is to ensure that you always have the most current version of Windows. This goal means installing the various updates and patches released by Microsoft, even when you deem the process to be a pain. It is. But you must ensure that the operating system has all the latest security updates required to meet any known or looming threats.

Checking the update status

Windows updates are downloaded automatically. You see an icon in the notification area on the taskbar indicating that an update is pending. In fact, your computer may restart automatically to apply the update, which can be upsetting when you leave the system on all the time and expect to return to your work as it was the night before.

You can delay a pending update to a more convenient time. In fact, Windows struggles to monitor when you actively use the computer, and any automatic restarts take place after this period.

To check for a pending update, follow these steps:

1. **Press the Win+I keyboard shortcut to summon the Settings app.**

2. **In Windows 11, choose Windows Update; in Windows 10, choose Update & Security.**

   If an update is pending, you see the Restart Now button. Otherwise, you see a button that reads Check for Updates.

3. **Click the Check for Updates button.**

   When an update is available, it's installed. But be warned that you may need to restart the computer. If so, the Check for Updates button changes its name to Restart Now.

It's common to restart the computer to apply an update. It's this restart that makes Windows Update a pain: You must save your work and close any running programs. Wait for the update to apply itself. Then you can reassemble your workflow.

>> Windows Update requires an Internet connection because the update is downloaded from the Microsoft mothership.

>> Most updates are installed in a matter of minutes. Major Windows updates take longer because they must restart the computer a few times.

>> Some updates are preview versions of Windows that can be installed ahead of time. These updates are optional.

>> Not all updates require that you restart the computer.

>> In Windows 10, you may be prompted to upgrade to Windows 11. Operating system upgrades are optional. If you don't want to upgrade, don't do it. But keep in mind that Windows continually pesters you about the upgrade.

TIP

>> Always check for a Windows update before you leave on a trip with your laptop. Install the update right away, because you don't know about your Internet connection at the destination.

>> When an update fails, you see the Retry button. Click it to attempt once again to apply the Windows update.

>> Some critical updates are installed automatically and cannot be postponed. The computer may even restart rudely without your permission, though outside of your normal working hours.

Postponing a Windows update

Updates are important, so install them as they appear. There are times, however, when you need the computer on for an extended period without interruption. In these rare cases, you can postpone Windows updates.

In the Settings app, on the Windows Update screen, look for an option to pause updates for a week. Or, you can select this item to choose a longer delay. But eventually, you must succumb to the update. Remember: This effort is about security.

When updates are paused, the Check for Updates button changes its name to Resume. Click this button to continue with regular Windows updates.

Exploring other updates and upgrades

It's easy to confuse the terms *update* and *upgrade*. People often confuse the words *naked* and *nude*, though a definite difference exists between update and upgrade.

An *update* is a tiny improvement to software. It might also be called a *patch*. An update may fix a bug or problem, or it can fine-tune some features.

Upgrades are complete revisions of programs. An upgrade presents a new release of the software, along with a new version number. For example, the latest version of Microsoft Office is an upgrade, not an update. The hop from Windows 10 to Windows 11 is an upgrade.

My advice: Update frequently. If the manufacturer offers a patch or a fix, install it as recommended. On the other hand, upgrades are necessary only when you desperately need the new features or modifications or when the upgrade addresses security issues.

REMEMBER

>> Updates are distributed by the manufacturer. Sometimes you're alerted in the program itself, although you may receive an email notice if you've registered the program.

>> Software updates and upgrades are downloaded over the Internet, installed just like software you download from the Internet.

>> If you're prompted with a UAC to accept the upgrade, click the Yes button or OK button. Even so, you must initiate the upgrade process in some way. For example, don't expect an update to arrive as an email attachment.

>> Not all upgrades are necessary, and they can often introduce new problems.

>> On the other hand, upgrades are necessary to stay current. For example, if you're still using DoodleWriter 4.2 and everybody else is using DoodleWriter 6.1, you may have difficulty exchanging documents. After a while, newer versions of programs become incompatible with their older models. If so, you need to upgrade.

>> You might discover that your software upgrade is incompatible with older versions of Windows. If so, you must upgrade Windows to use the new program.

>> In an office setting, everybody should be using the same software version. Everybody doesn't have to be using the *latest* version, just the *same* version.

>> To be *naked* is to be exposed. To be *nude* means that you're not wearing any clothes.

Your Privacy

Perhaps the most common question I'm asked is, "Why do you keep putting the orange juice back in the refrigerator when you know that the carton is empty?" But for the computer, the most common question I'm asked deals with computer privacy. People want to know what they can do to protect their privacy when it comes to using a modern piece of technology like a computer.

Locking the screen

If you plan on stepping away from your computer for even an instant, lock the screen: Press the Win+L keyboard shortcut.

Locking the screen doesn't sign you out of Windows. It's still running, and your programs are still humming along. But you must sign back into Windows to unlock it. Your information is safe.

Another way to lock the screen is to set a screen saver. Unlike the Win+L keyboard shortcut, the screen saver screen lock doesn't kick in until a given period of inactivity. Once it's active, however, you must unlock the screen — sign in to Windows — to regain access.

To set up a screen saver, or to confirm that a lock is in place, obey these steps:

1. **Tap the Windows key and type** Screen Saver **to see and choose the Change Screen Saver item.**

2. **Choose a screen saver from the Screen Saver button menu.**

3. **Set the Wait timeout value.**

   The screen saver you choose (refer to Step 2) takes over the display when you don't touch the keyboard or move the mouse for the given interval.

4. **Place a check mark by the option On Resume, Display Logon Screen.**

   This is the security setting you want.

5. **Click the OK button.**

To regain access to the computer, wiggle the mouse or tap a key on the keyboard to dismiss the screen saver. Type your account PIN or password, and the computer is unlocked.

>> Beware of downloading screen savers from the Internet. Though some are legitimate, most are invasive ads or programs that are impossible to uninstall or remove. If you download this type of screen saver, you're pretty much stuck with it. Be careful!

>> The computer's power management plan puts the monitor to sleep before the screen saver kicks in. See Chapter 18 for more information about the computer's power management plan.

>> Though screen savers can be amusing, this feature has a serious history. When the old CRT (glass) monitors were popular, images could *burn* into the screen's phosphor, rendering the monitor less than desirable. The screen saver would kick in to literally save the screen from the perils of phosphor burn-in. Today, it remains as an amusement, but also a form of security.

Reviewing Windows privacy settings

The Windows Settings app features a long list of privacy settings. These allow you to control which programs or apps have access to specific computer hardware and features as well as how your personal information is shared between apps.

To view the slate of privacy settings, heed these directions:

1. **Press Win+I to open the Settings app.**

2. **Choose Privacy and Security in Windows 11; in Windows 10, click the Privacy button.**

Look for the App Permissions heading. Below it you see a list of features, such as Location, Camera, Microphone and so on. Choose an item to see which apps are allowed or denied permission to use the feature. Or, you can disable the master control to prevent all apps from accessing the feature.

For example, choose Location and disable Location Services to prevent any app from accessing a laptop's GPS and other location features.

Be aware that apps request access even when you have denied permission to use the feature. You can choose to deny them again, but some apps are persistent. For example, the Camera app wants to use the computer's webcam by design. But if a game you downloaded from the Internet wants to use the camera, I'd be a bit cautious.

IN THIS CHAPTER

» Creating a backup copy

» Using File History to back up

» Configuring the backup schedule

» Backing up to the cloud

» Recovering an older version of a file

» Restoring files and folders

Chapter 22

An All-Important Safety Copy

L ife is risky in the digital realm. Not only are Bad Guys on the Internet looking to steal your data but all the information on your computer could also be suddenly wiped out by a nearby volcano. If not a volcano, some other disaster may befall your beloved computer. Or, you could one day accidentally overwrite a file only to find out that you cannot recover the original.

Don't be so hard on yourself, especially when you live close to an active volcano. Computer scientists have devised a clever way to keep a replica of your computer's stuff just for emergencies. All your files, documents, photos, music, and other items are safe, thanks to an all-important safety copy, a *backup*.

» Backup is the name of the process of creating a safety copy and also the safety copy itself. It's a noun-verb, like *fish* and *watch*.

» It wasn't a volcano, but rather an earthquake that destroyed my computer's hard drive once. Thanks to a recent backup, I was able to restore all my digital stuff.

Back Up Your Data

The backup process is part of your computer's security regimen. Not only is a backup copy good to have for earthquakes, volcanos, and building-size monsters but a business that suffers from a ransomware attack can often recover its files from an uncorrupted backup. You would think everyone would rush out and make a backup every hour! Some people do, but many don't bother — or they think that backup is a pain.

Part of the problem is that Windows doesn't prompt you to back up. Unlike other security issues covered elsewhere in this book, backup doesn't seem to be a high priority. It is. And implementing a backup system isn't the pain that it was in the last century.

>> Windows comes with backup software, including the File History feature and the ancient Windows 7 backup.

>> Microsoft also wants you to use cloud backup to its OneDrive service. See the later section "Using cloud backup."

>> Third-party backup programs are also available, most of which come on the external drive you need to carry out the backup process.

>> The other half of backup is *restore* — this process recovers files from the backup media, such as an older version of a file you've overwritten. The restore operation is covered later in this chapter.

Obtaining backup storage

Like all things in the computer universe, backup involves both hardware and software.

The software is provided by Windows in the form of File History backup or the antique-but-still-lovable Windows 7 backup.

The hardware must be provided in the form of an external drive: either a physical drive attached to the computer or some sort of network storage. The less technical option is an external drive. Yes, this hardware is required. Buy it. Don't get cheap on me, Dodgson.

>> If your computer lacks an external storage device, rush out and buy one. Ensure that the drive offers at least as much storage as the computer's primary mass storage device. A higher-capacity drive is better.

TIP

>> One benefit of obtaining an external drive is that it often comes with its own backup software. Yes, you can use this software in addition to Windows File History.

>> Laptops work best with portable drives — specifically, external USB drives that use only one cable: the USB cable. You can easily take the portable drive with you on the road.

REMEMBER

>> Also remember that laptops might benefit more from using cloud backup. See the later section "Using cloud backup."

>> Network backup works well, though I recommend you already have storage available on the network, such as a network drive. This drive can be connected directly to the network router or base station. Yes, this setup is more technical than a single drive attached to your computer.

TECHNICAL STUFF

>> If you use a network drive, ensure that it's mapped to the computer's storage system. Refer to Chapter 16 for details on mapping network drives (folders).

Configuring File History

The two backup utilities that come with Windows are the archaic Windows 7 Backup and the File History feature. Of the two, File History is better — plus, Windows 7 Backup is available only in Windows 10. (Well, it's also available in Windows 7, which isn't covered in this edition of the book.)

File History isn't activated on your computer, because it must be configured. This configuration requires that you inform the utility where to back up the files. An external drive is the best resource, as described in the preceding section.

To configure File History, obey these directions:

1. **Ensure that external storage is connected to the computer and available.**

   You can't avoid this step!

2. **Tap the Windows key to pop up the Start menu.**

3. **Type** file history.

4. **Choose the File History item.**

   In Windows 11, the Control Panel opens to the File History item in the System and Security Area. In Windows 10, the Settings app opens to the Files Backup subcategory of the Update & Security category.

If File History is active, you see the message "File History Is On" in Windows 11. In Windows 10, the master control toggle below the heading Automatically Back Up My Files is set to the On position. You're good. Otherwise, continue:

5. **Click the Add a Drive button.**

   Windows prowls for suitable locations, such as the external hard drive you added in Step 1. The results are displayed in a list.

6. **Choose a drive.**

   Select the drive you added in Step 1.

After you choose a location, Windows activates the File History feature. Continue reading in the next section.

>> File History duplicates copies of your files to the storage location chosen in Step 6. This process takes place automatically.

>> File History works on all your files and folders, but it does not back up program files or any part of the Windows operating system.

>> Third-party backup programs can be configured to back up all data, including programs and Windows. This feature is why I run a separate backup on my main computer in addition to File History.

>> If you leave your laptop turned off for a while or you disconnect from the File History storage device, you're reminded by a notification to reconnect and keep File History up-to-date.

Checking the backup schedule

The File History feature works automatically, but if you're like me, you probably don't trust computers, the same way you don't trust that the refrigerator door is truly shut. To confirm that File History is up and running, follow these steps:

1. **Follow Steps 1 through 4 in the preceding section to bring up the File History window.**

2. **In Windows 11, choose the Advanced Settings link on the right side of the windows. In Windows 10, click the More Options link.**

3. **Confirm the time interval for File History backups.**

   The default is hourly. Use the menu to choose an option other than Every Hour (the default). For example, on a laptop you bring home at the end of the day, you might want to choose Daily for the backup schedule.

4. **Ensure that backups are kept forever.**

The Forever option is the default. However, choosing Until Space Is Needed is better if you find the backup media getting full. With this option, older backups are removed to make room for newer ones.

If you need to back up right away, click the Run Now button on the main File History screen in Windows 11 (after Step 1). In Windows 10, after Step 2, click the Back Up Now button.

Yes, the refrigerator sounds an alarm when its door is open for an extended period. This alarm means nothing to teenagers sitting a few feet away.

Using cloud backup

Cloud backup uses the Internet as the backup "drive." In fact, Microsoft sorely wants you to use its OneDrive cloud storage for backing up Windows 11. You see a prompt urging you to do so in the Settings app. To further drive home the desire for OneDrive, the Office 365 suite of programs also prompts you to "back up" files on OneDrive. It's relentless.

The benefit of cloud backup is that files are backed up all the time whenever an Internet connection is available. For laptops, this type of backup is ideal. Plus, several cloud backup services exist beyond Microsoft's OneDrive, some of which pester you only half as much.

>> To use cloud backup, sign up for the feature and configure the backup. The process works all the time without your needing to mess with it.

>> Cloud backup often requires a subscription. It may be free for a limited quantity of storage. More storage results in a charge. Some services charge monthly.

>> Yes, you can use cloud backup in addition to standard backup.

>> Another bonus of cloud backup is that it may also feature file history. For example, OneDrive keeps previous copies of files.

>> Refer to Chapter 16 for more information on cloud storage.

The Restore Operation

Great duos go together: peanut butter and jelly, Tom and Jerry, politics and corruption. Add to the list the computer couplet of backup and restore. Like all great pairs, backup means nothing without its companion operation, restore. After all, what's the point of keeping backup files unless you can access them?

This section specifically covers using the Windows File History feature and its capability to restore files.

>> Though deleted files can be recovered from the electronic purgatory that is the Windows Recycle Bin, the restore operation is more exhaustive — especially when it comes to older files.

>> Any backup utility, such as the one that comes free on an external drive, allows you to restore an older version of a file as well as recover lost files and directories.

>> Cloud backup also offers restore, which is available through the cloud backup program on your computer or from the cloud storage website.

Restoring an older version

You can clobber a file by copying a new file to an existing file's location or by using an existing file's name when saving a new file. In both cases, you're warned of the file's impending doom. When you update a file, such as editing a list of people who owe you money, the older version is overwritten. To recover the original file in any of these instances with the File History feature, you conjure something called Previous Versions.

The Previous Versions tool works only when you've set up and configured File History. If so, follow these steps to recover an earlier version of a clobbered file. If not, weep bitter tears of woe.

1. **Locate the file you want.**

   If the file has been deleted, you can try to restore it from the Recycle Bin. If it's not found there, you need to restore it, as described in the next section.

2. **Right-click the File icon and choose Properties.**

3. **Choose the Restore Previous Versions tab.**

   A list of previous versions of the file appears, as shown in Figure 22-1. The list is the file's history, composed of older versions that can be recovered.

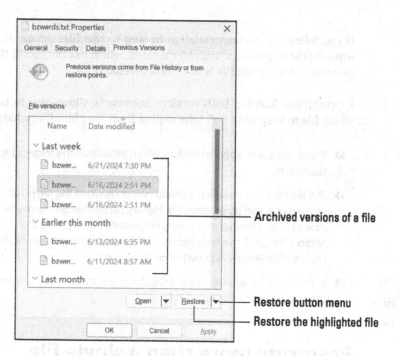

bzwerds.txt Properties   ✕

General   Security   Details   Previous Versions

Previous versions come from File History or from restore points.

File versions

Name	Date modified
∨ Last week	
📄 bzwer...	6/21/2024 7:30 PM
📄 bzwer...	6/16/2024 2:51 PM
📄 bzwer...	6/16/2024 2:51 PM
∨ Earlier this month	
📄 bzwer...	6/13/2024 6:35 PM
📄 bzwer...	6/11/2024 8:57 AM
∨ Last month	

Open ▼   Restore ▼

OK   Cancel   Apply

— Archived versions of a file

— Restore button menu
— Restore the highlighted file

FIGURE 22-1:
Perusing previous
versions of a file.

4. **Click to select a previous version of the file.**

Usually, the one you want is atop the list, the most recent.

5. **Click the Restore button.**

A menu appears with three options:

- *Replace the File in the Destination:* Choose this option if you want to overwrite any existing file with the older copy.

- *Skip This File:* Choose this option to ignore the operation and keep your existing file as is.

- *Compare Info for Both Files:* Choose this option to examine more details about the newer file that you're replacing with a backup.

6. **Choose the option to compare info for both files.**

I recommend that you keep and examine both files as opposed to obliterating the current one.

7. **Select both files.**

8. **Choose Continue.**

The same folder window opens in a new window — silly, but that's how it works.

If you follow my recommendation in Step 6, two files appear in the new folder window: the original and the older version, which has the text "(2)" suffixed to its filename. This second file is the one recovered.

I recommend keeping both versions because it allows you to better determine which file to keep or to pull information from the older file, whatever you want.

>> These steps also apply to folders, which include all the folder's files and any subfolders.

>> The file may not show any previous versions when the file is too new or hasn't yet been backed up or when File History isn't active on the media. Files you moved from other locations may not show a history. Files stored on Microsoft's OneDrive with copies available locally also may not show any file history. (File History is available on OneDrive.)

TIP

>> In Windows 10, you can choose the Restore Previous Versions command from the pop-up menu displayed in Step 2.

Restoring more than a single file

In addition to fetching the previous version of a file, you can use File History to recover multiple files or folders or everything you've saved and created on the computer. This trick isn't obvious. Follow these steps to reveal the secret — but don't tell anyone else!

1. **Tap the Windows key on the keyboard.**

   Up pops the Start menu.

2. **Type** file history **to show a list of matching results.**

3. **From the search results, choose the item Restore Your Files with File History.**

   The File History window appears, as shown in Figure 22-2. This location is where you can select individual files or complete folders to restore from the File History backup.

4. **Use the arrows to page through dates.**

   The arrows are illustrated in Figure 22-2. Use them to peruse older backups by date and time. The backup date and time appear atop the window.

File History backup date and time   Selected folder

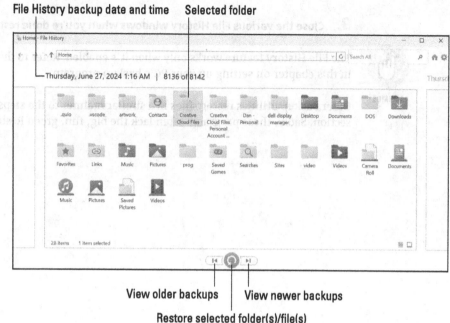

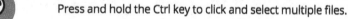

FIGURE 22-2:
The File
History window.

View older backups   View newer backups

Restore selected folder(s)/file(s)

5. **Choose a folder or file to restore.**

   Browse the files in the window just as though you would browse them on your computer. If you don't see the folder or file, open a folder on the screen. For example, double-click the Document's folder to view its contents.

   Page back and forth to find the exact file you want by date. If the file you want isn't in the folder, keep paging back through time. Eventually, it appears.

   Press and hold the Ctrl key to click and select multiple files.

6. **After selecting the file(s) or folder(s), click the big, fun, green Restore button.**

7. **Choose how to restore the file, if prompted.**

   The three options presented are the same as described in the preceding section. If you don't see the prompt, the files are magically restored to their original location(s).

8. **Select the option to compare versions.**

   The restore operation may take some time if you desire to compare versions. If you're certain that you want to restore the older versions without comparing, choose instead the option to replace the existing files with the backups.

TIP

9. **Close the various File History windows when you're done restoring files.**

REMEMBER

The File History feature works only when it's enabled. Refer to the sections earlier in this chapter on setting up your PC's backup program.

Other backup utilities restore files in a similar manner to the steps outlined in this section. Sadly, these programs often lack the big, fun, green Restore button.

Chapter **23**

Maintenance Chores

M aintenance is the thing that you know you're supposed to do but don't do and then later regret not doing. After all, as much as everyone would like to follow the manual's suggestion and winterize the lawnmower, we're not all Hank Hill. We forget. Then we suffer the inevitable consequences of living in a house with various pets and never knowing that the furnace has a filter that hasn't been changed in several years.

The good news is that computer maintenance chores don't involve messy liquids or any type of pruning. The better news is that, for the most part, the job is done by the computer. Only a handful of items are necessary for you, the human, to do.

» Windows comes with all the computer maintenance software (utilities) you need. I don't recommend obtaining third-party programs unless they perform tasks you desperately need.

» Avoid downloading "free" computer maintenance utilities from the Internet. Though some of them are legitimate, they're intended for advanced computer users (also known as nerds).

TIP

» Unlike with an automobile, you have no reason to take your computer to the dealer or a repair place for regular check-ups. Shun anyone who suggests such a program, which is often called a *maintenance contract* by some dealers. Your computer doesn't need it, and you don't need to pay for it.

Mass Storage Duties

My friend Jerry once made a living washing hard drives. I kid you not. He would go to large businesses, disassemble the drives, and wash them with special soap and water, and then he'd put the drives back into the computer. Those were the days.

Your computer's mass storage system needs no washing. In fact, do not wash the hard drive with anything. Instead, rely upon a few handy utilities to maintain all the drives in the computer system.

Checking storage

Your computer came supplied with oodles of room on its mass storage device. But like your closet or garage or that one drawer in the kitchen, eventually it fills up with all sorts of stuff. Before things become dire, check storage stats and potentially free up space on the computer's main drive. Follow these steps:

1. **Press Win+E.**

   This keyboard shortcut summons a File Explorer window.

2. **Choose This PC from the list of items on the left side of the window.**

   The default view for the This PC window lists storage devices attached to or available for the computer (including network drives). A graphical thermometer provides a quick overview of the storage situation for each drive.

3. **Right-click on a storage device, such as the primary hard drive, C.**

4. **Choose Properties.**

The storage device's Properties dialog box appears, as shown in Figure 23-1. It shows a chart illustrating drive usage and capacity, as well as the boring numbers that reflect the details.

When storage gets low, it's shown graphically. After Step 2, the drive's capacity thermometer shows red when the drive is perilously close to being full. When this condition occurs, it's time to act. Keep reading in the next section.

Freeing storage space

A good remedy for an overflowing drive is to run the Disk Cleanup utility. This program seeks out temporary files, digital leftovers, and other useless material that festoon a mass storage device like leaves and branches after a windstorm. Obey these directions:

Handy graph

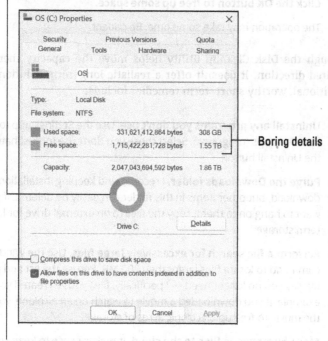

OS (C:) Properties   ×

| Security | | Previous Versions | | Quota |
| General | Tools | | Hardware | Sharing |

OS|

Type: Local Disk
File system: NTFS

Used space: 331,621,412,864 bytes   308 GB
Free space: 1,715,422,281,728 bytes 1.55 TB   ⟵ **Boring details**

Capacity: 2,047,043,694,592 bytes 1.86 TB

Drive C: Details

☐ Compress this drive to save disk space
☑ Allow files on this drive to have contents indexed in addition to
   file properties

OK   Cancel   Apply

FIGURE 23-1:
Checking storage
usage statistics.   **Don't do this**

1. **Pop up the Start menu.**

   Tap the Windows key on the keyboard or click the Start button on the taskbar.

2. **Type** disk cleanup.

3. **Choose the Disk Cleanup item.**

   The Disk Cleanup utility starts.

4. **Choose a drive from the menu, such as drive C or whichever drive is bursting at the seams.**

5. **Click OK.**

   The utility examines the drive, looking for useless and decrepit files. Soon, you see a list categorizing these files, along with the quantity of storage each category consumes. Some items are preselected in the list.

6. **Peruse the list of items to delete, placing check marks by various categories.**

   Pretty much everything on the list can go. Nothing on the list is worth keeping, especially when the drive is suffocating with files.

7. **Click the OK button to free up some space.**

   The operation may take some time. Be patient.

Though the Disk Cleanup utility helps move the capacity thermometer in the desired direction, it doesn't offer a realistic long-term solution for a full drive. Additional, worthy short-term remedies include:

>> **Uninstall any programs you don't use.** Use the Settings app to browse for installed apps (programs). Select those you don't use (or just hate) and click the Uninstall button.

>> **Purge the Downloads folder.** I recommend keeping installation files you download, but other items in this folder can easily be deleted. If you truly want to hang on to them, copy the files to an external drive for long-term storage.

>> **Perform a file search for excessively large files.** Use the Windows Search command to locate files larger than 200 MB. Peruse the list and purge those biggies you no longer need — specifically, files you've created yourself. For example, if you downloaded a movie to watch on an airplane, you can remove the movie to free up electronic acres of storage.

>> **Move humongous files to the cloud.** It makes sense to keep some larger files on the cloud, especially when you subscribe to various cloud services, such as Microsoft's OneDrive. These files are still accessible from the cloud (providing that an Internet connection is active), but they don't occupy storage on your computer.

If you can't free enough space, you need to obtain another storage device. You can add an external drive — but remember to use it! You can also replace the primary storage device with one of a larger capacity, though this operation is technical and may require you to hire an expert.

>> You can run the Disk Cleanup utility at any time. The drive doesn't necessarily need to be overflowing.

>> The largest file types are media files. Video files are especially girthy. A music library can occupy several Albert Halls of storage. Photo files aren't as voracious, but collectively they occupy a lot of storage. Moving these files to the cloud is an excellent way to keep them available while keeping local storage available.

>> If you download a movie to your laptop to watch on a flight, remember to delete the movie when the trip is over.

REMEMBER

WARNING

>> One solution you may see recommended is to compress the drive. The option is shown earlier, in Figure 23-1. Though this solution may work temporarily, it involves long-term complications that don't address the basic issue.

Checking for errors

Windows does its own error-checking for the computer's mass storage device, especially the primary mass storage device, drive C. This checking happens automatically. In fact, you may notice Windows performing a media check whenever you start Windows. This task is obvious when a problem is detected and you're alerted to the resolution.

So there's nothing for you to do. Yet you're still reading and, obviously, you see more text coming up — including some steps. Therefore, to manually run a media check, heed these directions:

1. **Open the This PC window.**

Press the Win+E keyboard to start the File Explorer program and choose This PC from the items listed on the left side of the window.

2. **Right-click the storage device you desire to check.**

It can be any storage device, from a thumb drive to the primary mass storage device.

3. **Choose Properties.**

4. **In the device's Properties dialog box, click the Tools tab.**

You see two tools available: the traditional file checking tool, once known as CheckDisk, and the defrag tool, both illustrated in Figure 23-2.

5. **Click the Check button.**

The storage device may not need checking. A prompt appears in that instance, which also reminds you that Windows automatically checks storage devices, even if you believed me when I wrote about this topic earlier.

6. **Click the Scan Drive button.**

Wait while Windows checks out the device.

7. **Peruse the results.**

8. **Close the window when you're done.**

If any errors are found, you may be prompted to correct them, though Windows fixes most errors automatically.

Tools tab

Check disk

Defrag

FIGURE 23-2:
Storage utilities.

Running defrag

The defrag utility is sheer genius. Developed in the late 1980s, it corrects a storage situation that drastically slows file access. I remember running a defrag utility on my PC back in the 1940s and being utterly blown away: Where it once took two days to access a file, after defragging the drive, it took only a few hours. O, how times have changed.

The defrag utility is still genius, and computers are much faster. But unlike in the old days, storage optimization runs automatically. You don't need to do a thing unless you're curious. And you are curious. So follow these steps:

1. **Press Win+E to summon a File Explorer window.**

2. **Choose This PC from the left side of the window.**

   You see a list of storage devices for your computer.

3. **Right-click on the primary mass storage device, drive C.**

   It doesn't matter which drive you right-click on. You choose the drive to optimize in Step 8.

4. **Choose Properties.**

5. **In the device's Properties dialog box, click the Tools tab.**

   Refer back to Figure 23-2.

6. **Click the Optimize button.**

The Optimize Drives window appears, as shown in Figure 23-3.

7. **Review the current fragmentation status of available storage devices.**

Because you may have doubted me, any drive that can be defragmented shows that Windows has already done so. In Figure 23-2, drive C was recently defragmented. Some drives — such as SSDs, thumb drives, media cards, and drives with a special format — cannot be optimized.

8. **If you insist upon moving forward, select a drive from the list.**

9. **Click the Analyze button.**

This button is unavailable for SSDs because the analyze process is unnecessary.

10. **Click the Optimize button to defragment the media.**

The process takes a while. A report is generated when it's complete.

Some drives can't be defragmented   Defragmentation status

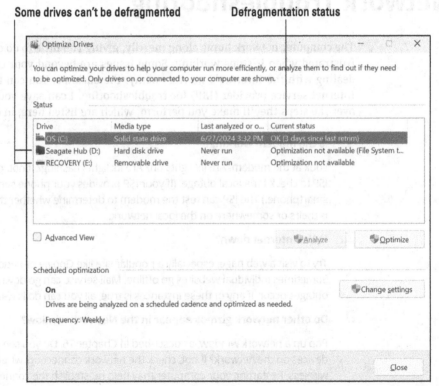

FIGURE 23-3:
The Optimize
Drives window.

Why bother with all these steps when the process is automatic or flat-out can't be done, primarily for older media, such as traditional hard drives? If the Optimize Drives window shows that the drive needs attention, give it a defrag.

WARNING

» Never, ever, run a defrag utility on an SSD, thumb drive, or media card. These storage media are damaged by the aggressive determination of the defragmentation process.

TECHNICAL STUFF

» *Fragmentation* is a technique whereby files are efficiently stored on mass media. Because files are created and deleted, "holes" exist in the media where the deleted files once were. Fragmentation splits files into pieces to fit into these holes, making more efficient use of the media. Even so, the process of collecting a file's several pieces is also inefficient. Defragmentation reassembles the files and fills in the holes. I'm sure a more technical description exists, which I am too lazy to write here.

Network Troubleshooting

The computer network hums along merrily, giving you little to do other than to be frustrated when it stops working. Some issues are beyond your control, such as dealing with the Internet's mortal enemy: the backhoe. You can try calling your Internet service provider (ISP) for troubleshooting. I can save you time by going over the steps they'll make you perform, which are listed here, in order:

1. **Is the modem working?**

   Look at the modem. Are its lights on? Are its lights flashing? If not, phone your ISP to check for a local outage. (If your ISP provides your phone service, use a smartphone.) The ISP can test the modem to determine whether the problem is theirs or somewhere on the local network.

2. **Is the Internet down?**

   Try to visit a web page, especially a popular site like Google or Reddit. Sometimes individual websites go offline. Mail service can go down. Internet outages occur. If any of these instances is true, all you can do is wait.

3. **Do other network gizmos appear in the Network window?**

   Pop up a network window, as described in Chapter 16. Do you see other devices on the network? If not, check the network connection, wired or wireless. Restarting your computer may help reestablish the connection.

4. **Have you restarted the gateway (router)?**

Unplug the gateway. Wait a few moments. Plug it back in. Restarting the gateway may "clear its head" and get the network back up.

5. **Have you restarted the entire network?**

The final troubleshooting step is to restart the entire network. Turn off everything: modem, gateway, any hubs or switches, and every network device. The devices include computers, tablets, phones, and printers.

Start with the modem. Turn it on first. Wait. Turn on the gateway. Wait. Turn on any switches or hubs. Wait. Turn on network devices. This process is tedious, but it often resolves network distress.

REMEMBER

Change is the number-one reason things go awry in any system. If you've added new devices to the network, updated software, or replaced hardware, that might explain why the network went hinkey.

TECHNICAL STUFF

Often, you must unplug a modem or router to turn it off. Don't bother looking for an on–off switch.

The Windows Do-Over

Sometimes I eat something and regret it later. If only I had a reset button — something to take me back in time, before the pain and noise.

Alas, humans lack a reset button, but Windows has one. And it's not just used for that questionable piece of pork.

If your computer suffers a dire mishap, or if you intend to sell it or give it away, you can reset Windows so that all your personal information is removed, programs uninstalled, and settings reverted to the time when Windows was freshly installed or upgraded.

Obviously, this operation is a drastic step. You don't reset Windows to fix minor ills. When necessary, however, obey these steps to reset Windows:

1. **Press the Win+I keyboard shortcut to bring up the Settings app.**

2. **In Windows 11, choose System; in Windows 10, choose Update & Security.**

3. **Choose the Recovery category.**

4. **In Windows 11, click the Reset PC button; in Windows 10, the button is labeled Get Started.**

5. **Choose whether to keep your files or remove everything.**

   If you choose Keep My Files, only Windows is unwound back to its original state. Otherwise, if you choose Remove Everything, the entire PC is reset.

   After you make the choice, Windows examines a few things and provides a summary of the operation and a confirmation message.

6. **Confirm that you want to proceed.**

   You cannot undo or cancel the operation after it begins.

7. **Proceed.**

   Sit back and wait.

After the process is complete, the computer restarts and Windows pops up its bright, cheery self. It asks the same questions it did when you first started your new computer. Yes, you are a complete stranger.

You can either proceed with setting up Windows again or turn off the computer. It's ready to be sold, traded, bartered, or simply left to die alone in a field somewhere.

General Cleaning

They say that up to 80 percent of the dust in your home or office comes from humans. Sloughed-off human skin cells land everywhere, even on your beloved computer — not to mention those several times you sneezed but were too busy typing to cover your mouth. Yes, humans are probably the first reason that computers must be cleaned. Your pets are number two.

Keeping it clean

Computers are robust beasts. They can go through a lot without cleaning. My gauge is when I can sign my name in the dust atop my desktop PC. Only then do I give it a wipe-down.

More important than dust is keeping the computer's vents clear. Especially if you have pets, use a vacuum cleaner to suck all the hair from the cooling vents. Your PC will thank you. The dog will recover from the sound of the vacuum.

For laptops, some minor cleaning is necessary after you've been out and about a few times. Use a soft cloth with a nonabrasive cleaner like 409 or Fantastic. Spray the cleaner on the cloth, and then wipe down everything on the laptop except for the screen. A damp sponge also works for cleaning a laptop. Be gentle as you wipe; try not to get any moisture inside the laptop.

TIP

WARNING

>> Consider washing your hands from time to time.

>> You can vacuum the vents on a desktop PC while it's on, but turn off a laptop before you start cleaning it.

>> Use a cotton swab to clean some of the gunk from the cracks.

>> Do not clean inside any openings. Never spray any liquids into those openings, either.

Vacuuming the keyboard

Every so often, I vacuum the computer's keyboard. The reason is that, despite any advice contrary, I do eat things like chips and pretzels while I work on the computer. Shame on me. Tender snack morsels love computer keyboards.

To suck the crap out of the keyboard, I use the little portable vacuum with either the tiny (toothbrush-size) brush or the upholstery cleaning attachment. This technique effectively vanquishes most of the crud. It's amazing to watch.

Some people prefer to clean the keyboard by using a can of compressed air. I don't recommend this method because the air can blow the muck farther into your keyboard. Instead, use a vacuum.

Cleansing the screen

It's considered polite to sneeze into a handkerchief or your folded arm. The reason for this behavior is that a human sneeze travels at the speed of sound and the spit vapor can spread outward up to ten feet. Yes, human beings are amazing creatures. So just imagine the terror under which the computer screen lives, knowing your potential.

You can clean the computer screen when it's powered on or off, though you see more of the yuck when the power is off. Wipe the monitor with a dry microfiber cloth. Don't use paper towels!

When the screen is particularly gross, use a cleaning fluid specifically designed for computer monitors. Especially for a touchscreen, using the wrong cleaner can damage the device, rendering its touch–powers useless or even making the screen difficult to see.

TIP

WARNING

- » Office supply stores carry special monitor and touchscreen cleaners as well as lint-free wipes. These items can also be used on your smartphone and tablet.

- » Allow a laptop's screen to dry completely before closing the lid.

- » Oftentimes, a laptop's keyboard creates a shadow stain on the screen. It's difficult to avoid and impossible to clean. To help prevent this shadow stain, place a soft, lint-free cloth — like one you'd use to clean the monitor inside the laptop — between the keyboard and screen when the laptop is closed.

- » Avoid using alcohol- or ammonia-based cleaners on a touchscreen! These harsh chemicals can damage the screen. Worse, they can render that expensive touchscreen monitor useless.

- » Never squirt any cleaner directly on a touchscreen.

6

The Part of Tens

IN THIS CHAPTER

» **Don't fear your computer**

» **Always save your work**

» **Back up your stuff**

» **Don't open or delete unknown files**

» **Don't fall prey to online predators**

» **Use antivirus and update software**

» **Be smart about upgrades**

» **Use the PC with proper posture**

» **Keep Windows up-to-date**

» **Always properly quit Windows**

Chapter **24**

Ten Computer Commandments

look nothing like Charlton Heston, yet I can picture myself descending from Mount. Io (that's a computer joke) to bestow upon you ten computer commandments. These directives are based on my experiences with computers and are in no way divinely inspired.

I. Thou Shalt Not Fear Thy PC

The computer isn't out to get you. It won't suddenly explode. It harbors no sinister intelligence. Honestly, it's rather dumb.

Knowledge is the key to overcoming fear.

II. Thou Shalt Save Thy Work

Whenever you're creating something blazingly original, use the Save command at once! In fact, use the Save command even when you create something stupid that you don't even want to save. Trust me — the computer's primary storage device has plenty of room for you to save your stuff.

You never know when your computer will meander off to watch NASCAR or chat with the wireless router across the street while you're hoping to finish the last few paragraphs of an important report. Save your work as often as possible. Save when you get up from your computer. Save when you answer the phone. Save! Save! Save!

III. Thou Shalt Back Up Thy Files

Nothing beats having that just-in-case copy of your stuff. The computer itself can run a backup program to make that safety copy, or you can duplicate your files yourself. Either way, that secondary backup copy can save your skin someday.

See Chapter 22 for information on backing up.

IV. That Shalt Not Open or Delete Things Unknownst

Here's the rule, written in modern English: Delete only those files or folders that you created yourself.

Unlike computer hardware, where sticky labels with red letters read Do Not Open, unknown computer files have no warning labels. They should! Windows is brimming with unusual and unknown files. Don't mess with 'em. Don't delete them. Don't move them. Don't rename them. And especially don't open them to see what they are. Sometimes, opening an unknown icon can lead to trouble.

V. Thou Shalt Not Be a Sucker

The Bad Guys are successful in spreading their evil, malicious software on the Internet because people let down their guard. Don't be a sucker for human engineering. Here's a list of ways you can avoid being a sucker:

>> Don't reply to any spam email. Doing so brings you even more spam. A popular trick is for spammers to include some text that says, "Reply to this message if you do not want to receive any further messages." Don't! Replying to spam signals the spammers that they have a "live one" and you then receive even more spam. Never, ever, reply to spam!

>> Don't open unknown or unexpected email attachments. Seriously, you're not missing anything if you don't open an attachment. Yet that's how human engineering works: The email fools you into believing that opening the attachment is important. It's not.

REMEMBER

>> No important information is sent via email unless you've asked for it. The government doesn't do it. Your bank doesn't do it. Overseas lotteries and foreign billionaires don't do it.

VI. Thou Shalt Use Antivirus Software, Yea Verily, and Keepeth It Up-to-Date

I highly recommend that you use antivirus software on your computer. Keep this software current. Refer to Chapter 21.

VII. Thou Shalt Upgrade Wisely

New hardware and software come out all the time. The new stuff is generally better and faster, and it's important to some people to be the First On The Block to have a new hardware gizmo or software upgrade. You don't have to be that person.

>> A new version, or *upgrade*, of computer software is necessary only when you truly need the new features it offers, when you need that new version to be compatible with your coworkers, or when the new version fixes problems and bugs you're experiencing.

>> I know plenty of people who stick with Windows 10 despite all the propaganda urging them to upgrade to Windows 11.

>> Buy hardware that's compatible with your PC. Especially when you have an older computer, confirm that the new hardware works with your system.

VIII. Thou Shalt Compute at a Proper Posture

Using a computer can be a pain. Literally. You must observe the proper posture and sitting position while you operate a desktop or laptop. By doing so, you can avoid back strain and the risk of repetitive stress injury (RSI).

>> Even if your wrists are as limber as a politician's spine, you might consider an ergonomic keyboard. This type of keyboard is specially designed at an angle to relieve the stress of typing for long — or short — periods.

>> Wrist pads elevate your wrists so that you type in a proper position, with your palms above the keyboard, not resting below the spacebar.

>> Sit at the computer with your elbows level with your wrists.

>> Your head should not tilt down or up when you view the computer screen. It should be straight ahead, which doesn't help your wrists as much as it helps your neck.

>> If you want to be truly trendy, don't sit at all while you use a computer. I don't! That's because I use a standing desk, where I stand up while I work. If you're game, this type of working environment is helpful for your spine and core. And, if you're timid, get a standing desk that adjusts its height so that you can sit down occasionally.

IX. Thou Shalt Keepeth Windows Up-to-Date

Microsoft keeps Windows continually fresh and updated. The updates fix problems, but they also address vulnerabilities that the Bad Guys exploit. In my book (the one you're reading now), updating is a good thing — but it's effective only when you use the Windows Update service regularly. See Chapter 21.

X. Thou Shalt Properly Shut Down Windows

When you're done with Windows, shut it down. Choose the Shut Down command from the Start menu. The computer automatically turns itself off. Avoid the temptation to unplug a computer to turn it off — unless the situation is desperate.

Refer to Chapter 5 for detailed Windows shutdown instructions.

IN THIS CHAPTER

» **Avoiding battery perils**

» **Using less battery power**

» **Cooling the battery**

» **Deactivating wireless radios**

» **Choosing a better power mode**

» **Using the battery saver**

» **Connecting to wall power**

Chapter **25**

Ten Battery-Saving Tips and Tricks

Without a battery, a laptop would be merely a tiny, overpriced PC. You need the battery to give the laptop its power of portability. There also comes a battery of battery issues, most of which involve squeezing the largest amount of life out of a limited supply of battery juice.

TIP

» Desktop PCs use a battery as part of an uninterruptible power supply. See Chapter 3 for details. Hardly any of the information in this chapter applies to desktops.

» Chapter 18 is chock-full of battery information. Refer there for further battery information.

SCARY LITHIUM-ION BATTERY TRIVIA

Lithium-ion batteries are what many of us humans aspire to be: smart and popular. But the lithium-ion battery has a scary side. Consider this frightening lithium-ion battery information designed to literally shock you away from any thought of messing with your laptop's battery:

- When a lithium-ion battery is overcharged, it gets hot. Then it explodes.
- The lithium metal in the battery burns when it comes in contact with water.
- The acid inside the battery is not only highly caustic, it's also flammable.
- I'm sure the acid is poisonous as well, but — golly — that last sentence had me at *caustic*.
- You cannot recycle a used lithium-ion battery, so don't ever think of buying or using a "recycled" battery.

Don't Drop the Battery, Get It Wet, Short It, Play Keep-Away with It, Open It, Burn It, or Throw It Away

Enough said.

Reduce the Screen's Brightness

To save a bit on battery life on the road, lower the brightness level on your laptop's screen just a hair — or perhaps as low as you can see. This reduction saves the juice.

TIP

The quick way to set screen brightness is to summon the Action Center: Press the Win+A keyboard shortcut. Use the Brightness slider to adjust screen brightness. This control might also be available on the laptop's keyboard as one of those Fn-key combinations.

>> Notebook-type laptops may sport brightness-setting buttons near the screen. Use these buttons to control the brightness.

>> Your laptop's power manager automatically dims the screen when the laptop is on battery power.

Keep the Laptop Cool

Beyond the screen brightness, another battery enemy is the laptop's cooling fan. You may hear it whir from time to time, especially when the laptop is busy doing an update or just starting.

Though the fan is a drain on the battery, it's a useful thing. You want the laptop to keep cool. When it warms up, the fan powers on and the battery drains a wee bit faster. To avoid this extra burden, don't set the laptop in a warm spot such as directly in the sun. Not only will keeping the laptop out of the sun's heat help with battery life, but avoiding sunlight also makes the screen easier to see.

Keep Memory Empty

A busy laptop is a laptop that requires lots of energy to do its thing, specifically the processor. Juggling multiple programs keeps the processor busy. A busy processor runs hot. A hot processor requires a cooling fan to activate. All these items add up to more drain on the battery.

To optimize battery performance, I recommend running only a few programs at a time. For example, you might be reading email in your email program, browsing the web, editing a document in your word processor, and keeping a game of Spider Solitaire going in another window. All this activity is unnecessary, and shutting down the programs you're not using helps save battery life — not a lot, but some.

TIP

>> It may seem trivial, but when you don't set a background image or wallpaper, and especially if you avoid the slide show wallpaper, Windows spends less time updating the screen. Time is battery life!

>> Watching a movie on your laptop doesn't consume a lot of battery power, especially when the movie is streaming from the Internet.

Disable Wi-Fi and Bluetooth

Your laptop's wireless radios — Wi-Fi and Bluetooth — place a subtle drain on the battery. Disabling these items may not gain you an extra hour of computing, but they won't drain the battery as quickly.

A fast way to disable both Wi-Fi and Bluetooth is to set the laptop into Airplane mode. See Chapter 19.

Change the Power Mode

Windows can optimize how the laptop's processor works, which is one way to squeeze more juice from the battery — but at the cost of slowing the system a tad. To change the laptop's power mode, follow these steps:

1. **Press the Win+I keyboard shortcut to conjure the Settings app.**

2. **Choose Power & Battery.**

3. **Tap or click the menu button by the Power Mode item.**

   You see three menu items: Best Power Efficiency, Balanced, and Best Performance.

4. **Choose Best Power Efficiency.**

In Best Power Efficiency mode, the processor works in a manner that reduces demand on the laptop's battery. Of course, this mode also means you're not seeing the best performance from your laptop. But when laptop power needs are dire, choose this mode.

REMEMBER

Don't forget to reset the power mode back to Balanced or Best Performance when battery usage isn't as demanding.

Understand That Batteries Drain Over Time!

No battery keeps its charge forever. Eventually, the battery's charge fades. For some reason, this topic surprises people. "That battery was fully charged when I last used my laptop six months ago!" Batteries drain over time.

Yet just because a battery has drained doesn't mean it's useless. You can always charge a drained or low battery. Plug in the laptop and it should be good to go in just a few hours, if not sooner.

Deal with the Low-Battery Warning

Thanks to smart-battery technology, your laptop can be programmed to inform you when the juice is about to run dry. In fact, you can set up two warnings on most laptops. The idea is to act fast on those warnings when they appear — and to take them seriously! Linger at your own risk. It's your data that you could lose!

Chapter 18 offers information on setting low-battery warnings.

Remember the Battery Saver!

Right there on the Action Center, you find the Battery Saver button. If you see the wee battery icon on the taskbar lose its solid coloring, press the Win+A keyboard shortcut and tap or click the Battery Saver button. Instantly, the laptop is thrust into battery-saving mode. Read more about this mode and how it helps in Chapter 18.

Plug the Laptop into the Wall

The best way to save the battery is to plug your laptop into a power source, a wall socket. This trick not only provides the laptop with a solid flow of energy but also charges the battery. Whatever will they think of next?

Chapter **26**

Ten Handy Laptop Accessories

The spending doesn't stop after you buy the laptop. Nope — many, many laptop toys are available for purchase. Beyond software are gizmos and gadgets galore. Some are standard computer peripherals, like media cards, but most are wonderful and useful items you can get to enhance your laptopping experience.

Yes, desktop PCs can have accessories as well, but not of the same quantity and cleverness you find with bonus laptop toys.

Laptop Bag or Travel Case

A handsome laptop traveling tote is a must. Chapter 19 offers some useful suggestions and recommendations.

External Storage

Obtain a USB-powered external SSD for your laptop. This portable storage device's purpose is to serve as a backup drive, as covered in Chapter 22. Even if you use cloud backup, an external hard drive or SSD comes in handy for file transfer and extra storage.

Cooling Pad

The ideal accessory for any well-loved laptop, especially the larger models, is a cooling pad. It's a device, similar to the one shown in Figure 26-1, on which your laptop sits. The *cooling pad* contains one or more fans and is powered by either the laptop's USB port or standard AA batteries. Your laptop rests on the pad, and the fans help draw away the heat that the battery and microprocessor generate. The result is a cooler-running laptop, which keeps Mr. Laptop happy.

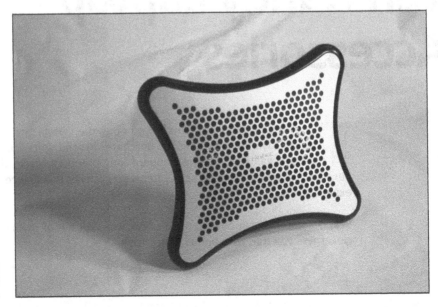

FIGURE 26-1:
A cool
cooling pad.

» Heed whether the cooling pad runs from the power supplied by the USB port or from its own batteries.

» If you're getting a USB-powered cooling pad, buy a model that has a pass-through USB port so that you don't lose a USB port when you add a cooling pad.

TIP

Laptop Stand

When it sits flat on a desktop or table, a laptop is too low for your arms and neck. To remedy this situation, obtain a laptop stand. Not only does the stand elevate the laptop to a more comfortable height, but the air circulation below the laptop also helps keep it cool.

» Many laptop stands are adjustable. In fact, they can compact into a small shape, which makes it easier to shove the thing into your laptop bag.

» An elevated laptop may be uncomfortable for you to type on. If so, remember that you can obtain an external keyboard. Set the keyboard on the desk but keep the laptop up high for better viewing.

TIP

Minivac

Useful for cleaning your laptop, especially the keyboard, is the minivac, or tiny vacuum. This item is found in most office supply stores, and many are portable (battery-powered). You'll be surprised (and disgusted) by the gunk the minivac can suck from your laptop.

Yes, some minivacs are USB-powered.

USB Lamp

Your laptop's screen is illuminated and even shows up in the dark. Sadly, some laptop keyboards don't light up. To help you see the keyboard as well as other important areas around your laptop, you can light things up with a USB-powered lamp.

The lamp plugs into a standard USB port on your laptop. It has either a stiff, bendable neck or a clamp so that you can position it. Flip the switch and let there be light!

>> Some laptops might already have built-in keyboard lights. A special Fn-key combination may be used to activate the keyboard lights. If this feature isn't available, get a USB lamp for your laptop.

>> Even when the keyboard is illuminated, a USB lamp helps you see things near your laptop, such as a notepad or reference or various crawling insects.

Full-Size Keyboard and External Mouse

I'm certain that you don't want to tote one around with you, but there's a measurable pleasure to be had when you're using a laptop with a comfy, full-size keyboard and a mouse. The mouse need not even be full-size; plenty of laptop-size mice are available.

>> Did I say *wireless?* If you really want to be free of those pesky wires, get a wireless or Bluetooth keyboard and mouse. Wires belong back in the office, not on the road.

>> Maybe you don't want a full-size PC keyboard. Perhaps you just need a numeric keypad? If so, buy a USB keypad for your laptop.

>> When you use your tablet PC as a tablet, consider getting a digital stylus or pen. It works a lot like a mouse; plus, it's a better input device for creating text on a touchscreen — much better than your stubby fingers.

>> Wireless gizmos need batteries. Along with any wireless gizmos, toss some spare AA or AAA batteries into your laptop bag.

REMEMBER

Privacy Screen Filter

Being in public with your laptop means that you're out amongst the rabble. Who knows which innocent coffee-sipper is secretly a Hollywood spy, eager to steal that blockbuster script you're working on?

To keep the snooping eyes at bay, get a privacy screen filter. These devices are composed of a thin mesh that hugs the laptop's screen. From straight-on, you see the information on the screen. Move away from the screen at even the shallowest angle and you don't see anything. That's why it's called a *privacy* screen filter.

The good news: Privacy screen filters are available in computer and office supply stores. Ensure that you know the laptop's screen size to buy the proper one. They're also available for desktop computers.

The bad news: These devices don't work well with tablet PCs. The screen interferes with your touch input. This hindrance might be okay for a while, and most tablets let you attach a keyboard, so it's a frustrating trade-off.

ID Card or Return Service Sticker

Way back when, your mom would probably write your name on your laptop, just like she wrote your name on your underwear. And, seriously, Mom: Who was going to steal my underwear? Did they do that in the old country?

My point is that your laptop is yours only because you keep it with you. What it needs is your name on it somewhere. For example, businesspeople commonly tape their business cards somewhere on the inside of their laptops, such as slightly to one side of the touchpad.

The idea here is not only to claim ownership of the laptop but also to pray that if the laptop is ever lost or stolen, it will be recognizable as your own. A good citizen will contact you and offer to return the found laptop that has your name emblazoned on an ID card.

>> While you're at it, attach a business card to other portable devices you might leave behind, like external storage, power supplies, and video projectors.

>> A better solution is to use a return service and take advantage of its tamper-resistant asset tags. Refer to Chapter 20 for more information.

Theft-Prevention System

The perfect gift for your dear laptop: some type of cable to keep it from walking off, one of those annoyingly loud my-laptop-has-been-moved alarms, or that special software that tries to "phone home" when the laptop is purloined. Ease your fears! Refer to Chapter 20 for more information on laptop security — specifically, these types of devices.

Chapter **27**

Ten Things to Throw in Your Laptop Bag

P ity the poor desktop PC. It has no bag. All the PC stuff you need is cluttered around the desktop because the system never moves. I suppose you could rent a U-Haul if you truly wanted to take it elsewhere. Don't forget the generator!

Unlike desktops, laptops are untethered and free to wander. Even so, you can't just hoist your laptop and waltz merrily out the door. No, you need stuff. What kind of stuff? Might I suggest ten things worthy of throwing (gently) into your laptop bag?

Yes, you need a laptop bag. See Chapter 19.

Power Cord and Brick

Sometimes I think, "Oh, I'm only going to be gone for an hour, and the battery lasts for six hours, so I don't need the power cord." Then something changes and I regret not bringing the power cord with me.

REMEMBER

Always take your power cord and its adapter, or "brick," in your laptop bag. You never know when you'll need it.

Mouse or Digital Pen

I figured I'd never forget my wee li'l wireless laptop mouse — until I did. I even toyed with the notion of buying another laptop mouse as opposed to using the touchpad for my entire trip. Since then, I've not neglected to keep the mouse in the laptop bag.

The laptop's pen or digital stylus is also an input device — one that probably costs more than a wireless mouse. Don't forget it, and especially don't lose it. If your laptop has a pen dock or clip, use it to keep the pen handy.

Screen Wipes and Cleaner

Go to the office supply store and buy some screen wipes. Ensure that they're safe for a touchscreen. Toss 'em in your laptop bag and keep them there.

WARNING

Don't confuse laptop screen wipes with eyeglass wipes. Eyeglasses can handle the harsh chemicals used in their wipes (typically, alcohol). Your laptop's touchscreen requires special wipes.

Laptop Lock

You purchased that laptop's antitheft device for a reason. Whether it's a cable you can connect to something solid or one of those loud, loud audio alarms, you probably want to pack it in your laptop bag. Refer to Chapter 20 for more information on laptop security.

Removable Media

Saving your stuff to the laptop's primary storage system often isn't enough. It helps to have an assortment of alternatives to get that information out of the computer, especially when your laptop isn't connected to a network for easy file transfer.

>> Label the media cards and thumb drives. This way, you can keep them straight.

>> I keep microSD cards in their tiny, plastic cases. They're more difficult to lose that way.

>> An external drive may seem a bit much, but if you adhere to a regular backup regimen, it's a must. Refer to Chapter 22.

Headphones

Consider two types of headphones for your laptop bag. First are the common earbud-style headphones, which you probably use on your cell phone. These are fine for a laptop and, if they feature a microphone, you can use them to Skype or for other voice input.

A second type of headphone is the more complex, full-size model. Also known as a *headset*, this headphone includes full-size ear cans and a separate microphone. I prefer this type of headset because it's more comfortable; plus, I have an irrational fear of earbuds getting stuck in my head.

TIP

>> My favorite headphones feature noise-canceling capabilities. Listening to music or watching a movie on my laptop is far more enjoyable in an airplane when I activate the headphone's noise-canceling feature.

REMEMBER

>> Airlines require that you use headphones when listening to music, watching a video, or playing a game during the flight.

Spare Batteries

I've looked, but I can't seem to find that hand-cranked portable mouse. I know I saw it on Amazon once. Or maybe it was Temu? Regardless, wireless pointing devices rely upon standard AA or AAA batteries. These last a long time, but it's best to be prepared. Keep one or two extra batteries in your laptop bag.

TIP

>> I use standard alkaline batteries in my wireless pointing devices. I would avoid using rechargeable batteries. They require a charger, and airlines ban certain types of rechargeable batteries.

>> Wireless Bluetooth gizmos let the laptop know how much charge remains. Visit the Bluetooth screen in the Settings app. Any active, paired device shows its current battery charge.

Office Supplies

Yeah, this is supposed to be the "paperless" age. Whatever. You still need a pad of paper and a writing implement, despite the redundancy and its overall anti-21st-century nature. I keep two pens, one highlighter, sticky notes, a small pad of paper, and a legal pad in my laptop bag. Although it's not intentional, my laptop bag has also collected various paper clips and rubber bands — plus, a stash of coins.

TIP

>> I throw my change into the laptop bag when going through airport security. The quantity has accumulated over time.

>> Another must-have item: business cards.

>> Also consider copies of your presentation (if you're making one) and perhaps some magazines or reading material.

>> Surprisingly, also available at an office supply store are a deck of cards, Band-Aids, aspirin, and other sundries. These too make excellent items to keep in your laptop bag.

Cables, Cables, Cables

Cables are good. When you can, bring any spare Ethernet, USB, or other type of cables you can muster. You might never use them, but then again, you never know.

>> Taking along a goodly length of Ethernet cable with your laptop is always a good idea. When a wired Ethernet port appears, you can instantly connect to the network without having to wait for or (worse) rent a cable.

>> A goodly length is about 6 feet.

>> A phone charging cable is also a handy thing to keep in the laptop bag. In fact, I keep a wireless charging pad in my laptop bag specifically for my phone.

Not the End of the List

You can pack your laptop bag full of so much stuff that the bag eventually weighs more than you do. Weight is the practical limit on what you can put into a laptop bag. The list is long, and gravity is persistent.

The items mentioned in this chapter are good to *always* have in your laptop bag. Add the other stuff as you need it. Or, when you're traveling, consider putting in your checked luggage the extra things you don't immediately need so that you're not toting their extra weight.

Chapter **28**

Ten Tips from a PC Guru

'␣ve been called a PC guru, though I don't seek this title. I'm just good at figuring things out and explaining how stuff works in an understandable and entertaining manner. I also screw up a lot, which has taught me some valuable lessons. Consider this final chapter in the book as my helpful advice, which I'm cheerfully passing along to you, whether you believe me to be a PC guru or just your run-of-the-mill nerd who can write good.

Remember That You're in Charge

You bought the computer. You clean up after its messes. You press the Any key (which is the Enter key). You control the computer — simple as that.

Think of your laptop or PC as an infant. You must treat it the same way, with respect and careful attention. Don't feel that the computer is bossing you around any more than you feel that a baby is bossing you around during those 3 A.M. feedings. They're both helpless creatures, subject to your every whim. Be gentle, but be in charge.

Mind Who "Helps" You

Nothing beats getting computer help when you need it. Most computer nerds enjoy helping beginners. Sometimes, they help you at no cost, though you shouldn't abuse a good relationship by becoming a pest.

REMEMBER

When you can't find help, use the support you paid for: from your manufacturer, computer dealer, software developer, and Internet service provider.

Above all, keep in mind that not everyone who tries to help you truly knows what they're doing. My advice is to avoid friends or (especially) relatives who offer to "fix" your computer when you haven't asked them to. This situation can lead to big trouble.

>> How do you know when you're being a pest to a computer-knowledgeable friend? I know the answer! When the only time you call is when you have computer trouble. Then you're abusing the relationship.

>> Treat your PC like your wallet. You wouldn't hand it over to your 5-year-old granddaughter, right?

WARNING

>> You may like your smart nephew Victor, but don't let him near your computer. Don't let the grandkids or out-of-town relatives "play" on the Internet while they visit. You'll thank me later.

Give Yourself Time to Learn

Things take time. No one sits down at a computer and instantly knows everything, especially with new software. True, the boss may have given you only a day to learn how to be clever with some new program. Such a task is unrealistic and unfair. If challenged, point to this sentence for validation.

It takes about a week to become comfortable with any software. It takes longer to truly figure out how it works, even if you receive a good tutorial on the topic. Honestly, I don't think anyone out there knows *everything* about a major software product. Don't set the bar so high that you can't leap over it.

Create Separate Accounts

Because I'm an insane member of computer nerd culture, everyone in my family has their own PC or laptop. You may instead be sane and have only one computer at home, the family computer. Everyone uses it. This situation often makes simple tasks like gathering email and bookmarking websites difficult. I have a solution!

Each user on the computer should have their own Windows account. This way, you can each keep your stuff separate. The issue is not secrecy but organization. Having one account for each person who uses the computer is better than having two or more people share — and mess up — the only account.

The same guideline applies to email: Get yourself separate email accounts — one for you and one for your partner or one for each human who uses the computer. This way, you receive only your mail, and you don't miss anything because someone else has read or deleted it.

>> Configuring a second account on Windows involves some arduous steps, the most egregious of which is that the second account holder must have an email address — even for a kid's account. That's just obnoxious.

>> Use the Settings app to add accounts. Choose the Accounts category, and then choose the Family option. Yes, this process can be frustrating, but it's a solid solution — especially when kids have access to the computer.

Mind What You Download

Even after years of experience, I fall victim to not heeding my own advice: Sometimes I'm in such a hurry to download a program from the Internet that I don't read everything. A box goes checked or unchecked, and the result is that unwanted software is installed on my computer.

The good news is that if you're quick, you can uninstall that software. If you don't notice — and it's easy to overlook — some software becomes embedded in your

PC. Not even antispyware utilities can remove it. That's because you *invited* the software in.

The solution is to slow down! Pay attention when you download or install software. Read *every* screen. Look for options and offers. Scan for a "skip" button or link. Install only what you need, not the bonus offers, toolbars, search engines, shopping assistants, or varieties of unwanted, loathsome programs.

Organize Your Files

Software developers have toiled endlessly to create a computer environment that fools you into believing that using a computer is fun and easy. It's not. Though working on a computer today is easier than in the text-mode days of the MS-DOS operating system, some complex computer science issues remain.

Number-one of all the basic computer science issues is file organization. You can live a digital life completely unfettered by any need to organize your files. The result is like living in a house without closets, cupboards, or drawers: Everything is everywhere. Some people like this setup, but it's far more effective to keep things organized.

>> Properly name files when you first save them. Be short and descriptive. Imagine yourself weeks or months from now trying to guess what's in the file, and then choose a good name.

>> There's nothing wrong with naming a file delete me or temp. This name portends future thrills for doing file hunting and removing files you no longer need.

>> Organize similar files into folders. Properly name the folders to describe their contents.

>> Use subfolders to further organize files.

Don't Reinstall Windows

A myth floating around tech support sites says that the solution to all your ills is to reinstall Windows. Some tech support people even claim that it's common for most Windows users to reinstall at least once a year. Such talk is rubbish.

You *never* need to reinstall Windows. All problems are fixable. It's just that the tech support people are urged by their bottom-line-watching overlords to get you off the line quickly. Therefore, they resort to a drastic solution rather than try to discover the true problem. If you press them, they *will* tell you what's wrong and how to fix it.

In all my years of using a computer, I have never reinstalled Windows or had to reformat the primary storage device. It's not even a good idea just to refresh the bits on the hard drive or whatever other nonsense they dish up. There just isn't a need to reinstall Windows, ever. Period.

If you enjoy this book and want to study more on fixing PC problems, check out *Troubleshooting & Maintaining PCs All-In-One For Dummies* (Wiley Publishing). The author does almost as good a job with that book as I do with this one.

Shun the Hype

The computer industry is rife with hype. Websites and pundits tout this or that solution, crow about new trends, and preannounce standards that supposedly will make everything you have obsolete. Ignore all of it! If you see the new thing advertised for sale, it's probably real. Otherwise, avoid being lured by the hype.

Keep on Learning

There's no reason to stop discovering new things about your computer. If you're into books (and you seem to be), consider getting another computer book on a topic that interests you. Bookstores, both physical and on the Internet, are brimming with titles covering just about every computer topic. Also peruse computer-related websites and online learning courses.

For example, perhaps you want to take up programming. I'm serious! If you enjoy solving puzzles, you'll probably enjoy programming. Or, maybe you want to learn how to get the most from a graphics program. In a time when people try to glean knowledge from mediocre (but free) information on the Internet, why not take time to truly educate yourself?

Remember Not to Take This Computer Stuff Too Seriously

Hey, simmer down! Computers aren't an important part of life. They're nothing more than mineral deposits and petroleum products. Close your eyes and take a few deep breaths. Imagine that you're lying on a soft, sandy beach in the South Pacific. Having just dined on tasty exotic food, you close your eyes as the sounds of the gentle surf lull you into a well-deserved late-afternoon nap.

Next, you're getting your feet rubbed as you sip a delectable and satisfying beverage. Soothing music plays as everyone who's ever said a bad thing about you in your life tosses you $100 bills.

Now, slowly open your eyes. It's just a dumb computer. Really. Don't take it too seriously.

Index

files
   about, 203
   accessing network folders, 206
   activating Network Discovery, 204–205
   cloud storage synchronization, 209–213
   deleting, 292
   integrating cloud storage, 211–212
   on local network, 203–209
   mapping shared folders, 206–208
   organizing, 318
   quarantined, 260–261
   sharing folders, 208–209
   sharing from cloud storage, 212–213
finding
   firewalls, 216–217
   printers in Windows, 161–162
   storage devices, 102
   web browsers, 195–196
fingerprints, for signing in to Windows, 48–49
Firefox (Mozilla), 195, 197
firewalls
   about, 216
   finding, 216–217
   warnings, 217–218
fixed storage device, 96
flash media, 95
flash memory, 84, 85
flying, with laptops, 238–242
Fn key, 123, 124–125
folders
   deleting, 292
   sharing, 208–209
forgetting Wi-Fi connections, 191
fragmentation, 284
Franklin, Benjamin, 227
freeing storage space, 278–281
frequency, of shutdowns, 68–69
front, of computer box, 23–24
full-size keyboards, 306
Function keys, on keyboards, 122, 125
future expansion, 23, 24

G

gateways, 182, 184
GB (gigabyte), 86
GHz (gigahertz), 79
gigabyte (GB), 86
gigahertz (GHz), 79
gizmos, USB-powered, 146
Google, 198
Google Drive, 210–211, 212
Google's Chrome, 195, 197
GPU (graphics processing unit), 109
graphics driver, 108
graphics processing unit (GPU), 109
graphics system
   about, 107
   adding monitors, 116–118
   attaching monitors, 110–111
   components of, 107–111
   display adapter, 109
   measuring monitors, 112–113
   monitor types, 112
   orienting monitors, 118–119
   reading monitor messages, 114
   setting monitor resolution, 115–116
   Windows controls, 115–119
   working monitor controls, 114–115

H

hard copy, 23, 155
hard disk drive (HDD), 95
hardware
   about, 12
   calculating requirements of, 15
hardware firewall, 216
HDD (hard disk drive), 95
HDMI (High-Definition Multimedia Interface), 110–111
HDMI (High-Definition Multimedia Interface) port, 36–37
headphones, 39, 174, 311
headset, 311
help, computer, 316
Hibernate option, 61–62

Control Panel, 55
  for mouse, 135
  for privacy, 266
  Settings app, 53–54
Settings app, 53–54
setup
  of laptops, 33–35
  screen savers, 265
  speakers, 172–174
shared folders, mapping, 206–208
sharing
  files from cloud storage, 212–213
  folders, 208–209
  web pages, 200
Shift+drag, with a mouse, 131
Shrink to Fit command, 199
Shrink to Page command, 199
shutdown
  about, 62
  configuration for, 65–68
  options for, 65–68
  Windows, 295
signing out, of Windows, 64
Simple Mail Transfer Protocol (SMTP), 202
size, of laptop bags, 236
sleep connectors, 142
Sleep mode, 60–61
small form factor (SMF), 20
small-footprint PCs, 21
SmartScreen, activating, 220–221
SMF (small form factor), 20
SMTP (Simple Mail Transfer Protocol), 202
social engineering, 257
software
  about, 12
  antivirus, 293
  registering, 247–248
solid-state drive (SSD), 95
sound output device, changing, 175
sound-generation hardware, 172
speakers
  about, 22, 38–39
  setting up, 172–174
Special button, on mouse, 130

speech-to-text feature, 138
speed
  of memory, 84
  processor, 79
spike, 41
spread, on touchscreens, 136
spyware, 259
SSD (solid-state drive), 95
SSID (service set identifier), 188
standards, USB, 142
standby connectors, 142
stands, for laptops, 305
Start button, 50
Start menu, accessing, 51–52
stealing images from web pages, 198
stolen laptops, 245–246
STOP (Security Tracking of Office Property)
      program, 247
storage
  about, 11
  checking, 278
  external, 304
  freeing up space, 278–281
storage, cloud
  about, 209–210
  integrating, 211–212
  options for, 210–211
  sharing files from, 212–213
  synchronization, 209–213
storage, mass
  about, 93–94, 278
  checking for errors, 281–282
  checking storage, 278
  connecting, 96–97
  freeing storage space, 278–281
  measuring, 96
  running defrag, 282–284
  technical terms for, 94–95
  types of, 95–96
storage cost, 95
strong password, 249
style, of laptop bags, 236–237
stylus, 132–134
subwoofer, 172, 173, 174

summoning System window, 80

surge, 41

surround speakers, 173

swipe, on touchscreens, 136

switch, 185

switching users, 64–65

synchronization, cloud storage, 209–213

system expansion

  about, 141

  expansion slots, 146–148

  USB port, 141–146

  using laptops as desktops, 152–154

  wireless connections with Bluetooth, 148–152

system security

  about, 255

  malware, 258–262

  privacy, 265–266

  Windows Security Center, 255–257

  Windows updates, 262–264

System window, summoning, 80

T

taskbar, in Windows, 50

TB (terabyte), 86

Technical Stuff icon, 4

techniques, for touchscreens, 136

temperature, of laptops, 244, 299

temporary storage, 84

terabyte (TB), 86

terminology

  for malware, 258–259

  for networks, 184–185

testing memory, 89–90

text, copying from web pages, 199

theft-prevention systems, 307

thumb drive, 97

time zone, 241–242

Tip icon, 4

toner cartridges, for printers, 157, 158

touch, on touchscreens, 136

touch keyboard, 137–138

touchpads

  about, 131–132

  on laptops, 28, 29

  setting options for, 135

touchscreens

  about, 135

  techniques for, 136

  typing on, 137–138

tower, 21

trackball, 128

tracking, on Internet, 196–197

transparency adapter, 171

travel case, 304

Trojan, 259

troubleshooting

  networks, 284–285

  printers, 166

turning off

  computers, 57–69

  frequency of, 68–69

  Hibernate option, 61–62

  locking Windows, 63–64

  restarting PCs, 63

  shutdown, 62

  shutdown options and configuration, 65–68

  signing out of Windows, 64

  Sleep mode, 60–61

  switching users, 64–65

  Windows power options, 58–60

turning on

  computers, 45–55

  laptops, 46–47

  PCs, 45–46

two, power of, 87

two-in-one. *See* PC tablet

typing on touchscreens, 137–138

U

UAC (User Account Control) warnings, 261–262

uninterruptible power supply (UPS), 41–43

universal resource locator (URL), 220

About the Author

Dan Gookin has been writing about computers since the reign of Charles II. He combines his love of writing with his gizmo fascination to create books that are informative, entertaining, and not boring. Having written over 170 titles with 12 million copies in print translated into over 30 languages on several planets, Dan can attest that his method of crafting technology tomes seems to work.

Perhaps his most famous title is the original *DOS For Dummies*, published in 1991. It became the world's fastest-selling computer book, at one time moving more copies per week than the *New York Times* number-one bestseller (though, as a reference, it could not be listed on the Times' Best Sellers list). That book spawned the entire line of *For Dummies* books, which remains a publishing phenomenon to this day.

Dan's least famous title is *Compute's Problem Solving with Sidekick Plus* (Compute! Books, 1989).

Dan's most popular titles include *Word For Dummies*, *Troubleshooting & Maintaining PCs All-in-One For Dummies*, and *C Programming For Dummies* (all from Wiley Publishing). His website is www.wambooli.com, which was once ranked 104,578,296th most popular website on the Internet.

Dan holds a degree in Communications/Visual Arts from the University of California, San Diego. He lives in the Pacific Northwest with his wife, children, animals, and various robots. He enjoys being sesquipedalian and inaniloquent.

Publisher's Acknowledgments

Acquisitions Editor: Steve Hayes
Senior Project Editor: Paul Levesque
Copy Editor: Becky Whitney
Tech Reviewer: Ryan Williams

Production Editor: Tamilmani Varadharaj
Cover Image: © Hispanolistic/Getty Images